The Ultimate Guide to
Shopping & Caring for Clothing

Everything you need to know... from blue jeans to ball gowns!

Steve Boorstein

The Ultimate Guide to Shopping and Caring for Clothing
Copyright © 2002 by Steven P. Boorstein

Boutique Books, LLC

PO Box 107
Glen Echo, MD 20812-0107

Includes bibliographical references, index, and glossary: First Printing, June 2002

ISBN Number 0-9717669-0-8
Printed in the United States of America

Publisher's Cataloging-in-Publication

Boorstein, Steve.
The ultimate guide to shopping and caring for
clothing / by Steve Boorstein. -- 1 st ed.
p. cm.
Includes index.
LCCN: 2002090812
ISBN: 09717669-0-8
1. Clothing and dress--Purchasing. 2. Clothing and
dress--Care. I. Title.
TX340.B66 2002   646'.3
QBI02-200279

10 9 8 7 6 5 4 3 2 1

To my parents: Beverly and Sandy Cohen and Edward and Ruth Boorstein, and my Sibs, Sharon, Nancy, and David

Information:

To book Steve Boorstein for seminars
To receive a Speaker's Package on Steve Boorstein
For information regarding discounts for bulk purchases

Please contact Boutique Books at 301.320.7292 or
sales@clothingdoctor.com or check the website at
www.clothingdoctor.com

Editor
Heather Dittbrenner
Jennifer Thompson—Publications Professionals
Barbara Boorstein—Final Edit

Cover Design
Michelle Marcello—Initial Brainstorming
Kathleen Kiely
Sheila Harrington—Studio 5 Design

Illustrator
Valery Bochkov

Photographer: Inside Photography
Richard Frasier—Frasierphoto.com

Cover Photography
Ken Weingart Photography: Female Image
Charlotte Mouton Photography: Male Image

Indexer
Kate Mertes

Computer Assistance and Preparation
Bevi Chagnon: PubCom

◆ *Acknowledgments*

I thank my wife, Barbara, my first-stage and final-stage editor and soul partner, and my two sons, Bryan and Ben, for all sharing my vision. Their unending support, patience, opinions, and good humor were as strong and spirited as my commitment and enthusiasm. Without them, it would have been a lonely two years.

I have so many people to thank that I'm afraid someone off-stage will "give me the hook." First, I wish to thank all of the people who worked with me at Parkway Custom Dry Cleaning for teaching me "almost" as much as I taught them, and to all of the valuable and committed customers who pushed me to achieve my best, through their trust, encouragement, and demands!

I wish to thank Mike Colen, owner of James Limited, for his calm, supportive energy, his excellent advice, his fashion savvy, and for the unselfish use of his fine Italian clothing for some of the pictures in this book. And Lisa Colen for her energy, insight, and interest. A nod to Joe Muscaro at James Limited for his help as well. To Barbara Gibson, a reweaver par excellence. To Rich Frasier, good friend and a great photographer, for his good nature and patient wisdom. He always felt this book had great potential, and he constantly reminded me to enjoy the fruits of my labor along the way.

Thanks to Kathy Charner for her excellent insights, guidance, and hand-holding. I wish to thank Jim Kirby at IFI for his technical advice through the years. He helped me put my own skills and knowledge into proper perspective. I would like to thank Jon Simon for giving me the time to write this book.

Thanks to Cary for his total calm and good wishes. Kim Addonizio, the poet, has been a true inspiration from my first written word. Her honest advice helped me get a grip on reality. Many thanks to Mark Ortman for his valuable advice. To Deborah Rechnitz for her uncompromising nature, and a warm thanks to the rest of the Eastern bureau for their needling and good humor.

A very special thanks to Lynda Carter, Judy Woodruff, Mary Margaret Valenti, and Mr. and Mrs. Marriott, for believing in me and my skills so deeply.

I wish to thank both John Olmstead and Noam Dworman for helping me realize my vision. This vision exposed another creative side of me that had lain dormant for too many years. To John Hallak for his infinite patience, wisdom, and wit. To Gary for always being there while I transformed myself into a writer.

◆ How This Book Is Organized

Part 1: *Shopping*

I started this book with shopping, and the options that we *all* have available to us—but that many of us never knew existed. I have a powerful appreciation for outstanding customer service and deeply believe that you deserve nothing less.

Part 2: *Basics for Men and Women*

Here I delve into all the "silent" components of the fabric of our lives—the buttons, linings, pleats, belts, stains, and a basic knowledge of fabrics. These are the stepping stones to knowledge, awareness and, ultimately, to gaining control of our clothing investment.

Part 3: *Steaming and Pressing*

The steaming and pressing of our clothing is as important (and perhaps more challenging) as the cleaning and washing of it. Most consumers know little about the subtleties of this part of the process—the "finishing" of a garment. But it is a key part of the maintenance and care of clothing. It affects every piece of clothing we clean.

Parts 4—6: *Shopping and Caring for Men's and Women's Clothing*

Now, on to the rudiments of buying men's and women's clothing: everyday clothing, formalwear, bridal gowns, leather, suede and fur, and clothing accessories. All the information comes together here like an "ensemble" when we begin to care for and clean these valuable possessions.

Part 7: *Home and Storage: Ironing, Closet Care, and Reweaving*

Good habits extend the life of our clothing. Rather than dispose of clothing due to wear, abuse, or old age, we can embrace the basics of clothing restoration. Whether we are repairing, reweaving, cleaning, or storing, our clothing deserves extra attention—it often beats buying new clothing!

Part 8: *What Is Drycleaning and How to Select a Drycleaner*

Drycleaning is required for much of the clothing that you wear. Drycleaning, and how to make the best of it, is a common thread running through the fabric of this book. Selecting a drycleaner can be an ongoing process as you search for the right fit. The chapter on selecting a drycleaner describes the scope of services available to you; helps you assess your needs; and provides you a basis by which to judge a drycleaner's performance.

Table of Contents

Part 3: Steaming and Pressing

Part 4: Women's Clothing

Part 5: Men's Clothing

Part 6: Unisex Clothing

Part 7: Home and Storage

Part 8: Drycleaning

◆ *Introduction*

We spend endless hours driving, shopping, and deciding on the right clothing, then altering, washing, and drycleaning our wardrobe ... it is an extension of our personality. No one wants to replace clothing; shopping is somewhere between a chore and a passion—and both require your time and money.

Literally speaking, there *is* no other book like this: It de-mystifies the art of shopping, caring for, and cleaning clothing while revealing information not always shared by clothing retailers, manufacturers, or drycleaners. This is not a tell-all book; it is meant to educate you and empower you. Finding who is at fault is not the focus—*understanding* is. The writing is friendly and informative, and it is *not* my aim to make it wordy or overly technical.

Shopping and caring for clothing is an ongoing theme that weaves its way through almost every chapter.

During the past twenty five years I have developed an intimate and committed appreciation for clothing. First, as a boutique owner, I was a buyer—and did everything else too. Later, as the owner of one of the most exclusive drycleaners in the country, I cared for clothing; helped repair, restyle and restore it; and gave shopping advice. I worked closely with buyers from boutiques and department stores, fabric specialists from world-renowned testing labs, and conservators from many institutions, including the Smithsonian Institution.

All this training helped educate me and open my eyes to the real need: helping people like you navigate your way through the many choices faced daily as you shop, care for, and clean clothing. We spend serious dollars on perishable clothing. There are "experts" on every possible subject—but where are the shopping and clothing-care gurus?

I am very excited to share all of these useful, time-saving, and money-saving tips. This book is reader friendly and can be used as a reference book. Some people have read it cover to cover, but most will "target read" as they shop and care for their clothing. Both approaches are valuable.

I hope you will enjoy reading this book as much as I enjoyed anticipating its value to you.

Steve Boorstein

Chapter 1

Shopping in the Retail World

Care Labels, Coping with Stores, Shopping by Appointment,
Interviews with Personal Shoppers

How many times have you walked into a store, been unable to get help from a salesperson, and roamed around aimlessly hoping for assistance? Of course, it depends on the type of store, but this experience is a familiar one for most of us. Once you've found a person to "help" you, he or she seems capable of finding a garment for you or locating a different size or color, but rarely openly shares important information, such as: fabric content, wearability, or care instructions. How many times have you asked, "Do you think it will shrink much?" all the while feeling almost silly about asking someone probably less informed than yourself? Wouldn't it be helpful to know what will happen to the garment after washing or drycleaning?

As a consumer, you need to gather the information yourself, know the questions to ask, and know where to find the answers. This is where I come in. In Chapter 2 you will learn about fabrics as they pertain to fabric *content* labels, but let's now examine what you can learn from *care* labels.

◆ Reading Care Labels

From my experience, too many people do not read care labels before they buy. Every garment that you purchase, by law, is supposed to have a sewn-in care label that supplies at least one safe method for cleaning. As a fabric-care specialist and sleuth, I've had the opportunity to experience care labels that are inaccurate, incomplete, and unsafe. You and your drycleaner should be able to trust the written instruction or international symbol on the label and assume that it provides a safe method for processing.

| Made IN ITALY |
| 95% Cotton |
| 5% Spandex |
| goat parts |
| **NO WASH IN WATER** |
| NO BLEACH |
| NO IRON |
| **NO DRY CLEAN** |

Label from a major
Italian clothing designer
How can this be cleaned?

Most "basic" wool suits, blue jeans, and cotton dress shirts have dependable care labels. It is not necessary for you to read every label as you shop, but most certainly you should before you buy. For unique garments—such as designer clothing, most outerwear, ski outfits, blended fabrics, and specialty pieces—I would suggest that you do not purchase a single garment without first reading and understanding the care-label instructions.

Instructions That Should Concern You

Do Not Tumble Dry/Air Dry Only

Show this type of care label to your drycleaner at the counter or attach a note for the delivery driver who picks up your clothes to be cleaned. Drycleaners have trouble with this instruction for two reasons: First, due to their experience, technicians don't routinely read every care label; and second, because most drycleaning machines clean and dry in one cycle, it is difficult to air dry a garment as a separate step. A "Do Not Tumble Dry" label usually appears on imported clothing, so be aware of this when you shop. Most clothing with this instruction will not be ruined if it is tumble dried, but some shrinkage may occur.

Warm-Iron Only

This label is an accurate warning for pressing acetate and other easily shined materials. It is also accurate for garments trimmed with beads, sequins, vinyl, snakeskin, and leather. This label also *wrongly appears* on many cotton dress shirts that clearly must be pressed with a very hot iron or on a laundry press in order to achieve a crisp finish. If you follow this label and use a warm iron on your dress shirts, they will look like you just slept in them!

Some poly-blended shirts *do* require a warm iron and have been melted or torn on a hot laundry press. You will have to police this yourself because 99% of the shirts sent to the drycleaners to be professionally laundered are completely compatible with a hot iron. If you do have a garment with a label that suggests a warm iron, be sure to bring this to the attention of your drycleaner so that he or she can make the proper care decision.

> **Common Labels**
> Some gowns and cocktail dresses that cost $500 or more have care labels that say, "Do not dryclean. Do not wash. Spot-clean only."

Do Not Dryclean, Do Not Wash, Spot-Clean Only

It's true. This type of label is very popular with formal dresses and garments adorned with beads, sequins, or fragile trims. Many of these garments, after proper testing by the technician and with your consent, can be drycleaned safely (usually in hydrocarbon; see Chapter 29). Many of these garments can actually be spot-cleaned only (without drycleaning), which may be sufficient if the stains are water based. Before you buy a formal garment like this, *read the care label.*

The care label may be tucked into the deepest recesses of the garment or sewn into a side seam, so be patient as you search for it. If you do not understand the instructions, try asking the salesperson for help. If he or she does not understand the instructions, then ask if the owner or manager is available. You could also call your drycleaner for guidance. If you still don't know the answer, make your best choice and make sure that the garment can be returned for a refund if it cannot be cleaned satisfactorily.

◆ Questions for Salespeople

Standard questions that apply to most clothing purchases will help you make the best of your investment. I would wager that you already have clothing in your closet that you don't wear because of the style or the color—why add improper fit, fragile elastic, or possible shrinkage to the list? Ask more questions.

▶ When buying a suit or a sport jacket, ask about fusible construction. (Pg. 83)

▶ Ask for extra buttons when you buy nice clothing because the buttons may not be available later. (See Chapter 3 on "Button and Trims.")

▶ When buying dress shirts, ask how much shrinkage should be expected in the collar. You would be surprised at the amount of progressive shrinkage in designer and custom shirts. (See Chapter 17, "Men's Shirts.")

▶ For expensive or unique clothing, ask for any care information the salesperson can share regarding washing or drycleaning. Ask the salesperson if he or she has heard any feedback from customers.

◆ Specialty Stores, Boutiques, and Department Stores

I'm sure that you have noticed a higher level of customer service at specialty stores, boutiques, and special departments within a department store. The clothing in these stores may be more expensive (though not always), but there is value in the service you receive. Good service saves time, provides better insight, reduces anxiety, and increases the value of your wardrobe investment.

Every time that you make an effort to build a relationship with the "right" salesperson, it pays off. You build continuity and familiarity, and you have someone on your side in a store that you like.

Shopping at smaller stores or at a certain department within a department store offers you the opportunity to build such a relationship. This type of shopping may be closer to your heart; you shop at fewer places and make better use of your time. You can start to do some shopping by phone, which saves you time and money. Make salespeople think about *you* and ask them to call when they receive new styles or when a garment that you ordered comes in. Share your taste with them. Great power is in this approach.

Avoid Inconvenience

How much running around do you do? You drive to a store or mall and put miles on yourself and your car. Then you may find that the size or color you want is sold out and can't be ordered. Just finding a salesperson to verify this information can exhaust you.

In Summary

Make the most of your time and shop smart. Read care labels, ask questions, learn more about fabrics, shop in smaller circles, run around less. Consider shopping by appointment or using a personal shopper.

◆ Shopping by Appointment

Don't tell me that you haven't agonized while shopping. Shopping is not always fun, is it? But it can be.

In specialty stores, boutiques, and department stores, you will find willing salespeople interested in the appointment concept. Instead of shopping piecemeal, with a suit here and a top there … think about wardrobes. (This concept works when you want to buy one special outfit as well.) As soon as you tell the manager or the appropriate salesperson what you want, then you will have their attention. What's in it for them? They have the opportunity to work with a single client for hours at a time, and you get their undivided attention and fashion sense. Salespeople crave this type of client. Many department stores—including Nordstrom, Saks Fifth Avenue, Neiman Marcus, and Bergdorf Goodman—promote this kind of arrangement.

Once you get past mainstream shopping (discount stores, discount department stores, and generic chain stores), the next level up offers many benefits. Men and women who can afford to make this small leap can experience shopping by appointment. With a little planning, a firm commitment, and a couple of hours, you can enjoy a service that few are aware exists.

Is It Worth the Investment?

Ask yourself these questions: How do you feel about the person who does your hair? Do you tell him or her what you like, what you think looks good? Do you ever ask for this person's opinion? He or she cuts, styles, or colors your hair—what about a trainer or someone who does body work on you? Pilates, yoga, or massage may be close to your heart. How much time and money do you spend on these aspects of your life? Shouldn't you relate on the same level to someone who sells you your clothing? You put this clothing on your treasured and pampered body, the clothing that completes you.

After thinking about the benefits of "shopping by appointment," this arrangement may sound like a sweet deal to you. It doesn't preclude you from "shopping 'til you drop" on your own whenever you wish, if that's what moves you, but there may be a place for this approach somewhere in your busy life.

◆ The Next Step: Assessing Your Personal Needs

Sit down, relax, and take some quality time (maybe in the restaurant at the department store where you shop) to ask yourself some questions. I think you will find that some of your answers may surprise you. At a minimum, you will learn some valuable things about your preferences; at best, you may be shocked at the clarity and power of your realizations.

▶ Assess your wardrobe needs. You've shopped your whole life, and you have some definite likes and dislikes.

▶ Write down your favorite colors and fabrics. Write down your least favorite colors and fabrics. Think about what people have commented on and complimented you on.

▶ Your body has probably found its natural weight by now—maybe not your ideal weight, but its natural weight (the one that you philosophically accept, even if your ego doesn't)—and you have a sense of what looks good on you. Or maybe you could use some fashion guidance, and that's all right, too. Write down what styles make you feel good.

▶ Do you have the interest and the inner strength to spend two to three hours with one salesperson? Is the time you will invest with this person worth any more than the hours you spend looking through racks and racks of clothes to find the right style at the right price?

▶ Have you had enough of the shopping rat-race, the traffic, the people, the time invested, the frustration of shopping numerous locations for hours on end and leaving with nothing or little of what you set out to find? Is it really worth all that?

After you have assessed your colors, fabrics, body type, personal preferences, and frustration level and have written them down, contact a boutique or two and a few departments that excite you and that you can afford. Go visit the appropriate

5

person and discuss your concepts. You will find that as soon as you express your interest—whether you need a wardrobe or a single outfit—the manager or owner will be very receptive. Pampering comes on many levels.

A Word About Personal Shoppers

I have had the pleasure of knowing many hard-working personal shoppers—mostly women. They are energetic and focused and really do have your best interest at heart. Many of the previous questions will prepare you for a relationship with a personal shopper. If this more personal approach is a good fit for you, personal shoppers will be with you during your shopping appointments, prepare clothing choices, and help you make those sometimes difficult assessments about your tastes and preferences. They can do more than just help with your wardrobe: they can reduce your other responsibilities—such as gift shopping for birthdays and special occasions—and free up more quality time for you to shop in peace.

◆ Perspective of Boutiques and Department Stores

The Salesperson's Perspective

Fine department stores such as Saks Fifth Avenue, Neiman Marcus, Barneys, Bergdorf Goodman, Nordstrom, and many more, all have their version of Couture, Finer Dresses, St. John Departments, and Fifth Avenue Club. Boutique shops such as Chanel, Versace, Hermes, Gucci, Yves St. Laurent, Brioni, and Jaeger, to name a few, also offer shopping by appointment. The same opportunity and pampering is available at many bridal boutiques.

Following are conversations with boutique owners and managers of designer departments, personal shoppers, and consultants. Their comments apply to both men and women.

This interview is with men's clothier Mike Colen of James Limited, located in Tysons Galleria, McLean, Virginia.

▶ **What kind of person would be interested in shopping by appointment?**
Very busy people, some affluent, many executives, certainly entertainers and people in the public eye, and people who value their time enough to budget it.

▶ **How does this service save clients time and aggravation?**
Many people actually have the time but can't envision spending it shopping. We try to make it a one-stop shopping experience, as much as our selection allows.

6

We offer drinks, wine, something to munch on. The environment reduces stress and opens their imagination, and they know that we are here for them.

▸ **What do people receive in these appointments?**

They get our undivided attention. They see the whole package. We coddle them, dress them, and let them learn about themselves. Many people have no idea of fashion trends, so we tie them into styles and make their wardrobe fit their lifestyle. We exchange personal information. We keep them in mind, e-mail them with updates, and send pictures of new styles.

▸ **How does this service change the way clients look at themselves?**

Most of these people already have confidence, but they really open up and share some interesting aspects of their personalities. They seem willing to discuss their lack of sophistication with regard to clothing sense. These are accomplished people, but unsure in this arena.

▸ **Do they gain a sense of control? Any epiphanies?**

I wouldn't go that far! Many of these people travel, and they shop in fashion centers around the world. They are happy to find that the "grass isn't always greener" elsewhere. We are showing the depth of our company in our selection and customer service.

▸ **Do clients begin and maintain a relationship with the fitter or tailor?**

This is very important. It's a very personal relationship. Fitters know the customer's body, their quirks and nuances: barrel-chested, one leg slightly longer than the other, where they carry their weight. We now have all their measurements. When they come in to shop, casually, and they find a shirt or slacks, they say, "You have my measurements; just do it."

▸ **How long does it take to build a wardrobe?**

It takes a few visits, a few seasons. There are basics, summer-weight wools and year-round weights. It is a philosophy as much as it is a shopping trip. It also involves a monetary investment.

▸ **What about trunk shows?**

We do them two times a season with different designers. It's relaxing to the clients: they drink, eat, talk, and shop. They can order the newest colors, fabrics, and styles the same day. It's great for people who don't fit well in off-the-rack clothing. It's exciting and rewarding.

▶ **How do people look at mainstream shopping after they have shopped by appointment?**

They are spoiled forever. Other cities and other stores lose a lot of their allure. Familiarity and personal care are very important.

This interview is with the Personal Shopper's Department at Neiman Marcus. This service is used primarily by women.

▶ **How does this service work, and can anyone take advantage of it?**

First of all, it is a free service offered to any customer who wants individual attention, whether buying one item or a wardrobe. We don't advertise it—most people come through referrals. The customer can call to ask about the service, or ask a salesperson on the floor. We meet with the customer in a comfortable private room that has a couch and a three-way mirror. The fitter will join us when we are ready.

▶ **What do you do for these customers? How do you prepare for meetings?**

The first meeting, which is often by phone, is spent asking customers about their particular needs: Do they want help with color selection and fabrics? Do they need fashion advice? Do they need an outfit for a special event? Some people are more open than others, so the information doesn't always just pour out. Once we have established the basics—height, coloring, and size—we begin the search for wardrobe and accessories.

▶ **Describe what kind of people use this service.**

Housewives, business people, people who travel, dignitaries. Some are young women in their twenties looking for the latest fashions. Some women are very sophisticated and use this service more for convenience and a sounding board rather than for advice. We have whole families: daughter, mother, and grandmother. They are very special to us—we get to know each member personally. They all sit together and support each other. We have people who have moved away or may be spending the winter away, but who still use this service because of the relationship we've formed and because we know their sizes and preferences.

▶ **How does this service save people time and aggravation?**

We will gather five or six dresses, shoes, and jewelry and have them ready when the customer arrives.

Sometimes we do walk the floor with them as well, especially in the beginning when we are getting to know each other. Sometimes people call and say, "I have twenty minutes to get a dress and shoes for a party tonight." We prepare a selection for them. We also get last-minute calls for gifts, especially from men. We find it, wrap it, and have it delivered if necessary.

▶ **Describe the relationship you develop with customers.**
We usually develop a rather personal relationship. If you think hairdressers hear stories... but I can't tell you any of them! Once there is a certain comfort level and familiarity, they trust the choices we make for them and we learn how far we can go fashion-wise. I have clients call me just to talk.

On the service side, when I work with clients long enough, I get to know their wardrobe intimately. If I am dressing someone who needs a certain blouse or skirt for an outfit, I will remind her that she has the perfect piece in her collection at home—she doesn't need to buy a new one.

▶ **Since we are on the subject, tell me more about "makeovers."**
Makeovers only represent 10% to 15% of the appointments, but it is an interesting experience. I have done this for men and women. Even though these clients are asking for the change, they generally fight it and it ends up a "split decision." We try a few things to see what works. Then the person goes to work and someone says, "What happened to you?" Then the person knows immediately if our instincts were right. One time I got a call from the person's friend who said, "He never looked better." Sometimes other men and women love the change, but the spouse does not.

▶ **How does this service change the way people look at themselves?**
They become more demanding! [Smiles] I have seen people come here self-conscious and introverted and watched them open up. This is important because sometimes along with the nurturing comes painful honesty, but I try to make it fun. The clients are appreciative because they know we care.

▶ **Do clients begin and maintain a relationship with the fitter or tailor?**
The fitter and the clients grow very close. There is little that the clients do not share with the fitter.

▶ **How long does it take to build a wardrobe?**
Some people have the capacity to spend long hours buying for different seasons, but most come two to four times a year. We do have clients come every

week to check in and they may buy a single piece, or they may just think about it for next time. But it takes time to build a wardrobe. This private approach helps them to buy clothing that they like and will wear. Sometimes we go to their home to help organize their closets and help them weed out clothing that they don't wear.

▶ **Tell me about trunk shows.**

Neiman's does trunk shows almost every day in one department or another. Designers and vendors introduce the clothing line to sales staff before the day begins. Then we have models and refreshments—it's very festive. The personal shoppers check their client list, make calls, and help them select fashions. They can buy that day, and the clothing is usually in the store in about four weeks.

▶ **How do people look at mainstream shopping after they have shopped by appointment?**

People become very spoiled and begin to expect this level of service wherever they go. Honestly, many people use both means to shop, but who wouldn't love the attention and pampering?

This interview is with Audrey Berlinsky, director of the Fifth Avenue Club at Saks Fifth Avenue in Chevy Chase, Maryland.

Ms. Berlinsky is very personable and has a real zest for her position. She feels that every client is special whether buying one piece or a wardrobe. "When a person crosses the threshold into the Fifth Avenue Club, they are to be treated like the Queen of England." And she makes no secret of this belief to her six clothing consultants.

▶ **How does this service work, and can anyone take advantage of it?**

Our clients are referred to us by other Fifth Avenue Club members. This may include daughters, friends, and business associates. Our six consultants work by appointment. We serve mostly women, but we do serve men as well. Our store in New York has a very successful Fifth Avenue Club for men.

▶ **What do you do for clients when you meet?**

In the first meeting with the client, we talk about lifestyle, what makes them comfortable, their individual needs, and their shopping habits. We "size up" the client: short-waisted, long-waisted, and any other particulars. We take note of likes and dislikes as we build a profile for each client. We are very perceptive. By the end of the visit, we know the client.

▶ **Describe what kind of person uses this service.**

In Washington, we serve people in the government, civic leaders, career people, young mothers—really a wide range of clients. Of course, travelers and busy executives also appreciate this service. This is truly a time saver, but more than saving time, it is the convenience and the personalized care that is the real value. We become a part of their lives.

▶ **How does this service save them time and aggravation?**

Most of the time we select ensembles for the client, which are waiting when they arrive. We can walk the floor together, but we usually know what they want. If they have a special request, be it a special outfit, or they want us to order them lunch, they can call us before their appointment. We may also show them something new that has just arrived. We can also set up an appointment to do their makeup while they are here. You can't beat this level of personal attention. We all need to be pampered now and then.

▶ **Describe the relationship you develop with the customer.**

We get to know our clients very well, as well as their family and spouses. When clients come to us, they know that they are getting qualified opinions, good fashion sense, and an up-to-the-moment glimpse of the ever-changing fashion industry. All our consultants have a retail background. Each day we have product knowledge meetings, and our consultants are very well informed on fabrics and the latest styles, from casual to couture. Our clients trust us. We guide them with honesty and integrity. If we feel that an outfit is not right for them, we will tell them so, and they respect us for that.

▶ **The Fifth Avenue Club has appointment rooms and offices and is teeming with activity. It feels like it has a life of its own.**

It does have a life of its own. We have a courier service; a computer room; a room for wrapping, packaging and shipping; a powder room; and a kitchen. We operate as our own entity. We have six clothing consultants who provide services from all the clothing, makeup, jewelry, and accessories departments. Each appointment room is soundproof and is equipped with a three-way mirror, fresh-cut flowers, a couch, and a TV/VCR to view the latest fashion lines.

We organize trunk shows, donate to charities, offer a selection of corporate gifts, send out invitations for trunk shows and special promotions, and mail out a semi-annual newsletter from the Fifth Avenue Club, called the *Fifth Avenue Club Line*, that informs the reader of the latest fashion news.

▶ **How does this service change the way people look at themselves?**

Women experience a degree of personal growth, some more than others. They become more open-minded as they are educated, and they gain the confidence to try different styles, often at our suggestion. When we have a private appointment room with clothing selected for them, it provides them a much greater opportunity to see themselves in outfits that they would rarely pick for themselves from a rack on the sales floor. Feeling better about yourself is what it's all about.

▶ **Tell me about trunk shows.**

We really believe in trunk shows. They are a great way to prepare people for the beginning of a season. If you're looking for something specific that you have not been able to find on the floor, you may find it during the show. Many of the pieces shown will not be ordered for stock, so the outfit can be truly different than what you see on the floor. If you're looking for a unique outfit, in a unique color, this is a good way to find it.

We have many social events in Washington each season. If the trunk show is attended well in advance of the event, the client can find the perfect dress, order it in the color she wants, know that it will be ready in three months, and be assured that she will have the right outfit for the special event.

▶ **Does the client begin and maintain a relationship with the fitter?**

The fitter is an integral part of the experience. The client and the fitter are very close, and the fitter is intimately aware of each client's body and fitting preferences. The consultant is there to offer advice and perspective as needed.

▶ **Saks has about sixty stores. Do the Fifth Avenue Clubs co-mingle?**

Each Saks Fifth Avenue has a "club," but there is no inter-store arrangement. If clients visit another club, they will be welcomed into a very familiar environment. The comfort and personalized service is evident in every store, though each club has its own director.

This interview is with Tina Sussman of "Personal Shopping" at Bergdorf Goodman in New York City.

The personal shopping department was started by Betty Halbreich more than twenty-five years ago.

▶ **How does this service work, and can anyone take advantage of it?**

We select single pieces, special occasion clothing, or complete wardrobes. We have thirteen personal shoppers in our department and each has an assistant. The service is available to everyone, at no cost to them. Most people inquire by phone. They can speak to our concierge to set up an appointment, or they can call the receptionist in the personal shopper department for an appointment. We probably get the most new clients through referrals by other clients.

▶ **What happens in the first meeting?**

Most of our clients are very busy, and it is more convenient for them to discuss preliminary information on the phone. During this first call, we get to know each other, develop a sense of their needs, and find out which designers or styles they currently wear. If they want to discuss a budget, we do that. We let everyone know that this is not an exclusive service—we provide services for casual clothing, accessories, party dresses and gowns, and even furs.

▶ **Describe what kind of person uses this service.**

Many of the clients are already Bergdorf customers but want a better way to navigate the store. This service is very appealing to busy people from all sectors: stay-at-home moms, businesspeople, people visiting on business and, of course, tourists. We have young teens who come in alone, very independent, to shop the fifth floor for jeans and T's, and trendy, funky clothing. We also have octogenarians. Many people come into the city just to shop at Bergdorf's. Because we offer so many services, they can "one-stop" shop, and then go back home.

▶ **How does this service save people time and aggravation?**

Most people make appointments, which is the most efficient way to use a personal shopper, but we do have "walk-ins" as well (especially tourists). With thirteen personal shoppers we usually have someone available to help them, or we will try to clear our schedule within an hour. If we cannot help them immediately, we ask them to come back after lunch. We also have restaurants in the store, and we often treat the customer to lunch while they wait.

We gather outfits and complete ensembles with all the accessories and have them ready for the client's arrival. We fit swimsuits, clothing for work, and pieces for special events. As personal shoppers, we can bring merchandise from every department in the store. We offer drinks and, depending on the time of day, breakfast or lunch.

With our newest service, we take merchandise and a fitter to the client's home. While we are there, we can refit other clothing in their wardrobe, survey their closets, and help them organize their clothing more efficiently.

▶ **Bergdorf Goodman is on Fifth Avenue in one of the best shopping cities in the world. What else sets you apart?**
We have a receptionist to greet the clients. Our meeting rooms have windows that face Fifth Avenue and 57th Street. Each room has a beautiful dresser equipped with shoes and accessories—everything needed for fittings. Our department has a small kitchen and a bathroom. Each personal shopper has an office that provides them the privacy and uninterrupted time to make client phone calls, focus on their client books, organize merchandise, and prepare for client meetings.

Most salespeople on the floor stay in one specific boutique or department, but we can provide the client with anything the store offers. We can pull things from the home floor, such as antiques and crystal. We can set up appointments for their hair and makeup, or arrange manicures and pedicures. We also prepare personalized gift baskets year-round for birthdays, holidays, and special occasions. With our assistance, clients can multitask and shop the whole store while they are in the middle of a fitting! What could personify Bergdorf's and New York City more?

We also have a special program for shopping at home. If clients have a Bergdorf charge card, we can send clothing on approval to try on at home, in their leisure. They have three days to decide, and then it is picked up by Federal Express. This service is great for our out-of-town clients, for people who don't travel well, and even for local clients who are too busy to come to the store.

▶ **Describe the relationship you develop with the customer.**
We become very close to our clients. We are invited to their homes and for special occasions with the family. We have seen many of their children grow up.

We e-mail and memo the client with fashion information and dates of events, and we acknowledge their special dates: anniversaries, birthdays.

The husbands count on us to help them with gifts and to keep them in touch with that part of their spouse's interests. The husbands enjoy meeting us, so they can put a face with a name.

▶ **Do you offer personal shopping for men's clothing?**
All of the personal shoppers work with men. We sell only women's clothing at this Bergdorf's, but we take the men across Fifth Avenue to the men's Bergdorf store and work with them there.

▶ **Tell me about trunk shows.**
Trunk shows give the client the opportunity to see the clothing before it gets to the store. They can order sizes from 2 to 16 and see one-of-a-kind designs in unique colors and fabrics. If they want a special sleeve length, or to change the cut of the neck, they can do that. They can also meet the designer. We had Oscar de la Renta here recently. The shows are very festive and, being in New York City, we often have the principal designer come to the show. The clothing is usually in the store in about two months.

This interview is with Donna Dorsch of the "Personal Touch" department at Nordstrom. She is based in McLean, Virginia, but the Personal Touch service is offered across the country.

The Personal Touch department was started around 1981, but the service existed in an informal capacity before that. Nordstrom believes in an entrepreneurial culture—if one store starts a program and it is successful, it often spreads through the company. Personal Touch is now available at most of Nordstrom's full-line stores.

▶ **How does this service work, and can anyone take advantage of it?**
The Personal Touch service provides one-on-one service to any customer who is interested. The service is not intimidating or meant to be exclusive. The wardrobe consultants have their offices and fitting rooms in the women's department of each store. To make an appointment, the client can call the Personal Touch department or just stop by while shopping. Customers are referred by other departments, friends, and relatives.

▶ **What do you do for clients in your first meeting?**
Most clients first contact us by phone. We talk about what they are currently wearing, find out what's on their mind, and what they want to achieve. We have a "formal consultation form" that we fill out with all of the client's vital information. We do some style profiling so we can start to select clothing for them.

For the first meeting in the store, we have potential outfits ready for them that were chosen based on our conversations. We tailor the selection to what we hear on the phone—for instance, a navy suit for work or a special dress for an occasion. We also bring accessories that we think complement the ensemble.

▶ **Describe what kind of person uses this service.**

There's a real need for this service. It's hard to find time to shop in between working, caring for children, and carpooling—especially for women just making it back into the work flow after maternity leave. People change jobs and have to adjust their wardrobe, be it casual or business casual. Maybe the person recently got a promotion and needs some help selecting more professional attire. We also do quite a bit of special occasion shopping for customers who often call in a rush, and then we prepare a selection of styles.

We are very busy with women who consider themselves hard to fit. Many women have concerns with their figure, sometimes unfounded, so we work together to find the most flattering clothing for them.

Our male clients find these conveniences especially appealing. Some men are shopping for suits, but others are making the transition to more casual work clothing and we help them find "dressy casual" that still looks professional. Women often shop for men, so men are comfortable with our consultants, and they get along great together. When the men come in for their appointment, we have preselected furnishings ready for them, such as shirts, ties, belts, and socks. Many men like to "target shop," get in and get out, so they are happy to have us care for them.

▶ **How does this service save people time and aggravation?**

Just having a consultant available to do the legwork and to gather clothing from throughout the store is almost convenience enough. Clients can park their busy day at the door, come into the fitting room relaxed, and let us do the work. The experience is a tremendous equalizer.

▶ **Describe the relationship you develop with the customer.**

Selecting and fitting clothing is a personal experience, and trust is a big part of that experience. Our consultants are intuitive—many were promoted from within our store because they have exceptional people skills. We offer the client our fashion sense, our undivided attention, and our honest opinion—and our clients respond positively to this. Our feeling is that "people shop with people, not with stores."

We get to know our clients and, in many cases, their family and extended family as well. Many mothers bring their daughters and we work with them, too. We talk with the mom about appropriate styles, and sometimes the parent leaves the daughter to work with us privately. We try to give the young girls and teenagers as much freedom as possible to express themselves. This is a great opportunity to teach them how to shop, to organize, and to be responsible. And it's a growing experience for the young ladies.

▶ **What other programs does your department offer?**

We encourage clients to bring their current wardrobe to us so we can assess and update it. We help them "accessorize," which can revitalize older outfits. We also offer complimentary "Wardrobing Seminars" to further the clients' fashion savvy. If clients are interested, we can chart all of their purchases and enter them on our computer. This information will allow us to mail out notices for in-store events with their favorite designer. If clients can't remember a certain purchase, we can check their history for a color or size to save them a return trip to the store. Or, if a friend or relative is shopping for a gift and wants to know what size the client wears, we can check the client's purchase history.

We do special-occasion shopping for both men and women. Some of our stores offer a "Holiday Wish List." Clients can enter preferences and we can check that list for suggestions, which makes gift selection easier—especially for the men! Three times a year we have sales, and all our Personal Touch clients will receive a personalized letter alerting them to the sale two weeks to a month in advance so they can call for an appointment. This advance notice applies to the "sneak preview" of new fall merchandise before it makes its way onto the sales floor.

For the customer's convenience, the phone operators at Nordstrom are kept abreast of our whereabouts: they know our appointment and lunch schedules.

▶ **How does this service change the way people look at themselves?**

Some clients come in with a preset image of themselves, and we help them reach their goal. Sometimes they surprise even themselves by making some definitive changes on their own. Others want guidance from the start, and over time they develop their own personal style. At the same time, we try to abolish the adage "a closet full of clothing and nothing to wear" by reopening their eyes to what they already own. Sometimes people haven't shopped for years, literally, and are looking for help. For them, we believe "a perfect wardrobe needs a perfect plan," and we help them develop that plan. The whole process is a growing experience.

This philosophy extends to the relationship clients develop with the fitter. At Nordstrom, some fitters may do the sewing as well. This relationship further cements the client's comfort and trust.

▸ **Tell me about trunk shows.**

We notify clients of the upcoming shows. Some clients come to the event, but many times we will actually shop the event for them. We prepare the selection along with accessories; then we call the customer to come in and try on the clothing. We send out trend reports to Personal Touch clients to give them a heads-up on coming fashions.

◆ My Take

It is clear to me that all the people interviewed are very committed to their clients. They love their work and are eternally patient. They are truly offering a unique brand of service—one that will continue to grow as the news gets out. My only goal in conducting these interviews is to convey what these people had to say. I did prompt some information from them based on my considerable experience with retail and based on the feedback I have received from shoppers.

In this section, I have conveyed options that are available to almost everyone, on many levels. The next time you feel that you're ready to throw in the shopping bag, think about these interviews.

The Ultimate Helper is in the back section of this book. That section has removable worksheets for *shopping guides*, bridal gowns, christening gowns, and leather and suede. Tear out the perforated sheets to take with you the next time you go shopping for clothing.

Chapter 2

Fabric Basics

◆ Identifying Fabrics — The Visual and Touching Experience

Touching can be an art form. When you shop, your eyes may initially draw you to the garment, but your hands immediately follow. Your eyes introduce you to the fabric; touching it completes the experience. Touching elicits a response, which in turn stimulates other senses and starts you thinking.

When I walk the floor of a clothing store and peruse the racks, my fingers are sending me messages. For example, acetate feels rough and synthetic, silk is soft and rich, linen feels flat and one-dimensional, a wool-cashmere blend is soft and luxurious, and rayon can feel like many different fabrics. If you think of clothing from a "tactile point of view," it sends you impulses. When you learn about fabrics, let your fingers tell you the following:

> **Wrinkle Warning**
> Wrinkled clothing should not be re-ironed or pressed if soiled. The heat that accompanies pressing may "set" stains and soil, making future removal difficult.

- ▶ **Acetate** — Thick texture, but it can shine when pressed, and it snags easily.
- ▶ **Silk** — Beautiful drape, but maintenance is high, and underarms can discolor in one wearing.
- ▶ **Linen** — Rich looking, but must be re-ironed every time it's worn.
- ▶ **Wool** — Usually soft and thick; most wool won't have to be pressed after each wearing. It is good for travel.
- ▶ **Rayon** — Great textures, but water sensitive; it can become spotted from raindrops.

See the difference this time through?

Learning fabrics can save you time when you shop and stretch your wardrobe dollar. That theme recurs throughout this book. Knowing which fabrics will wear well—which will pill, snag, or prematurely fade—will help you become more discriminating and more self-sufficient. (See "Fabrics at a Glance" at the end of this chapter.)

◆ Blended Fabrics

Blended fabrics open a new world of choices. They can make identification diffi-cult on first touch, but you can learn to recognize a blend, and you can check the fabric content label. Manufacturers use blended fabrics to attain a certain feel or texture, to make a pure fabric more interesting or useful, often to make a fabric more durable and, occasionally, to make it more affordable. Blends may also require more attention when cleaning and ironing, and especially during stain re-moval, so be aware of this when you shop.

Advantages of Blended Fabrics

Blends can aid in shape retention and can add body and drape. They also make beautiful materials.

Cotton-knit sweaters, as a rule, have poor memory retention. Repeated wearing or pulling on and taking off can cause the collar, cuffs, and waist to stretch out of shape. Washing and drying, or drycleaning, may help retighten the fabric in these troubled areas, depending on the type of weave, but many times it does not. Some cotton fabrics have more stretch and memory retention than others. If cotton knits were "blended" with some synthetic, such as Lycra or spandex, then this problem would not exist. Blending cotton with spandex has spawned a breed of "stretch-cotton" designs for casual blouses and slacks that are becoming a mainstay in the fashion world. The stretch materials used in these slacks help to produce a flattering line while simultaneously reducing "bagging" at the knees.

> **A Great Blend**
> The new cotton stretch jeans that are very popular have Lycra or spandex—a great blending of materials.

Keep an open mind as you shop, and consider the downfalls of certain fabrics. Try to see the patterns, recognize the trends in blends, and if you get burned, make a note to avoid that blend in the future. This is a new frontier, and the data are still forthcoming.

Downside of Blended Fabrics

The downside of blended fabrics is most evident in the restoration phase. Clean-ing and pressing bring out some of the problems with some blends, but the stain-removal phase is even more telling. Remember, not all blends are created equally.

Rayon, silk, and linen, as well as many synthetics, all have their quirks as fabrics, but at least they are pronounced and predictable (linen wrinkles easily, etc.). But when they are *blended*, sometimes the worst in each material becomes evident. In some garments, manufacturers have used four or five different materials, which can make drycleaning difficult. We do know that certain silk-linen blends and rayon-linen blends do not release stains easily and, on occasion, they have been literally impossible to restore after certain spills. These same stains, under the same conditions, have been safely removed in a 100% silk or 100% linen, unblended. Read the care and content labels before you buy. (See Chapter 1 for an in-depth view of care labels.)

◆ Common Fabric Problems

Some of the conditions listed here may not have a remedy, but at least you will recognize them when they happen and—one hopes—in many cases before they happen. These hints will definitely help you prevent damage to your clothing.

Color Loss
When fabrics lose color as a result of rubbing, bleaching, staining, or fading, there is usually no remedy. Drycleaners do have access to "dye pads," which they can use to add color back to the affected areas, but there are two problems: the color choices are limited, and the added dyes "wash out" each time they are drycleaned.

Deluster
When a fabric is rubbed with a dry or wet cloth, surface fibers are broken. These fibers lose surface dye and become abraded. If you look closely, you will see small "hairs" or fibers sticking up. Simply said, when you rub a stain in an attempt to remove it, you usually deluster the fabric permanently. Some drycleaners do offer mineral-oil treatments that help the fibers "lie down" to disguise the deluster. This can be quite effective but, like dye pads, the oil treatments also wash out the next time the item is drycleaned.

Dye Bleed
Although washable clothing may occasionally bleed from a spill or in washing, dye bleed is a more prevalent problem with dryclean-only garments. Water, in any form, can cause dyes to bleed: during hand or machine washing, from rain or snow, from drink spills (especially alcohol), and during attempted stain removal.

> **Misconception**
> Most people naturally assume that the best way to remove a stain is to grab the nearest napkin or towel, dip it in water, and rub until the stain is gone. *Never* rub, blot instead, and always think twice before using water, soap, or detergent.

Here are three examples:

▸ Striped, two-toned, and printed designs are susceptible to dye bleeding when they get wet. The darker or more vibrant the dye, the more likely it will bleed. Sometimes one color out of five in a particular print may be unstable. The manufacturer's responsibility should be to make sure the colors do not bleed.

▸ Many muted colors, upon closer examination, are actually two individual colors woven closely together. What looks like a gray "mix" is actually a blend of black and white threads (sometimes referred to as salt and pepper). Black dyes often have "extra" dye and, when wet, some of the extra dye can bleed into the lighter colors next to it.

If you spill a drink or use water to remove it, and the black and white threads become gray in that area, it is because the black dye has bled. If the area bled from water that easily, it will probably bleed when the drycleaner tries to restore it. Such unstable dyes make many stains difficult to remove. There is usually no cure for this type of dye bleed.

> **Spot Removal**
> If a spot or spill has water in it, it will probably need water to remove it. But many fabric dyes are water sensitive and occasionally bleed during stain removal.

▸ Most leather belts, straps, and handbags will bleed when wet. Depending on the color of the dye and the type of material the dye has bled onto, these stains can be difficult to remove and are often permanent. This type of dye bleed can be considered a dye-transfer as well. Be very careful with leather items in the rain and snow.

Dye Transfer

Dye transfer is different from dye bleed. With dye transfer, the "fugitive" (or secondary dye) comes from an outside source, not from the color woven next to it. Dyes can transfer when they are wet or dry. "Dry" dye transfer (such as from a shoulder bag rubbing) normally affects the surface of the garment and is easier for the drycleaner to remove than "wet" dye transfer (from a wet shoulder bag rubbing), which occurs from contact with water or perspiration.

Here are five examples:

▸ A strap from a briefcase or shoulder bag rubs along your shoulder or elsewhere, and it deposits a surface dye. This condition is more obvious with dark dyes on light clothing. Be aware of this problem in your daily routine.

▶ The waistband of a dark skirt, moist with perspiration, can transfer dye onto a white blouse that is tucked in. If you will always tuck in the blouse, however, this occurrence will be of little concern.

▶ When the dark lining of a jacket is wet with perspiration, it can leave purple rings on the underarms of a blouse or shirt. This occurrence is common at formal events. If the blouse is white or off-white, a skilled drycleaner probably can remove the fugitive dye.

▶ A formal black bow tie, wet with perspiration, can deposit dye onto the collar of the white formal shirt. This situation usually is an easy restoration for drycleaners.

▶ When a loose black sock or a dark item bleeds in the washer, it can cause dyes to transfer onto the rest of the load. This type of dye transfer is more difficult to remove; the dyes are wet, many colors are affected, and the clothing is not usually valuable enough for the drycleaner to get involved. Products are available to consumers that remove these dyes, but unless the garments are white, it is almost impossible to remove the dye or to remove it safely.

On the Bright Side: Most dyes that have transferred onto white garments can be improved. Drycleaners skilled in stain removal may be able to use a "dye stripper" to improve or remove the secondary dye. But dyes that have transferred onto colored garments are nearly impossible to remove.

Dye Fading

Once the dye on a fabric has faded, there is no remedy. Fading can occur from direct exposure to light, natural as well as incandescent or fluorescent. Dye fading can also be localized—such as just on the shoulder—from prolonged storage in the closet without protection. If the drycleaner packages your clothing with a paper "shoulder cape," leave it on until the next time you wear that garment. If the clothing will be in the closet for a prolonged period, drape an old cotton sheet over the top of your hanging clothing. This method can cover six linear feet at a time.

Fabric Pilling

Raw-silk jackets, sweaters, and knitted clothing are susceptible to pilling. These pills can be shaved, but each time they are shaved, the fabric thins. (See Chapter 22 for an in-depth examination of fabric pilling.)

> **Fact about Dying**
> Once it has faded, most clothing cannot be redyed back to life. "After-market" dye jobs are rarely acceptable in appearance.

Holes: Cotton and Linen

Just a few words about holes, but ones worth mentioning: cotton jersey polo shirts often develop small holes. This condition is common and should not be associated with poor drycleaning or washing practices. It has more to do with tensile strength and fiber construction. If you see holes appear after just weeks or a few months, consult your retailer.

Linen clothing, especially thinner linen, can develop holes prematurely. Linen is a strong fiber but is easily damaged by starching or creasing. Although most people prefer linen to have some starch to control the wrinkles, starch does cause the fibers to crack. This situation affects all colors, but the darker the dye, the more brittle the fabric. You will see holes form in black linen clothing much faster than they do in lighter colors.

Insect Damage

If you see small holes in your wool clothing that do not appear to be tears, they may be a result of insect damage. Insects are attracted to uncleaned clothing, especially wool and silk. Moths, silverfish, and crickets, to name a few, can do massive damage to clothing. Be sure to clean your clothing before seasonal storage, keep the clothing away from moisture and high humidity, and be proactive if you see any unfamiliar holes. Take the garment to your drycleaner to be assessed before you have a widespread problem. (See Chapter 28 for more on insect damage and proper storage.)

Snags

Snags are common on jersey, certain acetate, chiffon, satin lapels, and certain knitted fabrics. Some snags can be "pulled through" the fabric, and some can be stopped from becoming larger, but most are not restorable. Be careful with belts, watches, jewelry, handbags, buttons, and beads that have pronged settings because they all contribute to snagging.

Yarn Slippage

When a fabric does not stretch and then is stressed, the yarns will separate or tear. Silk, satin, organza, and chiffon are most susceptible to yarn slippage. If you have seen fabric separation under the arms, at the waist, along seams, and across the back of your clothing, it is usually yarn slippage. This condition also is an early sign that the clothing may be too tight in those areas. There is no remedy for this condition other than adding extra material to ease the fit in that area. Yarn slippage may become worse when the area gets wet with water or perspiration, which is commonly seen in the underarms of silk garments.

Weakened Fibers

Food stains, spills, sunlight, bleaches, scorching from an iron, and exposure to household chemicals can weaken fibers at an alarming rate. Depending on the type of fabric, stains such as ketchup, soda, juices, and oily stains, left untreated for weeks or months, can severely weaken a fabric and may lead to holes. Always dryclean or wash (whichever is applicable) stained clothing as soon as possible and try to identify the cause of the stain for your drycleaner.

◆ Synthetic Fibers versus Natural Fibers

Natural fibers include silk, wool, cotton, ramie, linen and, to some extent, rayon and microfiber.

Synthetic fibers include polyester, acetate, triacetate, nylon, acrylic, and many others.

Breathing

Natural fibers are cooler to wear than synthetics. They breathe better than synthetics, allowing air in and out. Some new exercise and work-out fabrics challenge this theory, but for casual and dress wear, natural fibers are still cooler.

Perspiration

Perspiration damages most fabrics. Natural fibers, especially proteins such as silk and wool, can change color under the arms after one wearing. Perspiration can also weaken natural fibers. Silk-knit sweaters react very badly to perspiration, and the odor can sometimes be impossible to remove. Most synthetics are more resistant to perspiration damage and color changes. (See Chapter 7 for preventive measures.)

Travel

Travel can really determine fabric selection. Nonwrinkle fabrics are readily available these days and may travel well, but many are not very flattering. Most synthetics, especially polyester, are also wrinkle resistant. Wool, long considered the best fabric for traveling, still remains an excellent choice. Selecting the proper weight garment for the appropriate weather will increase your satisfaction. If the clothing has been folded or placed in a wardrobe bag, hanging it up as soon as possible will help remove creases and relax wrinkles. Packing clothing with stuffing tissue, available at stores and shipping services, can be an excellent deterrent to wrinkles and creases.

Wear and Longevity

Nothing can challenge the longevity of synthetics. They are man-made and usually durable, but they are susceptible to processing problems, such as poor pressing and poor stain removal (particularly oil stains), depending on the fabric. Some synthetics do pill or lose their finish faster than certain natural fibers.

Storage

Natural fibers, especially proteins such as silk and wool, are very susceptible to insect damage. Fading from light exposure is a concern for all fibers. For long-term storage, consider a temperature-controlled environment for natural fibers. (Storage facilities are available through most full-service drycleaners.) If you store clothing yourself, remember to allow the clothing to breathe and be aware of moths, silverfish, and crickets. Synthetic fabrics have very few insect problems, but fading is a universal concern. (See Chapter 28 on storage.)

Note: For more information about how fabrics can be affected, see Chapter 8 on stains, Chapter 10 on finishing, and Chapter 28, which includes information on insects.

Fabrics at a Glance: Fabric Table

This fabric table is not based on a textbook. It is based on real cleaning, pressing, and storage experience from years of hands-on care. All fabrics should be cleaned before storing.

Fabric	Body & Drape	Stain Fragility	Deluster, etc.	Pressing	Insect Damage
Acetate	Has thick texture; good body	Protein stains; milk and certain foods	Rubbing will deluster fabric easily; snags	Needs soft pressing or will shine	No insect problems
Cashmere	Soft, rich drape	Hard-to-remove yellow stains; cannot bleach	May pill — depends on quality	Steam only	Moths, crickets, and carpet beetles
Chiffon	Beautiful drape; flows	Fragile—no home spotting	Do not rub; snags easily; yarn slippage	Steam and iron	Clean before storing
Cotton	Thin cotton wrinkles easily	Responsive to stain removal; dark colors are fragile	Durable but rubbing will chafe fabric	May need hot iron; be careful of shining	Silverfish and crickets
Cotton Knit	Can become stiff if washed	Coloring from foods are difficult to remove	Do not rub; will chafe fabric	Steam and block	Silverfish and crickets
Gabardine (Wool)	Good body; travels well	Stain removal is good, but protein stains are hard to remove.	Durable fabric; rubbing will affect dark colors	Shines easily from wear and poor pressing	Moths, crickets, and carpet beetles
Knits (Generic)	Good body; travels well	Stain removal good; milk, protein are difficult; spills are difficult	Snags easily; can unravel	Steam and block to shape	If wool, very susceptible

Fabric	Body & Drape	Stain Fragility	Deluster, etc.	Pressing	Insect Damage
Linen	Wrinkles fast; travels poorly; crisp with starch	Colors are fragile; color loss is common	Color fades from rubbing; black and navy fabric prone to holes	Needs hot iron; starch will stain dark colors; could wrinkle permanently	Silverfish and crickets
Microfiber (Generic)	Good body; travels well	Protein stains; milk, soda	Can deluster, but durable	Soft press; tends to shine	Silverfish and crickets
Organza	Firm drape; creases can be permanent	Very fragile; cannot spot too aggressively	Deluster; yarn slippage; do not rub	Needs careful ironing; steam	Susceptible
Polyester	Good body; travels well	Most stains are removed easily; oily stains may be difficult	Durable; dark colors may fade	Steams easily; most press without shine	No real concern
Rayon (Many varieties)	Good body; most travel well	Water stains; spills; protein sensitive!	Reasonably durable	Soft press and steam	Silverfish
Satin	Rich drape; travels well	Sensitive to perspiration; spot protein and spills on reverse side	Can deluster easily; snags	Iron on reverse side and steam; can shine	Moths and crickets
Silk (Crepe de chine)	Rich drape; most travel well—add tissue	Perspiration; perfume; protein stains	Can deluster easily; snags, yarn slippage—especially underarms	Soft press and steam; be careful of double-thick areas	Moths and crickets—especially raw silk
Taffeta	Firm drape; must add sizing	Perspiration; perfume; protein stains	Can deluster easily; snags	Hand iron and steam; careful of double-thick areas	Moths and crickets

Fabric	Body & Drape	Stain Fragility	Deluster, etc.	Pressing	Insect Damage
Velvet	Good body; travels well; do not fold without tissue	Almost every stain is damaging; water-based and perspiration are the worst	Do not rub when wet, will crush pile easily	Steam only; cannot iron or press	Be careful with silk velvet
Wool (Flannel, fine)	Good body; travels well	Protein stains and perspiration	Durable, but still susceptible	Soft press to avoid shine	Very prone to damage; moths, crickets, and carpet beetles; check well for insects; **must** clean before storage!

―――――――――――――――――

People spend hours reading and researching before they purchase stereo equipment, televisions, automobiles, and other high-priced possessions. Clothing can last longer than many of these items, and can be just as expensive, relatively speaking; but where is the research when it comes to shopping and clothing-care?

Developing your knowledge of fabrics and their care can be an invaluable addition. Imagine walking up to a rack of clothing armed with all this information. The experience will change your buying habits forever. Your hands and eyes will not fail you!

―――――――――――――――――

Chapter 3

Buttons and Trims

Buttons can "make" an outfit. Often, clothing manufacturers and designers create an element of obsolescence by making buttons unique to each garment or ensemble. New York City has stores that sell only buttons. Some collectors disassemble vintage clothing, keeping the buttons and discarding the rest. As with other topics, I have plenty to say about buttons.

◆ Button Styles

Fabric-Covered Buttons

Covered buttons can be fragile depending on the material used. Most are covered with the same fabric as the outfit—silk, crepe, satin, and so forth. These buttons rarely break, but they do fray or tear. They can fray from the friction in drycleaning, and if they are not protected, they eventually become bare in areas. If extra material can be found inside a pocket or cuff, and the "shell" of the button can be opened and reclosed, a good seamstress or tailor can remake a button. If the button cannot be opened, new shells are available in various sizes and can be purchased from a fabric store.

Frayed button

Wrapped and Glued Buttons

Buttons that have been wound or wrapped are more fragile than covered buttons. These dome-shaped buttons, that look as though they have been made with wound rope, are usually glued together. When these buttons fray on the edges, they eventually unravel as the glue begins to dry out and then each layer unfolds like a snake rising from a basket during the Indian flute song. These layers can sometimes be reglued with some success. Buttons that are assembled with wax are more likely to unravel than the glued counterparts are.

Wrapped buttons unravelled

31

Note: Have wrapped or glued buttons removed before drycleaning because dry-cleaning solvents usually dissolve glue and wax. Some of the glue can bleed onto the garment and then can be difficult to remove safely.

Shell and Pearl Buttons

Shell buttons have become a mainstay in clothing design. They can be designed in many shapes, sizes, colors, and textures. They are expensive and often unique. They can be wafer-thin and scalloped, thick and round like a coin, oblong with uneven surfaces, or virtually any shape the designer wants and can afford to make. Shell buttons can be dyed to match an outfit, brushed or buffed to a desired texture, and emblazoned with a design or logo. All of these beautiful creations lead to one conclusion: These buttons are fragile and often not replaceable.

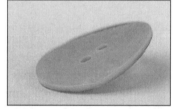

Scalloped wafer-thin shell button

Pearl buttons are typically shaped like a ball, occasionally oblong, and are usually seen on wedding gowns. They are also used for trims. These buttons, which are not "real" pearls, can peel from wear, friction, and drycleaning solvents. They are easier to replace than shell buttons and should be available at most fine fabric stores.

Brass-Colored Buttons

Brass buttons are used on all types of clothing, but especially on jackets. These buttons can be solid brass, brass coated, cast, or hollow. The solid buttons are rich looking, heavy, and difficult to maintain. The shanks are soldered or cast, and they can break easily. They can lose their finish from normal wear, exposing the gray metal base. If solid buttons are not properly protected prior to drycleaning, the soft alloys can change shape and in one cleaning look old or worthless. Brass buttons can be embossed with designs and logos, most notably done by Burberry of London, Gucci, and Ralph Lauren.

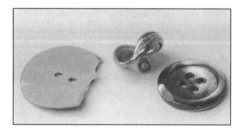

Cracked shell and peeling brass-plated button

Ironically, the "fake" cast buttons, hollow and light in weight, are much more durable. Hollow buttons do not look as formal or rich, but they can be cast in any shape, embossed with any design, and are less expensive. If you *gently* tap a button on a front tooth or a tabletop, you can hear and feel the difference between a hollow and a solid button.

Inlaid Buttons

Buttons with inlaid stones or chips, either glued or set inside bezels, are fragile and heavy. They are truly a work of art and should be treated as one. Some are mass-produced "zirconium-type" buttons with settings that are more easily replaced, but most buttons of this genre are unique. Stones and chips do fall out of settings and need to be reglued. Replacing a missing or damaged button that will match the set is difficult and sometimes impossible. Pronged settings may have exposed jagged edges that can snag clothing. Feel the edges of the setting to make sure that this will not happen to your clothing. Although this may sound extreme, the edges of the setting can be lightly sanded with an emery board to soften metal burrs and minimize damage.

Plastic Buttons

You may be surprised to hear that the plastic button may be high maintenance as well. Although most plastic buttons are durable, some are unique and fragile in design.

Basic plastic buttons found on most suits, pants, and casual wear are made in common shapes and colors. Black buttons are easily replaced at the button store and at the drycleaners. The problems start when the buttons are dyed to match a fabric, are thin-ridged opposed to rounded, or are attached to imported or designer clothing. Because the buttons are plastic, most consumers and most drycleaners have come to automatically assume that the buttons are durable or replaceable.

When buttons became a design issue that distinguished one designer from another, plastic buttons became as individual as shell buttons. Most imported and designer clothing is now outfitted with unique buttons, many of which are made in shapes and shades specific to the outfit. Each season the buttons change and replacement of one button often necessitates replacing the whole set.

Shirt Buttons: In the Laundry

Finer dress shirts made by Brioni, Borelli, and other high-end designers have ultra-thick shell buttons that are difficult to replace. Only a handful of laundries in the country will have these buttons available, so get a bagful when you purchase these types of shirts. (For more on men's shirt buttons, see Chapter 17.)

◆ Button Breakage and Protection

Why Buttons Break

Shell, brass, glass, inlaid, and some plastic buttons are susceptible to chipping, cracking, and breaking. Shell buttons, depending on design, can be as fragile as glass. Brass buttons can lose their finish and become misshapen and battered, and plastic buttons with raised edges can chip badly, exposing the white core underneath.

Protecting Buttons

Drycleaners use various types of gadgets to protect buttons during cleaning. The most widely used method is to wrap thick aluminum foil around the buttons, but this process is marginally effective. Many cleaners are using a Velcro® enclosure the size of a ravioli. (I tested, manufactured, and marketed the Velcro version, referred to generically as hook and loop, and I sold it around the world until a larger company knocked it off and began selling it.) The hook-and-loop version has been rock solid, and it has satisfactorily protected many of the buttons that at one time had to be removed and resewn before and after cleaning.

Protecting buttons during cleaning should be a routine process, but too often the cleaners are not in touch with this nuance. Use this knowledge to your advantage.

Buttons to Be Concerned About

▶ Very thin or scalloped shell buttons, which are fragile to begin with, may chip or break from the agitation in cleaning, regardless of protection.

▶ Buttons between the sizes of a quarter and a fifty-cent piece, which are heavier than a fifty-cent piece, may wiggle their way out of the Velcro protector.

▶ Heavy domed buttons, typically made of a metal alloy, are prone to shifting in the Velcro protector and may become damaged.

▶ The cleaning solvent may cause glued-on stones and chips to become loose.

▶ Leather-covered buttons may bleed or fade. They can be tested before cleaning.

Bottom Line: Buttons that are unique, expensive, painted, large, heavy, or odd shaped should be judged on a per-case basis. For these buttons, removal is probably the safest approach.

◆ Melting, Fading, and Resewing

Melting

Plastic buttons have been known to melt in drycleaning solution, but it is more common for a plastic button to become tacky or dull. The heat from a shirt pressing machine, which is hotter than a drycleaning garment press, can melt the small plastic "domed" button sometimes used on tuxedo shirts.

Bleeding

Some dark plastic buttons bleed during steaming and pressing. We had a crème silk blouse with dark purple buttons, and moments after the steam was used to remove wrinkles, the dye bled under each button onto the silk fabric. We removed the buttons, used a dye-stripper, and recleaned the blouse (fortunately the blouse was white and could be stripped). Wooden or painted buttons occasionally bleed during the finishing process as well.

Fixing Dye Loss and Fading

Cleaning solvent can fade buttons and cause dye loss on parts of buttons. Redying buttons is not an option, but they can be touched up with colored markers. This method can be a long-term solution with porous buttons, but some buttons may need to have the marker reapplied after each cleaning. Leather buttons that have faded can also be touched up this way.

Plastic buttons that have faded or dulled can have a mineral or vegetable oil applied that may restore the depth of color. Small chips on ridged buttons can sometimes be touched up with a marker, and if it is a small enough chip, the white core can be effectively disguised.

Removing and Resewing Buttons

Before button protectors were used, some drycleaners spent several hours a day removing and resewing buttons. This process is expensive and time-consuming, and the repeated use of sewing needles in the same area weakens fibers. Some button holes are fragile and constant handling during sewing can damage them.

▸ Buttons should be removed and resewn by a skilled person. They should be resewn in the same manner in which they were originally sewn.

▸ If the button has a long, sewn shank, as do many overcoat and inside suit buttons, bring this to the attention of the seamstress so that it can be replicated.

▸ Buttons are occasionally misplaced after being removed.

▸ If you are unsure if a button should be removed, consult your drycleaner. If there is any uncertainty, go ahead and remove the button. It's the prudent decision.

Missing and Extra Buttons

Buttons disappear in the oddest ways. Sometimes a button is loose and falls off without your knowledge; buttons can be lost or broken in the drycleaning process; shanks can break during resewing. At times like this, you will wish you had an extra button.

◆ Let's Go Shopping: Buttons

When you shop for finer clothing, be sure to check for extra buttons. You may find an extra button or two hanging from a care label, from the zipper, in a pocket, or sewn to an inside seam. If there isn't one, ask the salesperson to order an extra button or two at the time of purchase. The more unique the button, the more necessary it is to have an extra. If you think that one will be obtainable six months later, think again. On behalf of our customers, and occasionally to get ourselves out of a jam, we have called, written, and sent samples to designers and manufacturers for button replacements.

> **Extra Buttons**
> If you need to call a designer for an extra button, ask for the *alteration* department and offer to send a sample or a fax with a picture.

This method has worked about one-third of the time. It can be a hassle, and it requires persistence. The more trendy or fashionable the outfit, the less successful the chance for replacement. Smaller boutiques are usually more responsive to missing-button requests and, on occasion, they can find an extra button loose in a "button box." Department stores are becoming more helpful and may have more "pull" with the designer. Either way, it is easier to request extra buttons at the time of purchase while the outfit is still in season.

Hint: If you do have extra buttons, designate a place in your jewelry box or dresser drawer where you can put all your extra buttons. If you are unable to find an extra button, there are many button stores in New York City. One of the best known stores is Tender Buttons, and they have a huge selection (212-758-7004).

◆ Trims, Beads, and Sequins

Trims can be attached to clothing by glue, wax, or thread. Trims are rarely governed by the care labels attached to the garment; you may have seen the label that says, "Dryclean-only—exclusive of trims." This situation makes care for these items a separate challenge. Trims are often made of materials different from those on the body of the garment, which is an immediate tip-off that there may be a problem in cleaning.

Trims: Glue or Wax

Glue and wax used on trims can soften, bleed, or disintegrate in drycleaning—some glue disintegrates in water as well. When you purchase a garment with a trim, check it closely for construction materials. These glues and waxes are commonly used on children's dresses that have belts and bows, on formal dresses with flowers and pearls, and on trims at the collar and neckline.

Look within the flowers and bows and around the base of the trim to see if any threads are visible. It is common to have a blend of glued and sewn construction. If you do not see threads woven through the trim, then you can be reasonably certain that an adhesive of some type has been used. If this is the case, check the care label again and speak to a customer service representative for help.

Emblems and crests on jackets, blazers, and trendy designer garments can also be suspect at times. Most are made properly, but a cursory inspection is suggested. Look for dark dyes, pronged settings, and/or glued stones, beads, and metallic threads.

Beads and Sequins

This category is deep, dark, and deceitful! Beads, pearls, and sequins present a tremendous challenge to drycleaners. These fancy adornments are rarely protected by care labels, can be wildly unpredictable in solvents and water, and can rarely be tested successfully enough to make the technician comfortable. Fortunately for the cleaning industry, many drycleaners are now using a mild hydrocarbon solvent that has been successful with most of these trims. Drycleaners that are still using Perc, a more aggressive solvent, are very careful when accepting clothing with trims and beads and may refuse to process certain items. Your best defense is to buy this type of garment from a reputable store. (See Chapter 29 for more on solvents.)

Beads, pearls, and sequins have a multitude of characteristics that may be affected by drycleaning and finishing:

▶ Beads can lose color, change color, or become tacky. They can bleed onto other parts of the garment, or they can completely dissolve.

▶ Hand-painted beads, typically made of wood, may fade but rarely bleed.

▶ Sequins that are flexible or bendable are more colorfast than rigid sequins. Dry-cleaners can test the rigid sequins before cleaning and can usually trust the results.

▶ The pearls that are typically used on bridal gowns and specialty pieces are usually safe in cleaning, although the larger pearls peel faster than the smaller ones. Painted pearls should be tested before they are drycleaned.

▶ Flexible sequins that are flat can curl from direct steam.

◆ Designs: Painted, Raised, and Embossed

Hand-painted clothing, tie-dyed clothing, and garments purchased at art fairs can be surprisingly colorfast. Store-bought garments with care labels are very dependable. Paint that is "sitting" on the surface of the garment may crack, but it rarely bleeds. Raised or embossed paint, such as that used on dots, stars, and lettering, has proven to crack or separate in cleaning. Athletic team or "letter" jackets that have a fabric body with dyed leather sleeves have shown some cracking on the sleeves during cleaning and usually need to be redyed.

◆ Let's Go Shopping: Trims

Check care labels closely when purchasing any clothing with trims, beads, or sequins. Check trims for pronged settings and jagged edges, glues, waxes, and all precariously attached parts. Any unusual designs may create problems, so ask the salesperson for guidance before purchasing, especially if the outfit is expensive. Beaded garments commonly come with an extra packet of beads and sequins. If your garment does not have such a packet, inquire at the time of purchase because you may need extras in the future.

Important Note: If a specialty garment is considered a cleaning risk for any reason, it can probably be spot-cleaned and pressed (oily stains require more care). Spot-cleaning is a legitimate alternative: a garment does not always have to be immersed in solvent to be "cleaned."

◆ At the Cleaners

Check clothing for loose threads and dangling or missing beads and secure those before cleaning. If this is the first cleaning, ask the clerk to examine the beads and sequins to advise on any probable dye bleeding, fading, or melting.

If the garment has trims that are attached by wax, alert the clerk. The garment can be cleaned in a net, and after the wax disintegrates and trims fall off, the seamstress or tailor can reattach them by thread. Bows, belts, and accessories that are poorly attached, or that can be removed and do not need cleaning, should be taken home with you.

If the drycleaner believes your garment is too fragile to clean, and you trust this judgment, consider spot-cleaning. This process can freshen up the underarms and neckline and remove small, obvious stains.

Before you dress for a formal event, or wear a cherished outfit, check to make sure that all the buttons are securely attached—especially if the buttons are heavy. Too often, buttons fall off during wear and are not noticed until it is too late. It will take only a moment to check the buttons, and it may save you the heartache and hassle of replacing a complete set.

Chapter 4

Women's Accessories
Scarves, Bows, Flowers, and Sashes

Accessories can be an important part of an ensemble. They need care and cleaning just like full-sized garments, and in some instances they require more attention. Some of these "moving parts," as I affectionately refer to them, are small or removable and can be easily misplaced. Belts are also an accessory and are discussed in detail in Chapter 6.

This chapter is devoted to the care and maintenance of various fabrics and designs.

◆ Scarves: Silk

Scarves are a mainstay in our wardrobe. They are worn by both men and women as an accent to an ensemble, for warmth, to protect the collar from body oils and cosmetics, and sometimes as a companion.

Silk and Other Fragile Fabrics

Silk scarves with multicolored printed designs often have water-soluble dyes, which means that they may bleed when exposed to rain, perfume, perspiration, or spills. It's ironic that scarves, which are often used to protect clothing, can be damaged by the exact elements from which they are protecting clothes. And what's more baffling is that little can be done to avoid this problem.

When a silk print scarf bleeds from a water-based stain, the affected area generally cannot be restored. Multiple colors make it nearly impossible to remove some dye stains without damaging the other dyes. Larger scarves have layers of fabric that "flow" into folds around the neck, and if dye bleeding does occur, it is often hidden within the folds. Because dye bleed is common with silk, I suggest you accept it as a necessary evil.

> **Stain Inspection**
> At the end of the day, under bright light, inspect your scarves for stains. Check closely for dye bleed as well.

Home Care

Expensive scarves such as those made by Hermes, Gucci, and Chanel are best cleaned professionally. You should not try to remove stains from silk scarves by using soap and water, particularly scarves with printed designs. Solid colors can be hand washed, but the texture may change and the colors tend to fade. If you do have makeup stains or body oil stains, then you should have the scarves cleaned within a few days. Do not inadvertently put the scarf back in the drawer because the next time you look at it the stains may be set.

If you have only makeup stains and you plan to wear the scarf again soon, then you can probably wait a week, maybe two.

Care for Pleated Scarves

A few designers are making scarves with "accordion pleats" that are very beautiful, a true work of art. The problem with accordion-pleated silk scarves is that the pleats are often removed by water. This means that if you get the scarf wet or so badly stained that the cleaner needs to use an abundance of water to improve the stains, then you run the risk of losing the pleats in that area. It is very difficult to have this type of scarf re-pleated.

◆ Scarves: Other Fabrics

Wool scarves are dependable in all colors. Camel, cashmere, mohair, and other wool blends are very stable. They should be cleaned as needed, but certainly at the end of the season to protect them from insect damage. Special fabrics, such as rayon and acrylic, are also dependable. Some are washable; check the care label.

Chenille

Chenille scarves are soft and shimmery but are very water sensitive. Liquid spills of all varieties can change the nap, which may dull the finish permanently. The scarves can unravel and snag easily. Chenille scarves should always be drycleaned unless otherwise specified.

Velvet, Chiffon, and Taffeta

Velvet is extremely water sensitive and the nap is easily crushed when wet. Velvet is a formal pile fabric and should be worn with care. Silk chiffon is one of the most fragile fabrics made. It also is weaker when wet, which makes it susceptible to yarn slippage. This condition is difficult to improve. Taffeta has firm body and drape, it is a strong weave, and stain removal is manageable. Taffeta must, however, have sizing added after cleaning to restore the body and drape.

◆ Bows, Flowers, and Sashes

Bows and Flowers

These accessories tend to pick up small spots and spills, especially when attached to a child's dress. If they do not have stains and appear to be properly shaped, it is best to remove the accessories from the garment before cleaning. If they do need steaming or pressing, remove them from the garment and make sure the drycleaner writes them up as a separate piece so that they will not be misplaced.

Bows and flowers can often be spot-cleaned (stain removal without immersion), which is the best way to retain the body, shape, and drape. If they are over-cleaned, you may have a drooping flower or a flat bow.

Sashes

A sash usually comes sewn on as part of the garment, tacked on by a stitch, or held on by loops. Sashes usually "fly in the wind," so they get into everything: plates of food, drinks, makeup, and any other accidents waiting to happen. After wearing, be sure to inspect the sash well and have it cleaned and spotted as needed. If it does not need cleaning or pressing, then don't do it. If you are concerned that the color won't match after the garment is cleaned, don't be; it's a rare occurrence. If the color does change, then you can have the sash cleaned as well.

◆ Specific Stains

Perfume

Perfume is the "invisible" killer. Perfume stains can go virtually undetected until they have turned a pale yellow, at which point it is sometimes too late to remove the stain entirely. For this reason, identifying the stain for your drycleaner is very important.

Cooking Oils and Fruits

Splatters, squirts, and drips from cooking oils and fruits are often invisible when they occur. If left alone at room temperature, however, they can oxidize or caramelize and turn yellow. Yellow is often a sign that discoloration is permanent.

> **The Apple Story**
> Take a bite of an apple, leave it for five minutes, and look at the result. This discoloration mirrors the way a stained garment looks after being stored for a few weeks or months.

◆ At the Cleaners

Inspect your scarves for makeup, lipstick, dye bleed, and invisible stains (to catch them before they yellow). Silk scarves are often hand sewn along the edges and occasionally need to be re-stitched. Remind the clerk that the edges are to be rolled, not pressed flat.

Bows and flowers should be hand spotted and hand ironed, if possible, to minimize distortion. If they must be cleaned, ask to add extra sizing so that they will look fresh and full. Sizing will help the flower petals open up and will keep bows from flopping over. Sashes should be inspected for food stains and makeup, and the edges should be soft pressed to avoid shine.

Chapter 5

Pleats, Textures, and Linings

Pleated garments are stylish and flattering, but they are expensive to maintain. This chapter teaches you aspects of construction, how they affect your choices when shopping, and how to care for pleated garments on a daily basis.

◆ Before Shopping

Pleat Styles

There are three primary pleat styles for skirts: knife, box, and accordion. Knife pleats are the most common. They are sewn into place at the waist, or a few inches below, and the stitching sets the lines or creases for the pleats. Box pleats are less common, but are also stitched into place. Accordion pleats are rarely sewn in from the waist, may have 75 pleats around the skirt and, when spread apart, look like the musical instrument of the same name. This type of pleat can lose its pattern because the pleats are not sewn into place like they are with knife pleats. Skirts made of polyester fabric often have "permanent" knife or accordion pleats that have a "memory" (these pleats are often "heat-set") and require only steaming after cleaning. Any additional ironing during "touch up" would be minor.

Designers also use pleats to accent the front of a blouse, along the sleeves, down the back, and on collars and cuffs.

Are Pleated Garments High Maintenance?

Soft woolens and some rayon fabrics can be worn more than once without re-pleating. Silk, linen, and other similarly fragile fabrics will need to be ironed after each wearing. This fact means that unless you iron them at home, there will be regular trips to the drycleaners. Most pleated garments will need more work on the seat and back areas. Sitting on a chair and leaning against a chair back can wrinkle pleating. If the seat or back of the skirt is moist from perspiration, then the fabric can develop hard wrinkles. This problem can further diminish the possibility of wearing the skirt or blouse again without ironing it first.

Cost of Pleating

Because pleat pressing is done by hand, the price for drycleaning any pleated garment will be higher than drycleaning a garment without pleats. Some drycleaners still charge for each pleat, but most charge by the garment. Box pleats are the easiest, followed by knife and then accordion pleats. The price may also be adjusted according to the length—above the knee or below the knee. The price may increase based on the fabric—soft wool being the easiest, and silk, linen, and gabardine being the most time-consuming and difficult.

◆ Let's Go Shopping

When you shop for clothing that has pleats, consider the cost of drycleaning. Pleats are nearly impossible to iron at home, and most fabrics require a commercial steam iron rather than a typical home-style electric iron. (See Chapter 25 about irons.)

When you look at a pleated skirt on the clothing rack, hold the sides of the skirt down near the hem, spread the hem open like an accordion and see how wide it has become. A typical knee-length pleated skirt opened this way can be five feet wide, and every pleat that you see will have to be hand ironed.

Accordion pleats are the most time-consuming, the most difficult, and the most expensive to iron.

Before you buy a pleated garment, you should check the sewing construction at the top of the pleats as well as down each pleat to make sure that each pleat is secure and even. If pleats are crooked they will only become worse with wear.

> **Cost of Pressing**
> Knife pleats can increase the cleaning price by 30% to 50%. Accordion pleats could be double the price or more.

Important Incidentals

Just because a garment is being sold in a reputable store or boutique, or is made by a well-known designer, does not guarantee that it is easily serviceable. Some garments have pleats with no sewn-in pattern and no memory. This type of garment can lose the pleat pattern from wearing, from water, and sometimes from cleaning or steaming, and it may not be restorable.

> **Survival Care Tip**
> Before purchasing designer clothing with unusual pleating patterns, inquire about care and maintenance.

While these garments represent the minority, the condition is all too familiar. More common are crushed pleats on the seat of accordion-pleated silk skirts that lose their line or pattern and are nearly impossible to completely restore.

Note: The buyer for the clothing store is not necessarily at fault for purchasing difficult and sometimes unserviceable garments. Buyers are not mind readers, and manufacturers do not make it known if the care and maintenance of a garment may be difficult or expensive. That issue is not the buyer's specialty.

Ironing: What Does a Properly Pleated Skirt Look Like?

Each time a pleated skirt or dress is pressed, the pleats must be hand ironed to have a sharp, clean finish. A pleat should have little or no impression from the pleat next to it. Each pleat should be flat, straight (not wavy), and as wide or narrow as the one next to it. This is true for all pleats unless they are designed to be uneven. Not all pleats will be perfect because the outcome also depends on the quality of the fabric and the quality of the original sewing.

◆ Textures

The Crinkle-Wrinkle Look

Many garments have a crinkle look: not quite pleated, yet not quite flat in texture. This type of finish can be perishable. Cotton, rayon, nylon, and polyester fabrics are commonly used for this type of crinkle finish. When you buy a garment with a crinkle look, read the care label closely and take note of the ironing instructions. Can the garment be drycleaned *and* washed? Can it be ironed, or should it be only air dried to maintain the crinkle look? Does it need some special care to restore the crinkled texture after cleaning?

Story Time ...

After managing my drycleaning business for many years, I finally purchased it. On my first day of ownership, a few hours after settlement, I was in my office, my feet up on my desk, drinking champagne and enjoying the moment, when one of my finishers came into the office with a blouse she was having trouble ironing. She showed me a polyester blouse with wrinkles all over it. I asked if she had already tried to remove the wrinkles with a hot-head press, and she nodded yes. I flippantly suggested that she try a shirt press, which is also a hot-head press but much hotter because it is designed for cotton dress shirts. I told her to spray a little water on it before pressing, and I went back to my champagne and balloons.

A week later, one of the clerks came into my office with that same blouse. The customer said that the blouse used to have wrinkles and now it didn't. The customer also said, "The blouse is ruined." It was beautifully ironed, no wrinkles. I read the care label, which said something like, "Use low heat in ironing" or "Do not iron."

I called the customer. She was a regular, and she trusted me implicitly. She said it was new, it was an Issey Miyaki, it was the first time it had been cleaned, and it had cost $300. I didn't argue. I found her another one in a size 2, I gave the "ruined" blouse to my most petite employee, and I moved on.

That was the first "crinkle-wrinkle" garment that I had ever seen. I believe Miyaki was the first to design them, and since then the industry has seen thousands of them in various forms. Had I known then what I know now, I would have re-wetted it, balled it up into a wrinkled mass, and allowed it to air dry. This process works most of the time.

The moral of the story is this: Read all care labels closely when you shop, particularly when purchasing clothing with unique designs or textures. Then share the information with your drycleaner so that the garment can be processed properly.

Note: Many crinkle garments, depending on the fabric and dye, can be twisted like a towel you are wringing out, tied at each end, and allowed to dry. Or you can twist the garment and place it in a nylon stocking to air dry.

◆ Linings: Everything You Need to Know

Most linings are made of rayon or acetate. Silk lining, which is more fragile than synthetic lining, is typically chosen for high-fashion and custom-made clothing. Think of lining as a utilitarian item that protects the outer fabric or shell. It gives the garment body and allows clothing to slide on easily. It reduces friction, which in turn reduces pilling on fabrics with a nap. Lining in slacks, especially the half lining in men's slacks, helps to prolong the life of the pants fabric and to reduce the wear inside the thigh area. Linings also take abuse from wear; they fade, discolor, and occasionally tighten up.

Shrinkage and Stretching
Most lining material is stable or has been preshrunk. Sometimes a lining is sewn and attached to the hem of a garment. When a jacket or coat hem puckers or ripples, it is because the outer shell of the garment has tightened or drawn up. When a lining shrinks it is usu-

> **Lining Fact**
> When a lining is pulled, it weakens. If a jacket or coat is too tight, seams can pull and stitches can break. Inspect the lining hem occasionally as well.

ally the result of becoming overwet from rain or from wet cleaning. Drycleaning solution has little moisture and rarely causes shrinkage.

Other lining materials, such as cotton and wool, may not be as stable. When these linings *do* stretch, they can bag or droop below the hemline. If the lining is wet from rain or perspiration, and then worn in that condition, the lining will probably stretch.

Fading and Discoloration

People are constantly surprised when they notice fading or discoloration in the lining of their clothing. A lining can change color because of prolonged exposure to light, because of perspiration, or because of dye transfer from the garment worn underneath. Perspiration is the most common reason for discoloration. If the color change is under the arm, it is easy to equate the two, but perspiration can also affect the back, sides, and collar. The lining in the upper thighs and crotch area of a pair of slacks can fade from perspiration, urine, and discharge, which chemically may cause the lining to weaken and eventually deteriorate.

Deterioration

If a lining is too tight, then it becomes stressed. The tension pulls on the seams, which either tears or thins the lining material. This problem occurs with skirts, upper-body wear, and the crotch of slacks.

Belts, buckles, metal buttons, and jewelry can all contribute to deterioration of a lining. These objects rub against the same areas of the lining each time you wear them. Repeated friction thins and frays the lining and, over time, holes may develop. This is often a surprise. If you give the lining an occasional cursory inspection, then you may see the chafing in time to identify the object that is causing it.

Customers have expressed their dismay in regard to this deterioration, often assuming that the drycleaning process caused it. The process may speed the deterioration because of the agitation, but it does not cause it. The same is true of lining hems that fall because of faulty stitching, wear, and poor seam binding or fusing. The drycleaning process may aggravate the condition, but it rarely causes it.

Tears from Stress and Faulty Stitching

Lining usually tears from stress because the garment is just too tight. The underarms, inside collar, back vent, kick pleat, and area across the back are the most affected areas. The underarm area often could benefit from better sewing, but kick pleats are typically too long and too tight from the start. Falling hems are usually a result of faulty stitching or poor fusing materials. The stitching inside the sleeve cuffs and inside the hem of slacks is often weak and poorly finished, which also contributes to dangling linings. Retacking these hems should be an ongoing part of normal maintenance.

Lining Restoration

We have seen linings come into the alteration department with every affliction imaginable. In each case, we must decide if they should be repaired, patched, or replaced.

Minor Repairs

The underarm area can be reinforced with better stitching, or you can have underarm shields sewn in that will strengthen the area and help guard against perspiration damage (very effective with jackets and overcoats).

When a lining pulls away from the seam, you should assume that it has become too tight. Simply resewing it will not help the problem; it will probably just tear again. It may need an additional piece of lining material added—perhaps as much as a half inch to an inch.

Vents in dress and overcoat linings tear regularly and reinforcement is usually satisfactory. Torn kick pleats, however, should not be automatically retacked without first assessing the condition: Should extra material be added to allow more lateral movement? Should a triangle of fabric be added to the top of the vent to reinforce the area? If a simple tacking is done and it tears again, then it could become a much more involved repair.

Patches

If an area of the lining is badly torn or shredded, then it is usually more cost-effective to add the material needed to patch it rather than waste the time to restitch it. This type of repair is appropriate and effective. If the area is not visible, then matching the color is not necessary and any swatch will do. If the area is visible, then ask the tailor or seamstress if he or she has fabric to match. If not, then a piece of new lining material can be purchased to match the color and texture. If you are concerned about it looking piecemeal or cheaply patched, then ask the seamstress to replace a complete panel with the closest color and texture so that it will look more aesthetically pleasing.

Relining

If an area is too large to patch or is too weak from deterioration, but the garment is worth restoring, then complete relining is probably the best option. Relining a jacket, coat, or slacks, especially if there are pockets or vents, requires a true artisan. But there are choices you must make, and they require some thought.

▸ First, you should know that relining can be expensive. Relining a jacket can cost between $75 and $150, depending on the type of lining and the amount of detail. Slacks can cost $75 and an overcoat can cost $150 to $200. (All figures are estimates.)

▸ You may want to consult with the seamstress or tailor before automatically choosing to use the same lining material as the original. Ask these questions, of yourself and of the seamstress, to help you assess your next move:

a. Did the first lining wear out prematurely?

b. Am I particularly rough on my clothing?

c. Would a heavier or more durable lining be more appropriate?

d. Does the seamstress have relining experience and samples to show?

A Few More Details about Relining

▸ Recognize that the texture of a lining can change the body and comfort of the garment.

▸ If the garment is fragile, of a particular design, or very feminine, then you should select a lining that will enhance the drape and add a luxurious feel. You would not want to choose a lining that should be used for an overcoat.

▸ Is there an additional charge for higher-quality lining?

▸ Discuss the stitching. Will it be sewn by hand or by machine? Is the style of the stitching or the finishing around the pockets of concern to you?

▸ If there is an embroidered monogram on the lining; can it be duplicated?

▸ Finally, discuss how long it will take so that there will be no misunderstandings.

Pleated skirts can be expensive to shorten. If the waist needs to be altered as well, then the seamstress or tailor may be able to shorten the skirt from the waist instead of from the hem. By doing the waist and the hem at the same time, you may be able to save some money. Most pleated skirts are shortened from the hem, but if the hem is very wide, and many can be double or triple the width of the waistband, the alteration will be more expensive.

Chapter 6

Removable Accessories
Collars and Cuffs, Belts, Underarm Shields, and Shoulder Pads

◆ Collars and Cuffs: Cleaning and Care

The collar and cuffs on an outfit require extra care to keep them looking fresh. If they are the same color as the garment, then the soil may not be as noticeable, but most two-toned or removable collar and cuff sets are designed in white, which presents a special challenge. Removable sets are usually attached to the garment by buttons, snaps or, occasionally, Velcro®.

Fabrics and Soil

The collar can become soiled from perspiration, makeup, body oil, jewelry oxidation and, occasionally, dye transfer from another garment. The cuffs have similar concerns, but are mostly affected by general soil from tabletops and perspiration. A dark-colored garment is often worn once or twice without a thought for the white collar or cuffs. When it's time for drycleaning, the soil suddenly becomes much more obvious. Because of the time that has passed, which could be two weeks or more, the soil can become much more difficult to remove safely, particularly perfume stains.

Perfume is initially invisible but, over time, can turn a muted yellow. Once it turns yellow, it has begun to oxidize and removal is severely hampered. Soil removal is easiest on white cotton, linen, and polyester fabrics. Silk, wool, rayon, and specialty fabrics create a much greater challenge.

> **Soil Control**
> Drycleaning is usually not as effective as wet cleaning on collar and cuff soil. Both processes may be limited by the colorfastness or fabric of the garment.

Removable Collars and Cuffs

It is necessary to thoroughly inspect and possibly clean your collar and cuffs after *each* wearing. When you have a garment with removable collar or cuffs, you might not be cleaning the collar and cuffs every time that you clean the garment. For this reason, collars and cuffs that are attached by buttons, snaps, or Velcro are often more soiled than those that are sewn onto the garment. At first glance, the collar and cuffs may appear to be clean, therefore intentionally separated from the garment when it's time for the trip to the cleaners; but remember, they soil as easily as those that are permanently attached.

Fabric and Design

Removable pieces are generally made of silk, cotton, or acetate. They are usually designed in white, while the rest of the outfit is often a darker color. These accessories are typically attached to dryclean-only garments, which implies that the collar and cuffs should be drycleaned as well. Because the collar and cuffs are not always cleaned with the garment, they become more soiled.

How Collars and Cuffs Become Soiled

Let's examine what challenges these white accessories must endure to remain white.

A white collar, whether it is sewn on or attached by buttons, absorbs body oil, perspiration, makeup, lipstick, perfume, squirts from fruit, and any other errant spill on its way to your lips. If the collar has absorbed even one of these stains, and is overlooked and placed back in the closet, then it may become permanently discolored. It's that easy.

White cuffs are almost the same as a sewn-on napkin. They can get into everything that your hands do. They absorb the same stains that collars do, plus soil from desktops and food from restaurant tabletops. If you have French cuffs, they can develop a dark line on the edge.

> **Soil Sense**
> Dark garments are typically worn twice before cleaning, compared to white garments, which should be cleaned after each wearing. Where does this leave the white collar and cuffs?

Drycleaning and Wet Cleaning

Drycleaning

Drycleaning works very well on oily stains that are detected soon after they occur. The gray soil lines, some of the food stains, and most of the makeup can be greatly improved by drycleaning and special spotting. But perspiration, perfume, and some of the food stains may still remain after drycleaning and may require *wet cleaning*.

Wet Cleaning

Although wet cleaning is the most appropriate process for the removal of water-based stains and any remnant of general soil, not all fabrics are suitable for this process. If you've ever washed a silk garment, you know that the texture usually changes. Silk and acetate fabrics, which are most commonly used for collars and cuffs, can shrink and become rough from wet cleaning. If the collar and cuffs change size or shape, then they may not reattach properly to the garment.

Oily stains are rarely improved by wet cleaning, so drycleaning should be the first process. Wet cleaning before drycleaning may severely limit the future removal of oily stains.

> **Wet Cleaning**
> Wet cleaning is a water-based method used to clean clothing that would normally be drycleaned. This process often is aided by the use of special bleaches. (See the Glossary for the complete story.)

Bleaches—Everyone's Answer-All

Bleach is not a soap and should not be used as a soap substitute. It is most effective when whitening and removing the "last trace" of a stain.

Most color-safe bleach is safe on most fabrics. Chlorine is rarely used by professionals and should *never* be used on silk, acetate, or wool because it will permanently turn the fabric yellow. (This applies to all colors, including white.) Silk can be spotted and wet cleaned, but is limited by the types of bleach that can be used.

White cotton, however, can usually withstand all types of bleach at the proper strength, and can be effective on perfume stains even after yellowing has begun. (For chlorine, use the ratio of one ounce of bleach to one gallon of water.)

The best remedy for stain removal is early detection, identification, and regular cleaning. This may sound like overkill, but neglect will shorten the life of these accessories and could remove them from the ensemble permanently.

What *You* Can Do

▶ After you undress at night, inspect the collar and cuffs in bright light. If you are too tired, be sure to do it first thing in the morning. If stains are visible, do not let them go untreated.

▶ If you perspired or wore perfume, you should have the removable collar drycleaned.

▶ If there is no "visible" staining from the perfume, then point out the area to the drycleaning clerk so that the cleaner can spot it appropriately *before* the stains appear from the heat used in pressing.

▸ If you feel confident about hand washing and air drying a removable set at home, pre-treat the pieces with a gentle soap such as Woolite® and follow the instructions. Then lay flat or hang to air dry. If you see gray soil lines, prespot them with soap and lightly scrub them with a *soft* toothbrush.

▸ If the collar and cuffs are made of silk, then be careful when assessing the type of soil. Many stains that are oily in nature, such as makeup and body oil, may not be removed with soap and water and should be drycleaned before wet cleaning. (See Chapter 8 for stain identification skills.)

▸ If the collar and cuff set is two-toned, then do *not* wet clean it. These items will probably require drycleaning because most two-toned fabrics that bleed in water are usually safe in drycleaning.

Collars and cuffs need extra attention to keep them white. If you've been diligent about maintaining them, then prespotting and drycleaning should be all they need. If they do need wet cleaning to remove heavier soil, then be firm about your expectations when speaking to the cleaner. Just a thought: if the cuffs require wet cleaning but the collar does not, then the shades of white may not match after the process.

Note: If a collar or cuffs has been discolored or ruined by stains, a skilled seamstress or tailor should be able to remake a set. Matching fabrics may be a challenge, but it is an excellent option available to you.

◆ Two-Toned Clothing (Color-Blocked)

I would like to address those garments that are designed with two contrasting colors close to each other and that are *not* removable. An example would be a dark-colored dress with white cuffs, white pocket trim, a white strip down the front placket, or any other similar design. See how prevalent these types of garments are the next time you shop for clothing. Here is a list of concerns:

▸ Dark clothing is often worn twice before it is drycleaned, compared to one time for most white clothing. This means that the light portion of the dark garment will show more soil than the rest of the garment.

▸ Dark clothing is usually drycleaned with other dark clothing. If a garment has a white collar or cuffs or light trims and is drycleaned with the "dark load," then the drycleaner must do something special to keep the white parts white. Drycleaning on its own is not necessarily equipped to keep white trims white; they need more. (Some cleaners may clean trimmed garments in a separate cycle.)

▶ In an effort to keep the white parts white, water-based spot removers and bleaches must be used on the white areas only. If the bleaches touch the dark areas during these attempts, the dark color may lighten or actually lose color.

▶ Water-based stain removers can loosen the dark dyes, especially with silk fabrics, and cause them to bleed onto the white trims. This is a common occurrence, one that severely limits stain removal.

Caring for Two-Toned Clothing: What *You* Can Do

▶ After wearing a two-toned outfit the first time, closely check the trims and contrasting colors.

▶ When you undress at night, inspect the collar and cuffs in bright light. If you are too tired, then be sure to do it first thing in the morning. If stains are visible, then do not let them go untreated.

▶ If you perspired or wore perfume, then you should have the outfit drycleaned within 24 hours.

▶ If there is any evidence of soil, then have the garment drycleaned immediately. Built-up soil from repeated wearing can become exponentially worse. Twice is much more damaging than once, and three times may be an insurmountable challenge. It may be days or weeks before you wear the outfit again, which means body oil and food can oxidize, making stain removal very difficult.

▶ When you shop, think about the maintenance necessary for two-toned clothing. If you are aware of the challenge it poses to you and your drycleaner, then you may be more respectful of the limitations.

Note: I have written hundreds of notes to customers over the years about why their white trims have become "dingy." The majority of our customers were very understanding, but by reading this book you have the opportunity to avoid these problems.

◆ Belts

Belts require extra care to keep them clean and to remain an integral part of your ensemble.

Belt Construction

Many belts are "faced" or covered with the same fabric as the garment. Most belts of this type are *not* intended to be drycleaned. Belts that are constructed with a hard backing made of plastic or paper products can soften or turn brittle in drycleaning solution and are only meant to be spot-cleaned.

Some belts are made with glued layers, which can also present problems. During drycleaning, glue can bleed through to the front, or it can dissolve, causing the belt layers to separate. The layers can also bubble during spot removal.

Many belts have fancy hardware, such as brass or porcelain buckles or leather trims. A Gianni Versace belt we saw recently was made of flexible, "fake" razor blades that were sewn to the waistband of a pair of slacks. Two blades were broken when they were brought to the cleaners and, as careful as we were, two more came apart in cleaning. (They were subsequently stitched back together, which made them stronger than the original construction.)

Cleaning and Care for Fabric Belts

It is best to inspect fabric belts each time after wearing. If there is a stain or if the fabric is frayed, then take it to your drycleaner sooner rather than later.

▸ Water-based stains can often be improved by spot cleaning, which is not an immersion method. Oily stains are more challenging, and though they sometimes improve, you should not expect miracles.

Spot Cleaning
Items are often spot-cleaned to avoid immersion in drycleaning solvent.

▸ If the stains are new and not too large, then the technician can limit the amount of chemicals and steam required to spot-clean the stained area. It is usually the hot steam that affects the glues on the back of the belt.

▸ If the belt fabric has frayed, then the seamstress or tailor may be able to retuck the material or perhaps add a stitch or two.

Home Spotting
Spot-cleaning belts can be very tricky because it is hard to flush out the chemicals and the soil. If you do it at home, then test a small area before you start.

▸ If the belt has no backing and can be drycleaned or wet cleaned, then assess the fragility of the hardware and have it removed if necessary.

▸ Specialty belts, such as designer creations with ornamentation, are best spot-cleaned or not cleaned at all. Ski belts, especially the Bogner brand with the brushed silver buckles, should never be cleaned in a machine. If needed, hand washing will probably be safe.

Note: Bogner has been very consumer friendly and has always sent buckle parts and toggles as needed. (See Chapter 23 on outerwear.)

Leather and Suede Belts

Each belt or sash must be judged individually. Most leather and suede pieces are high maintenance and difficult to remove stains from. They are usually spot-cleaned rather than immersion cleaned. (See Chapter 24 for the complete picture on suede and leather cleaning.)

▸ Suede, nubuck, and dyed leather belts, regardless of color, may present serious challenges during stain removal.

▸ Some leather and suede belts have a natural skin as a backing, as opposed to plastic or paper, which may allow them to be drycleaned (immersed).

▸ Oily stains, though, are very difficult to remove by spot-cleaning.

▸ Spot-cleaning is a common approach with leather and suede belts. This type of stain removal, though limited compared to immersion cleaning, often provides acceptable improvement. When you purchase a belt made of leather or suede, you will have to compromise on stain removal at some point along the way.

▸ Be sure to inspect the belt closely after each wearing to assess its condition. You get the most benefit from spot-cleaning by catching the stains in their early stages. It may be expensive to have the belt spot-cleaned each time you see a sizeable stain, but waiting will surely compromise longevity.

◆ Underarm Shields

Underarm shields are very useful and often necessary for silk clothing. I have seen hundreds of silk blouses, dresses, and formals ruined by perspiration. Because perspiration can become highly alkaline and silk is easily damaged by alkalinity, the fabric under the arms can change color in just one wearing. For blouses and other single-ply garments, color changes can show through to the outside layer. Many silk blouses have been relegated to "under-the-jacket" status because of discoloration. (Acetate, wool, rayon and other fabrics are also sensitive to perspiration.)

Perspiration damage can be diminished or avoided by the use of underarm shields. These shields also protect linings from discoloration and the fabric weakening that accompanies the damage. Many men's jackets have underarm shields, which have proven to be very effective.

Sewn-in Shields

Sewn-in underarm shields are shaped like a half-moon and are sewn, by the manufacturer, into the underarms of many high-quality garments. These shields are not removable, so they should be spot-cleaned each time the garment is drycleaned. This type of shield is usually made of the same material as the lining.

Snap-in Shields

When a shield is attached "after market," it can be sewn in permanently, like the manufacturer's, or it can be a snap-in style. Snap-in underarm shields allow the shield to be removed, hand washed, and snapped back in. Snap-in shields are usually made of cotton, which is lighter and more flexible than the sewn-in type and is a better choice for delicate and sheer garments. Both types of shields can be used on sheer fabrics, but snap-in shields require fewer stitches and may be more appropriate. Check them out.

◆ Shoulder Pads

Shoulder pads are intended to be a flattering addition to blouses, dresses, jackets, and coats. Their size is usually determined by what's in fashion at the time. They are made from many different materials—especially from men's to women's clothing. Some pads require more maintenance than others.

Size

It is not possible for every pad to fit every person, so a pad that may enhance the garment for one person may negatively affect the next. It is important to remember that shoulder pads can be removed, altered, cut down, or exchanged for a more appropriate size.

Note: When shopping, do not let poorly fitting shoulder pads keep you from buying an outfit. But remember that if the pad is changed or removed, then it may affect the fit of the garment. If the pads feel lumpy, or shift while at the store, then have them corrected or replaced before you leave.

Velcro® Strip Shoulder Pads

Shopping

Shoulder pads that are attached with Velcro® strips are convenient because they can be removed each time the garment needs to be cleaned. With regard to design and comfort, be sure that the Velcro strip does not show through to the outer layer of the fabric. On thin and sheer fabrics, the strip may show through as an impression, which is not flattering.

Snap-in pads may shift on the shoulder more than Velcro pads, but they are more suitable for thin or delicate fabrics. Velcro pads can easily be changed to a snap-in style by a seamstress or tailor. The pads can then be easily removed for cleaning and snapped back in afterward.

Velcro® Strip Pads in Drycleaning

Velcro pads should be removed before drycleaning for two reasons: First, the inside of the pads can be made of many different materials, some of which may disintegrate in cleaning or become lumpy. Second, the Velcro strips that hold the pads to the outfit are often glued to the pad instead of sewn. If the strips are glued, then the glue may dissolve and separate in the cleaning solution. If this problem occurs, then it will be necessary to find the strips or to make new ones; then the strips can be sewn to the pad permanently.

Permanent Pads

A sewn-in pad is usually secure with minimal, if any, shifting. High-quality clothing, almost unilaterally, has quality pads made with good materials. This does not mean that the pads won't need to be altered or removed; it simply reduces the possibility of shifting and bunching. Both men's and women's jackets may have problems with shoulder pads slipping into the lining and down the sleeve, but the slippage does seem to be more prevalent with women's clothing.

Permanent Pads in Drycleaning

Because permanent shoulder pads cannot be removed before drycleaning or washing, it is important to examine their stability occasionally so that you can alert the drycleaner if the pads have shifted or become lumpy. Here are three preventive care tips:

> **Rarely Considered**
> If you carry a backpack, briefcase, or wardrobe bag across your shoulder, you are putting tremendous pressure on the shoulder pads of your jacket. This weight and friction can distort the shoulder pad area and also cause the fabric to shine.

▶ The drycleaner could put safety pins through the pad, which will join the layers and reduce shifting. Pins can be removed after cleaning.

▶ You could have a few stitches sewn into the pad to reduce bunching or shifting.

▶ The cleaner can use a fabric gun to insert a nylon "staple," which would also stabilize the pad during cleaning. (The fabric gun is the type used by retailers to attach price tags and cards that dangle from most new clothing.)

Note: If the pads do shift or become lumpy, the finisher (presser) may be able to resteam and block them back to shape. In a worst-case scenario, the pad can be opened and repaired or replaced.

I've spent quite a bit of time talking about Velcro shoulder pads. Do you know how Velcro was invented?

"In 1941, George de Mestral and his Irish pointer were hunting game birds in the ancient Jura mountains of Switzerland. All day long, he had to pull off sticky cockleburs clinging to the dog's coat and his own trousers. De Mestral marvelled at the tenacity of these hitchhiking seedpods that were difficult to disentangle from animal fur or woolen cloth. That evening, this Swiss engineer placed a burr under a microscope and was stunned to see that the exterior of the seedpod was covered with masses of tiny hooks that acted like hundreds of grasping hands. De Mestral wondered whether it would be possible to mimic nature and create a fastener for fabric. When he succeeded he gave the creation a memorable name by splicing together the first syllable of two French words: velour (velvet) and crochet (hook): Velcro."

Excerpted from a great book, Allyn Freeman and Bob Golden's *Why Didn't I Think of That?*

Chapter 7

Silk and Satin
And How They React to Perspiration, Hair Spray, and Dye Bleed

I know from my years in drycleaning that silk, in all forms, presents challenges on many levels. It can be expensive, it soils and stains easily, and it is at the higher end of the cost spectrum for drycleaning services.

Women, and men to a lesser extent, often complain about the sensitive and often short-lived nature of silk blouses, shirts, slacks, skirts, and dresses. Specialty items, such as silk outer jackets, overcoats, and formals, have their own distinct problems.

Knowing about silk from the service end makes me particularly attuned to your concerns. This chapter will answer many often-asked questions, as well as many that *should* be asked but haven't been. This chapter speaks about clothing for women, but everything said about silk applies to clothing for *both* genders.

◆ Silk

In our society, silk has an aristocratic aura. Better-quality silk offers a beautiful drape, a luxurious feel, and intimate comfort. There is, however, tremendous disparity in quality, reflected in most cases by price. Lower-quality silk may have a comparatively poor drape and a rough-hewn feel, and it may present more of a challenge during stain removal. Keep in mind that silk—merely because of its reputation as a quality fabric—is not above reproach. Be discriminating when you shop.

Plain Silk
Some call it crepe de chine, and most silk blouses and dresses are made of this thin, finely crinkled or pebbly fabric. It is the most common type of silk you'll see. It should be less expensive—quality being relative—than the same blouse in sueded silk or silk satin. Many formal gowns are made of plain silk, but most have a thicker ply for a more formal drape.

I would like to point out, clearly, that "cheap" or less-expensive silk garments that have poor drape are more difficult to remove stains from than are those of quality silk. Because silk is a difficult fabric to maintain, it is better to make the investment in better quality if you can afford to.

Sueded or Washed Silk

Sueded silk can often be identified by the "nap," which can sometimes be brushed up and down in much the same way a real sueded leather garment can. The nap is more noticeable with dark colors. The material has a very soft feel, a flowing drape, and a resistance to wrinkling. Two-piece outfits, though, are sometimes made from mismatched bolts of fabric. If the difference is noticeable at the time of purchase, then it will be very obvious after cleaning. All the conditions mentioned in this section about silk are especially true for sueded silk.

> **Sueded Silk**
> If you love the fit—or the color is special—buy the garment, but treat it with care.

Simple Truths about Caring for Sueded Silk

▶ Stain removal is exceptionally difficult because dark dyes are very unstable. Simple stain removal of most water-based stains, such as a soda stain, is very difficult because of the unstable dyes. The mere attempt can cause a blotchy area of color loss, producing dark and light shades around the original spot.

▶ It takes a very skilled technician to remove stains, especially hair spray. Some oily stains that are "easy" to remove from crepe de chine and satin are not at all routinely removed from sueded silk.

▶ Only white and off-white are considered low maintenance and require a less-skilled technician.

▶ I would heartily recommend, especially for darker shades, that you have all pieces of an ensemble cleaned together to ensure color consistency.

> **Stain Removal**
> You should never try to remove stains from sueded silk. Such removal requires the proper tools and the proper training.

Note: Many consumers have refused to buy sueded silk fabrics. In the best of circumstances, they are lush looking and have a comfortable feel and excellent drape, but not all makers use the best-quality material. In worse cases, the material can be ruined by one stain catastrophe.

Satin

Satin is actually a type of weave. It is thick and lustrous. Well-made satin has fabulous drape and exudes an aristocratic aura. Of silks in the mainstream-clothing market, satin is most often seen in blouses and formals. Because of the lustrous nature of the weave, most satin garments have beautiful drape, regardless of price.

All silk fabric is subject to snags, color loss, and *deluster*, but satin, because of its rich weave, tends to show any minor damage. (See Chapter 2 about these problems.) Watchbands, jewelry, fingernails, and zippers can catch the fabric and snag it. Color loss, from rubbing a stain ever so slightly, will permanently mar the surface. Satin should be treated only by a quality drycleaner. Ironing at home is also more challenging than it is with other types of silk.

> **What is Deluster?**
> Deluster is a condition that occurs from rubbing a fabric and breaking the fibers—causing a change in the sheen and possible loss of color.

◆ How Silk Is Damaged

Perspiration

Silk blouses, shirts, jackets, dresses, and other upper-body garments are worn for everyday use in professional offices, for casual lunches, formal events, and nights out. Silk is a protein fiber, and it is easily damaged by alkaline chemicals that are present in perfume, hair products (especially hair spray), household cleaners and, most specifically, perspiration. (Perspiration turns very alkaline when left untreated.) Silk is also damaged by chloride salts, which are present in foods, perspiration, and some deodorants. Chloride salts also cause fabric deterioration, which is especially common under the arms of silk garments.

The common thread affecting all people is perspiration. People in all walks of life perspire, some more than others. (A few claim that they do not perspire, but they are definitely in the minority.)

> **Fabric Fragility**
> Satin is more fragile than crepe de chine or sueded silk. It can deluster very easily, hampering perspiration removal.

This condition means that in an average day or night, a person may perspire under the arms, at the waist, in the upper thighs, and at the cuffs and collar. This perspiration can, and will, affect the color and the strength of the fabric. I'm sure that every woman, at least once in her life, has noticed a color change and perhaps some fiber deterioration in the underarm area of her silk blouse.

Color Changes from Perspiration and Perfume

Here are examples of the color changes to silk that may help you recognize the signals early enough to do something about them.

▶ White turns yellow.   ▶ Red turns purple.
▶ Green turns yellow.   ▶ Navy turns purple.

Dye Bleed and Dye Transfer

▶ When the waist area of a silk blouse becomes moist from perspiration, a few things come into play. If you are wearing a blouse untucked, with a belt around the waist, then the moisture may cause the belt to bleed onto the blouse. If the blouse is light in color and the belt is dark, then there may be noticeable dye transfer on the waist area of the blouse.

▶ On occasion, the waistband of a skirt or slacks, wet with perspiration, may bleed onto the blouse that is tucked in. Again, color contrast and the fabric content of the skirt or slacks may contribute to the problem. If the blouse is white or off-white, then the dye may be removable. If not, continue to tuck it in to hide the non-removable stain.

▶ When the dark lining of a jacket is wet with perspiration, it can leave purple rings on the underarms of a silk blouse or shirt (very common at formal events). If the blouse is white or off-white, then there is a good chance that a skilled drycleaner can remove the wet, fugitive dye that has transferred on to the blouse or shirt.

▶ A formal silk bow tie, wet with perspiration, can deposit dye onto the collar of a white formal shirt. This problem is usually an easy restoration for most drycleaners.

> **Real Situation**
> If the dye bleeds from a belt onto a blouse, who is responsible? Should the person who sold you the belt have alerted you first? Should the belt withstand contact with moisture and perspiration without bleeding? This reality has no easy answer.

On the Bright Side: Most stains from dyes that have transferred onto white garments can be improved. If your drycleaner is skilled in the art of stain removal, then a "dye-stripper" may be used to improve or remove the fugitive dye.

Unfortunately, dyes that have transferred onto colored garments are nearly impossible to remove safely.

Perfume

Perfume is the "invisible" killer. Perfume stains can go virtually undetected until they have changed the color of the silk, at which point it is sometimes too late to remove the stain entirely. For this reason, identifying the stain for your drycleaner is very important.

Hair Spray

Hair spray ruins more silk clothing than people know. Because the spots seem harmless at first, if they are seen at all, and the assumption is that the marks will come out in cleaning, people are lax about them. The fact is that they are nearly impossible to remove from crepe de chine and silk satin, and are impossible to completely remove from sueded or washed silk.

> **Stain News**
> Hair spray damages silk and other fabrics. It is especially damaging when it comes out in "spurts" instead of a mist, which makes it much harder to remove safely. Always spray hair *before* getting dressed.

Yarn Slippage and Fabric Separation

When a fabric doesn't stretch and then there is stress on the fabric, the threads will separate or tear. If you have seen fabric separation under the arms, at the waist, along seams, and across the back of your clothing, it is usually yarn slippage. Separation is also an early sign that the clothing may be too tight in those areas. You may want to consider adding extra material to relax the fit and to remove stress from the area. Yarn slippage may worsen when the fabric is wet with water or perspiration.

▸ Inspect your silk garments at the underarms, back, waist, and inside the crotch.

▸ Hold the garment up to the light and look at the areas where the silk has thinned and separated, leaving little "spaces." These spaces are the result of yarn slippage. If the underarm is wet and if you reach hard for something, then the fabric may separate rather than stretch. Something has to give; sometimes it's the fabric and sometimes it's the seam.

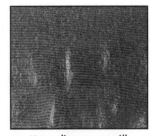

Yarn slippage on silk

▸ Instead of stretching in the way nylon or Lycra does, silk will tear, and there is no remedy for this condition.

Yarn slippage and yarn separation can sometimes be improved by carefully re-aligning the threads one at a time with a sharp pin. This type of restoration can be time-consuming, but it may offer some improvement.

Deluster: Rubbing Silk

What happens when you rub silk while trying to remove a stain? If you would be satisfied to merely accept my word that rubbing causes damage to silk, and if you promise not to do it, then you can skip this section!

Rubbing a fabric will almost always break the surface fibers, which creates lighter areas and makes the area look like the dye has faded. The condition is usually permanent. It takes the proper equipment and a skilled "spotter-technician" to properly remove stains without delustering the fabric. Under ideal conditions, the removal will still be subject to the five stain-removal conditions (see Chapter 8, page 75). Rubbing will usually rough up the fabric and cause color loss, but will rarely remove the stain. If you have a seemingly minor spill in a public situation and you feel that you must do something, then do not rub, only blot with a dry white cloth.

Delustered silk (magnified)

You may not "see" any damage occurring while you rub, but in 99% of the cases, you are upsetting the fibers, and you will see the color loss and the deluster after the fabric dries or after drycleaning. The color loss that remains is often in a prominent place, which will compromise the garment forever.

What Can Be Done?

In some cases, though not often enough to consider it an option, a blend of mineral oil and cleaning solvent can be applied to the delustered area. This application will sometimes improve your *faux pas* enough to disguise it. The mineral-oil application is time-consuming and fleeting because it rinses out in every subsequent drycleaning and then must be reapplied. In some cases, it is the only possibility for restoration, but you should not count on it. Try to refrain from doing spot removal on your delicate fabrics.

Snags

Snags do occur and they are generally not restorable. A seamstress or tailor can sometimes "stop" the run from growing. Look at the belts, watches, and jewelry that you wear, and be mindful of the part they play in snagging fibers.

> **Mineral Oil**
> When your hair is damaged and you apply conditioner, it helps the hair lie back down and it restores the sheen. Mineral-oil treatments help the broken fibers of silk lie back down, restoring a sheen to the rubbed area.

◆ How to Avoid Damage

▶ First, always apply deodorants, perfume, and hair spray *before* you dress. Hair spray and perfume often contain alcohol and other chemicals that can permanently damage silk, satin, rayon, and other fabrics.

▶ You can experiment with various deodorants and antiperspirants (there *is* a difference) to see how they react with your body and which ones keep you the driest. The underarm stain at the end of the night can be a combination of deodorant, perspiration and, occasionally, dye.

▶ If you tend to perspire more than the average person, then you may want to consider putting in washable, snap-in underarm shields before you ever wear the garment. (See Chapter 6 for more on shields.) This way, you can protect the silk and also have a method of cleaning the shields after wearing. These shields are actually a very good idea and worth the time and money.

▶ If you are not willing to use shields, or if they cannot be sewn into a particular garment, then consider visiting a bathroom when you begin to perspire, to blot under your arms with a paper napkin, in order to allay further damage. I know this sounds a bit crazy, but it will preserve your silk blouses.

> **Perspiration**
> If you know that you've perspired, then you must have the garment drycleaned or hand washed to combat the color change. If you do not, then it will almost certainly discolor.

What More Can *You* Do?

▶ When you undress at night, reflect on the activities of the day (it's said that this is a form of meditation) and, in good light, inspect your clothing for stains.

▶ If you remember perspiring to the point of dripping, then examine the area to see if there is any dye bleed or discoloration.

▶ The discoloration may be a thin ring under the arm, so inspect it closely. Depending on your physiology, what type of deodorant you use, and what you had to eat, you may see a much larger area affected.

▶ If you do not attend to the underarm area, then it will most likely be permanently affected, which can mean that you can no longer wear this blouse openly and freely without being self-conscious of the underarms. The stain may relegate this blouse to a support piece in your closet, and you will need to wear a jacket or cardigan over it.

▶ Be sure to have your garment cleaned within 48 hours to give yourself a fighting chance of saving it. If the drycleaner is very skilled, then a color change can sometimes be reversed by using the proper chemicals in the proper order.

▶ Remember, perfume stains can go virtually undetected until they have caused a color change, at which point it may be too late to remove the stain entirely. Therefore, it is important that you identify the stain each time that you take the garment to the drycleaner.

Note: Perspiration, hair spray, and perfume are all water based, and drycleaning *alone* does very little to remove these stains. Be specific when going over your garments with the drycleaning clerk.

◆ Let's Go Shopping

When shopping for silk, remember the importance of fabric drape. This factor may be the key to your long-term satisfaction. If there are snags on the garment already, it may be a sign of fragility. If you are buying a beaded or sequined garment, then check the sewing and trim closely, and recognize that ornamentation with sharp edges can contribute to snagging. I know you are buying the "look" first (perhaps with an ensemble in mind), and then comfort, but try to slip in some pragmatic thoughts as well.

> **Shopping Hints**
> See Chapter 1 for great shopping tips, and refer to them for every important clothing purchase.

◆ At the Cleaners

Inspect your silk clothing closely for stains, perspiration, perfume, and hair spray. Be sure to point out the "invisible" stains that you remember. If you have cuff links or removable shoulder pads, then be sure to take them home, unless the drycleaner will replace them for you after pressing. (Shoulder pads need not be cleaned.)

If you did rub an area, then tell the clerk. You will be helping the drycleaner immensely by pointing out the stain and the subsequent color loss. The cleaner may be able to improve the affected area with a mineral-oil treatment.

If you have specific concerns about the pressing of your clothing, or if you want to share subtle, style preferences such as wanting a rolled collar, rounded sleeves, no creases, soft pleats, or rolled hems, then now is the time speak up. If you wish to have your slacks hung from the waist (typical with most silk slacks), then now is the time to tell the clerk. (See Chapter 10 about hangers.)

Chapter 8

Stains and Their Treatment
Identifying, Removing, and Surviving Stains

◆ Determine the Nature of the Stain

How many times have you taken a napkin, dipped it in water, and tried to remove a stain? Almost everyone does it—even I have on occasion, and I know better. That just shows how common a practice it is. Yet it is a dangerous practice, and people do it without knowing or considering whether it is a water-based stain or an oil-based stain.

This chapter is an invaluable reference guide for home washing and drycleaning tips. It may even save you the heartache and expense of having to replace perfectly good clothing.

> **1st Simple Rule**
> If the stain contains anything oily, then it will probably not come out with *water*. That knowledge is half the battle.

Stains can be oil soluble (dissolves in drycleaning solvent), water soluble (dissolves in water), what I call co-stains (which contain oil and water), or insoluble. If you do not know the origin of the stain, then you should always assume that it is oily in nature. It is the safest assumption. Remember, *most oily stains do not wash out with soap and water,* and they are often "set" by soap, water, or heat.

Treating an oily stain as a water-based stain is the worst mistake you can make.

Examples of Oily Stains

Oily stains include salad dressing, gravy, cooking oils, meat juice, butter, lipstick, car grease, certain inks, and typewriter correction fluid.

> **2nd Simple Rule**
> If the stain is water based, then it will probably not come out in *drycleaning*. It must be spotted separately. That's the other half of the battle.

These types of stains are most safely removed in the drycleaning process. In most cases, they cannot be removed safely with plain water, soap and water, most home spotters, or club soda, without risking damage to the color or the fabric. (Polyester has a tendency to hold oily stains, making them particularly difficult to remove.)

Many tablecloths are washed at home because we believe it to be the right remedy —only to notice two weeks later that the clear, oily stains from the meal have turned yellow. The yellowed areas are the remains of aged oil stains that could not be removed during washing.

Note: If you take the time to think about it, many stains contain some degree of oil: splatters from cooking, spills, soups, sauces. Do not be surprised if small spots remain on your washable clothing. These are probably the oily parts.

Water-Based Stains

Examples of water-based stains include drink spills (including alcohol), certain inks and felt-tip markers, certain foods—such as fruits and most foods with sugar (cake icing)—blood, perspiration, breast milk, and discharge.

Co-Stains

Co-stains are generally of an oily nature with water-based ingredients or some food coloring. These may include chocolate, mustard, beets, certain paints, certain inks, typewriter correction fluid, and medicines. Co-stains first need to be treated with an oily-stain remover and then drycleaned. After cleaning they are treated with a water-based stain remover for food coloring or other residue.

Insoluble Stains

Insoluble stains are stains that cannot be dissolved. The most common example is super glue. This type of glue, among others, is almost impossible to remove and, once it has set, may never be removable regardless of the type of fabric. Some stain removal is inhibited by the type of fabric and the color, as opposed to the nature of the stain itself.

A soda stain can often be pre-spotted and removed from most wool and cotton, but that same stain may not be removable from certain rayon or rayon blends because of the sizing in the fabric. Lastly, time can set stains permanently, rendering them insoluble.

Two examples of Insoluble Stains: A stain that has yellowed from age that cannot be bleached due to the type of fabric, or cannot be removed with bleach. Or an oxidized (aged) oil stain that does not respond to stronger spot removers. An oxidized oil stain typically "wicks" out into the fabric, forming a cross.

Note: See "Stain Care 'At a Glance'" at the end of this chapter.

◆ You've Identified the Stain; Now Treat It

This section addresses washable clothing versus drycleanable clothing, and water-based stains versus oily stains, and how the stains are affected by choosing one technique over another.

Dark clothing is most susceptible to color loss when treated. Light clothing, especially white and off-white, is most susceptible to rings and discoloration. Treating fragile, dark-colored fabrics at home, such as silk, satin, taffeta, polished cotton, and linen, should be considered off-limits. Even professionals who are trained in spot removal are at a severe disadvantage without the proper tools and equipment. On these fabrics you should only blot stains with a dry, white cloth. Do not wet the stains or try to remove them. Never rub the fabric.

Care Label Sense
Care of a dryclean-only garment is noted on the care label. Although some clothing with this label can be washed, drycleaning is a good rule to follow.

Water-Based Stains on Washable Clothing

If the clothing has a wash label, then it implies that the colors are stable. If you have a water-based stain on this type of garment and you cannot wash it immediately, then blot it dry to absorb the spill, and stop there. In most instances, applying water to a water-based stain is the right thing to do, although it can get messy. If a ring forms or the stain spreads, though it may look bad, it may be a good sign because it shows that the stain does dissolve in water.

Hand or machine washing should break up the ring and "flush" the stain through the fabric as it agitates. This process should remove the rest of the stain safely. Remember, sugar-based stains, such as "squirts" from fruit, should be washed within 24 hours to avoid yellowing.

Oily Stains on Washable Clothing

There is no "on-the-spot" approach for the removal of an oily stain as there is for a water-based stain. Dry blotting is all you should do. Some products, such as Prell® shampoo and Lestoil®, may aid in the removal of car grease and other oily stains by lubricating the stains during machine washing. All fabrics should be tested in a small, discreet area, and you must be patient when testing. (Natural fibers release oil stains better than polyester and other synthetic fibers do.) You may resist

Safety First
When rubbing a fabric with a dry or moist cloth (be it washable, dry-cleanable, light, or dark), one thing is almost certain: the color will probably fade and the fabric will become rougher.

sending your washable clothing to a drycleaner, but drycleaning solution has a natural affinity to oil stains and most fresh stains come out easily in the process.

Water-Based Stains on Dryclean-Only Clothing

Unlike water-based stains on washable clothing, if you get a ring on dryclean-only clothing, or the stain spreads after you apply water, then the problems will not "flush" out in the drycleaning machine. This type of staining can ruin the majority of drycleanable fabrics because of the sizing and the sensitive dyes. The only safe method for treating a water-based stain on a dryclean-only garment is to blot with a dry, white cloth and then dryclean it.

> **Stain Emergency**
> If you get a spill and you must do something, blot, but do not rub. A clean, white cloth is usually a safe bet. Do not apply water or club soda.

If you apply a moist cloth to a stain on a dryclean-only garment, two things can happen: the fabric surface can become rough, causing the color to fade, or a ring can form that may be impossible to remove. Because there is virtually no water in the drycleaning process, neither the stain nor the ring will be removed.

Oily Stains on Dryclean-Only Clothing

I consider it careless and dangerous for you to attempt removal of oily stains from dryclean-only clothing. Granted, drycleaning services can be expensive, but so is *replacing* the clothing in question. Count to ten before you ruin a good outfit. There is no safe way *yet* for you to remove oily stains from fragile clothing.

Whether you're in a restaurant, at a friend's home, or on an airplane, do not attempt removal. You have almost no chance of improving the garment and an above-average chance of ruining it.

Note: Many times an oily stain is invisible at the time of the spill or splatter. The first thought is, "It doesn't show—don't bother." If the stain does surface in two weeks' time, then it may be impossible for the drycleaner to remove. If you see an oily spill, then have the garment drycleaned.

◆ Survival Techniques

Everyone, at one time or another, has tried unsuccessfully to remove a stain. Without proper knowledge of fabrics, dyes, stains, or the science of stain removal, you have a great chance of doing more harm than good.

This chapter can be of greater service to you by teaching what *not* to do than by trying to teach you the necessary stain-removal techniques to cover every situation.

Lipstick, grease, makeup, spills from food and drink, and some inks may wash off your hands and face with soap and water, but they are rarely removable from clothing in the same manner.

Stain removal is subject to roughly five conditions:

▶ Origin of the stain

▶ Size of the stain

▶ Type of fabric and nap

▶ Dyes that make up the fabric

▶ Amount of time that the stain remains in the fabric

Rubbing Fabric—A Very Dangerous Thing to Do

Rubbing a stain with a napkin or a cloth can upset the nap, break the surface fibers, cause chafing, possibly separate the fibers (yarn slippage) and, depending on the dyes, cause severe color loss and deluster (changing the sheen of the fabric, which is usually permanent). Most of the time I recommend blotting with a dry, white cloth. If I seem like a broken record, it's intentional.

Stains Gone Bad—Improperly Treated

When there is a stain disaster, stand back, assess, count to ten, and refer to this section of the book. It sounds simple, but it is sage advice.

If you are trying to remove a stain and it looks like the fabric might be damaged, then *stop*, blot it, jot down what you did, and take the garment to your drycleaner. The cleaner is trained to assess these problems. The more remedies you use, the more harm you may do—and the harder it is to restore. Out of concern and frustration, consumers try many things in an attempt to remove stains. This practice compounds the problem, makes retracing the steps difficult, and limits the eventual stain removal by trained technicians.

Some tricks of the trade can be used to restore damaged clothing, but most are marginal and temporary.

> **Stubborn Stains**
> Oxidation is the term used to describe the process of an oily stain turning yellow. Safely removing this type of stain yourself is nearly impossible.

A Word about Home Spot Removal on Oily Stains

You can apply whatever stain remover you wish, but do it at your own risk. I have yet to see a store-, TV-, or magazine-purchased stain remover work properly on oily stains.

If it takes the drycleaning industry six months or more to train a spotter to remove stains from fragile fabrics, then how can a remedy in a bottle work for the public at large? There is not enough small print on the package to cover every circumstance. Nor can one given chemical in a bottle remove every type of stain on every type of fabric.

◆ Stain Care "At a Glance"

Water-Based Stains on Washable Clothing

Perspiration, drink spills, and non-oily stains can be washed out of most washable clothing. Stains with food coloring from punch, chocolate, or mustard may need further attention such as pre-treatment or rewashing. In some cases, the residual food coloring may require a color-safe bleach.

Oily Stains on Washable Clothing

There's really no home remedy for most oily stains. Some oily stains may improve in washing with the help of lubricants, but most will probably need drycleaning. If the garment has already been washed, then let it air dry to avoid heat.

Water-Based Stains on Dryclean-Only Clothing

If clothing can't (or shouldn't) be washed, then blotting the stain with a dry, white cloth, before drycleaning it, is the safest approach. If you still question this advice, re-read the more detailed section in this chapter or call your drycleaner.

Oily Stains on Dryclean-Only Clothing

I'm sorry, but I still can't recommend a safe home remedy. Drycleaning is the only solution. Stay tuned to my website for further technical advancements in stain removal (and other great news): **www.clothingdoctor.com.**

Chapter 9

The Finished Product
Steaming, Hand Ironing, Machine Pressing

"Finishing" is the term that professionals use for the final process. A garment can be finished in three ways: it can be steamed, which is the lightest and softest approach; it can be hand ironed, which allows a firmer finish while still addressing the details and nuances; or it can be pressed, which uses a manual or air-operated press that imparts the most "body" and the firmest finish. In many cases, all three processes are used, and all three are referred to as "pressing" or "finishing."

◆ Steaming

Steam is used throughout the finishing process. Most pressing machines have steam that pours out of both the top and bottom surfaces. Although some drycleaners do use electric irons (mostly for shirts and some linens), most hand irons are steam operated, are safe on most fabrics, and do not scorch clothing.

Most pressing stations are also equipped with steam-operated puff irons (called "puffs"). Puffs are available in different shapes and sizes and are designed to steam hard-to-reach areas of garments, such as shoulders, elbows, and collars. Puffs are also used for subtleties and details, such as bows, overlayers, pleats, and puffy sleeves. Puffs provide a good addition to the pressing machine by softening and rounding the edges some-times left by presses and hand irons.

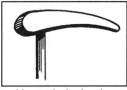

Different-shaped puff irons for shoulder pads, body, sleeves

Advantages

Restoration

Steam can restore shape, body, and softness to fabrics. It helps to remove the sheen from many garments that have become shined from wear or poor pressing. A finisher usually has a puff iron to restore lumpy shoulder pads, to remove creases from a sleeve, to roll a pleat, and to soften hard wrinkles in difficult-to-reach areas of a garment.

Improved Body, Texture, and Subtleties

Steam can soften a stiff or poorly finished garment. If a wool suit has been drenched by rain and needs softening or stretching, steam often can restore it. If slacks have been creased when they were supposed to have been rolled, steam and a hand iron can often remove the hard lines, depending on the fabric. Steam can keep a fabric soft and supple. Many high-grade fabrics must be steamed—not pressed—to remain rich and lustrous.

Shaping

Knits need to be steamed and sometimes blocked to shape. Steam allows the finisher to reshape sweaters that have become tight in areas, to reblock garments larger, or to "ease out" certain sensitive areas, such as the hips and bust. In some cases, steam can help tighten areas that have become stretched, such as the neck, waist, and cuffs. The operator must also be careful when steaming acrylic garments because they can be stretched *out* of shape, too. Be aware of that if you use a home steamer.

Disadvantages

Certain trims, elastics, buttons, and fused (glued) fabrics can be affected by steam if they have not been manufactured properly or if the steam is misused. Sequins can curl, beads can melt, pearls can peel, buttons can bleed, and elastic can stretch. If the care label says the garment can be drycleaned, then, unless stated otherwise, both the garment and its trims should withstand the steaming process.

Many garments have been fused in areas, and occasionally these bonded areas can separate and bubbles will appear after steaming. This is a hotly contested issue among manufacturers and drycleaners, but the belief is that if the fusing has been done properly, then the steam will not affect the garment. (Many fused garments do process well.)

◆ Hand Ironing

Hand ironing is an "old-world" approach still used by many drycleaners. Most mainstream drycleaners do some hand ironing, but most prefer machine pressing because it is faster.

Advantages

Most fine clothing needs hand ironing. If you have a garment with details such as pleating, overlays, pocket flaps, bows, beads, uneven surfaces, or double-thick layers, then you should request that these areas be hand ironed to protect them from shining and wrinkling.

78

Hand ironing can virtually eliminate most of the finishing problems associated with machine pressing.

Hand ironing and steaming enable drycleaners to avoid shining fragile satin lapels and gabardine fabrics, reduce unsightly seam impressions, eliminate flattening of soft woolens, and protect against damaging special hardware or trims. If every garment could be hand ironed, most would look perfect. Some cleaners out there are still doing the lion's share of their work this way, but you have to seek them out. For your better clothing, it is a worthy hunt.

Disadvantages
One real disadvantage of hand ironing, to you as a customer, is that it *is* a more expensive service. Drycleaners consider it to be a slow and unprofitable way to finish a garment. Another disadvantage is that it is difficult to impart a necessary and hard finish on certain fabrics, most notably linen. Finally, a hand iron is also limited in its ability to press the wrinkles out of some washed clothing.

◆ Machine Pressing

Most presses come in two varieties. The utility press provides a softer finish and is used for most woolens, sweaters, silks, and soft cottons. A "hot-head" press provides a firmer press and is used for men's dress shirts, linen, hard cotton, and some ball and bridal gowns.

Advantages
If you have a pair of slacks that need a sharp crease, a badly wrinkled linen outfit, a badly wrinkled satin ball gown, or a "sleepy" looking raincoat, machine pressing can restore the body and lines to the garment. It is also the most economical way for the drycleaner to finish clothing. Machine pressing enables the presser to produce two or three times more pieces per hour than hand ironing.

> **Firmest Finish**
> Hot-head presses have a chrome surface and are very good for providing a crisp finish.

Disadvantages
Most pressing machines cannot address the details that many fabrics require; they tend to overpress pocket flaps, vents, and double-thick and uneven surfaces. They can cause button impressions and leave impressions on pleats. Many delicate fabrics are almost impossible to press without some shine. Gabardine, acetate, and satin are difficult to press without shining the fabric permanently. Because of this problem, using steam puffs and a hand iron is often required for these fabrics in order to achieve a clean, professional finish.

◆ In Summary

If you are concerned about details and nuances, then ask about your drycleaner's philosophy on soft-pressing. Cleaners do not want to harm a valuable piece of your wardrobe or sour their relationship with you, nor do they want to pay you for a damaged garment. Communication is the key. Don't be timid when it comes to maintaining your wardrobe investment.

Chapter 10

Finishing Problems

Wrinkles, Shine, Bubbles, Creases, Hangers

My years in the clothing and drycleaning businesses have shown me that many people wonder why some clothing wrinkles so badly, shines, or develops bubbles. And they wonder why drycleaners can't get straight which slacks have creases and which don't. Common questions—sometimes difficult answers.

◆ Wrinkles

Problems

You may wonder why some clothing comes back from the drycleaners with wrinkles after you just paid to have it pressed. Sometimes the clothing has been sitting on a rack or conveyor for too long, causing "breaks" and areas that look "tired." Sometimes a part of a garment looks like it hasn't been pressed at all, as if the presser or the inspector missed it (which is very rare). The truth is that most of the time wrinkles are there because of the nature of the fabric.

Velvet, silk, cotton and particularly linen are fabrics that wrinkle easily. Perspiration, coupled with pressure from sitting in a car or at a desk for hours, can cause deep and sometimes permanent wrinkling. The lower back, elbows, stomach, seat, and collar tend to wrinkle the most. The wrinkles that do not come out in finishing are considered "hard wrinkles," with linen being the worst offender. The heat and pressure required to remove certain hard wrinkles, in some cases, could actually damage the fabric.

Hard wrinkles can be so severe that machine pressing—even with a hot-head press, which offers the most aggressive approach—may not remove all the wrinkles. (Remember, velvet cannot be pressed, only steamed.)

> **Texture Variation**
> When one area of a garment is smooth and the space next to it is rough, the rough area probably has been missed by the finisher. This area may be referred to as "rough-dry." This condition is most obvious on cotton, linen, and satin.

81

Resolutions

You can help reduce the minor wrinkles and breaks by picking up your clothing from the cleaner soon after it is ready. You can also help by hanging up your more susceptible garments at the end of each day of wear instead of depositing them in a pile for the next trip to the cleaners.

You pay a price by wearing a linen outfit or thin cotton on a humid summer day; it may be cool and thin, but hard wrinkling is inevitable. If you want a linen or a thin cotton to be crisp, then you can ask the cleaner to add starch or sizing. This process will help in the short run, but it will ultimately wrinkle just as much. It's best to approach linen the European way, which is to wear it soft and allow the wrinkles to become part of the personality of the piece.

If you receive clothing back from the drycleaners with wrinkles in the troubled areas, consider the challenges a drycleaner faces before you assume that the condition has been overlooked. If you are still dissatisfied, then do not hesitate to return the garment for a second look.

> **Starch Talk**
> Be very careful when spraying starch on linen garments. It can cause spots and permanent stiffening. This condition is especially dangerous on deep colors, and usually cannot be improved during drycleaning.

◆ Shine

Problems

You've probably seen shine on outfits, particularly on darker colors. It shows most prominently on seams, lapels, and pockets.

Gabardine, acetate, and triacetate fabrics tend to shine from friction and pressure. All three fabric types will shine on the thighs from sliding in and out of a desk, on the elbows from the top of a desk or a counter, and on the seat of the slacks from sliding in and out of a car. Gabardine is a high-maintenance material (technically a twill), and in time *all* gabs will shine with normal wear. This situation is something to consider when selecting a sport jacket, slacks, or suit.

> **Travel Advice**
> If you are forced to use an unfamiliar drycleaner when you travel, then be certain to clearly voice your concerns. When you use a hotel concierge, you do relinquish most control.

If a gabardine is machine pressed during finishing, then it is guaranteed to shine prematurely. If any of these fabrics are pressed too hard, then they can begin to shine badly even in the first pressing. Soft pressing is the key to longevity.

Resolutions

Use common sense when buying one of these high-maintenance fabrics. If you're buying work suits for everyday wear, then think about 100% wool. (Wool blends that contain a synthetic fabric will *shine* faster than 100% wool.) Just being aware of the pitfalls of these fabrics will help you prolong their life.

When these fabrics do shine, either from normal wear or from poor pressing, a skilled finisher can sometimes reverse the damage by steaming and brushing. If the shine was caused by poor pressing, then be sure to clearly convey your dissatisfaction to the manager. Unfortunately, many delicate fabrics are poorly pressed at some point and do need this type of restoration.

> **Hand Ironing**
> If your garment does have a problem with shine or fusible bubbles, then a cleaner who specializes in hand ironing can be of tremendous value.

◆ Fusible Bubbles

Fused construction is a method used to bond two layers of fabric (or facing) together. This method is used in the production of jackets and coats. Fused construction is used universally by manufacturers of clothing, from casual to couture. This method is usually effective, and it produces a clean, smooth surface.

Problems

You have probably seen the results of poor fusing on a navy or black sport jacket, but you may not have known the name or the cause. The two layers separate in areas, typically on the front panel, and small bubbles form. The bubbles look like raindrops sitting on glass. This condition is most common with gabardine, though I have seen it occur with acetate and some silk and satin, but rarely with soft wool.

There is an ongoing debate between drycleaners and manufacturers regarding the cause of the separation. Drycleaners feel that the adhesives are of low quality or that the fusing process is poor, and the manufacturers think that the cleaner is using too much steam or is pressing with too much heat. I would like to point out that while both parties may be correct to some extent, why then are so many fused jackets still perfectly fine after being pressed twenty times? I believe, however, that low heat and minimal steam do provide the best care.

Resolutions

Each time that a jacket is pressed, either by machine or by hand, the fabric is heated and the adhesive may be affected. If bubbles do appear, then the finisher should try to reheat the adhesives with the iron to reset them, in an attempt to smooth the area. Sometimes the layers reseal easily and the separation never shows; other times the bubbles reappear after the area cools. If the bubbles cannot be removed by re-pressing, then it may be possible to peel back the interfacing, separate it, and re-press it. This process is tricky and requires a skilled seamstress or tailor and an experienced finisher, but it has worked many times for us.

If this approach is not possible or the result is not satisfactory, then the drycleaner may be part of the solution. Depending on the age of the garment and the status of the drycleaner's relationship with the retailer, the cleaner may be able to facilitate a return to the manufacturer for repair or replacement. It is not necessarily the drycleaner's responsibility to go the extra mile, so judge the situation accordingly.

◆ Creases

I am certain that you have had slacks returned from the cleaners with a crease where there was none, without a crease when there was one, and occasionally with multiple creases. (I have even seen new slacks with double creases.)

Most drycleaners have a difficult time regulating this issue. When a pair of slacks has a hard crease, it is obvious to the staff, and the slacks are routinely returned to you with a crease. Drycleaners prefer to crease slacks because it is faster than steaming in a "soft roll" or pressing them without a crease.

When a pair of slacks is received by the cleaners with a soft crease, or if it is badly wrinkled from being in a bag, the crease is not always obvious, and this is where the trouble begins. But if the cleaners do get the crease right, then they may ultimately fold it over a hanger when perhaps it should be hanging from the waist, either sideways or faced forward. It would help if the customer could make his or her preference clear.

Types of Creases and Issues

No Crease

We have returned slacks to customers with no crease, as they requested, and still managed to hang them wrong. Customers have told me that if the slacks are hung from the waist with the slacks facing forward, opposed to sideways, it makes the legs "bowl" out and causes the wearer to look fat. If you prefer to get your slacks back with no crease, you should clarify which way to hang them.

Soft Crease

A soft crease is a subtle thing. Depending on the material, which may or may not hold a soft crease, the crease should be rounded with no hint of a conventional hard line. Silk, linen, and acetate fabrics can usually be soft creased by merely hanging the slacks from the waist, facing sideways.

Crease

A sharp crease is tidy and professional looking. Creased slacks should have only one crease. The crease should be sharp, but not like a knife, unless that's your preference. If you're changing from "no crease" or a "soft crease" to *a crease*, then be very deliberate about the decision. On most fabrics, once it's creased, it is permanent. Make sure your preference is known, and recognize that pleated slacks are the most difficult to re-crease properly.

Hard Crease

Some people want hard creases on their slacks, but many fabrics turn white or fade in the creased area. It may not happen the first time that they are creased, but it is imminent, and there is no going back. Dark colors may be affected the first time they are hard creased, and the discoloration is immediate.

Double Creases

Finishers are supposed to follow the original crease line when they press, and there should only be one line to follow. A second line (a double crease) is sometimes present because the slacks have been badly pressed either at home or at some point by a drycleaner. When there are two crease lines, the finisher must make a decision to either steam out both and start over, or to follow the best line. Unfortunately, with most fabrics, once a crease has been pressed in, it is impossible to remove all remnants of the incorrect crease. Soft wool is the easiest to correct and restore.

> **Creasing Facts**
> Many drycleaners are pressing 25 to 50 slacks an hour and, at that rate, extra creases can occur. Slacks must be positioned by hand and carefully aligned to avoid double creases.

What to Do

I mentioned that it's hard to tell if a wrinkled pair of slacks has a crease. It is also difficult to tell *after* the slacks come out of the drycleaning machine, and certainly after wet cleaning. Be specific and tell the clerk. If you use a pick-up and delivery service, then send a note with your clothing. The cleaners will "flag" the slacks and do their best to make sure you get what you requested.

Resolutions

When you shop for slacks, be sure to check them closely for multiple creases before you buy. Be careful when you iron at home and when you travel. And be selective before sending your clothing to an unfamiliar cleaner or when using a hotel concierge service.

Note: The crease problems are an issue for custom and specialty cleaners and run rampant in average and high-production drycleaning plants throughout the industry. It is not my intention to disparage any drycleaners, but this problem has been an ongoing issue at almost every industry meeting I have attended for the last five years.

◆ Hangers

The choice of what kind of hanger to use or how to hang slacks can affect how they look. When slacks are hung from the waist, they are usually attached to the hanger by pins. You have no doubt struggled with these pins more than once. They can ruin a good manicure in a snap. They also put pinholes in the waistband of fragile materials and crush the nap of velvet and other sensitive fabrics. Many drycleaners have seen the trend toward uncreased slacks, have started listening to their customers, and have begun using "clip" hangers instead of pins to hang slacks from the waist.

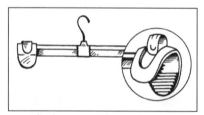

Clip hanger with rough ridges

This change has given way to different styles of clip hangers. In the beginning, there were only clips with ridges, which held slacks and skirts securely but deposited unsightly impressions on the waistband. These hangers could not be used on delicate fabrics. Now the industry is starting

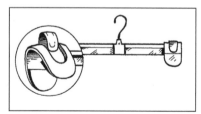

Clip hanger with a smooth soft-grip

to shift to soft-grip clip hangers which have a flat surface suitable for blue jeans, silk slacks, and even velvet. These hangers should help get your slacks back to you in the manner that you wish.

I suggest that you share this information with your drycleaners if they are not already using soft-grips. It will help them, and it will help the environment if they recycle the hangers. You can help by returning the clip hangers each time you visit.

All the do's, don'ts, and subtleties of finishing that I have mentioned in the past two chapters are important practices used at quality drycleaners. But more importantly, these insights afford you a rare glimpse at a part of the "process" that is seldom shared with consumers.

If you had to know just one part of the drycleaning process, it would be "finishing." You now have the knowledge to communicate with your cleaner in a positive and informative manner.

Chapter 11

Women's Clothing
Construction, Shopping, and Care

Women's clothing is often adorned with fragile, decorative buttons, delicate pleats, angle-cut lapels, "bones" in the bodice, stand-up Mandarin collars, full-skirt linings, and narrow vents. Women's fashion provides a wider forum for designers' expressions due to constantly evolving fashion trends, and there are more fabrics and fabric blends to work with than in men's wear. The challenges that men face when shopping for a wardrobe pale in comparison.

There is no question that women's clothing presents a broader range of problems and requires greater attention to detail. In fact, silk and satin fabric—which touches most women's wardrobes through scarves, accessories, and clothing—has so many nuances that I have given them a chapter of their own (Chapter 7).

After reading some of these chapters, you will shop with new awareness. You will see how different a rack of clothing will look to you, the details that your mind will register, the questions that you will ask, and the answers that you seek.

Chapter 1 on "Shopping in the Retail World," Chapter 2 on "Fabric Basics," and Chapter 3 on "Buttons and Trims" are all worth reading before shopping. You can use them as a reference anytime you have a question, especially the "Fabrics at a Glance" in Chapter 2, for specifics about the most common and fashionable fabrics.

◆ Save Time, Money, and Frustration

Time: You can reduce the amount of time it takes for you to shop and reduce the amount of return visits to the store. If you shop for yourself and other family members, then clothing returns become a regular and accepted way of life—but you can do better.

Money: Each time you return to a store, it costs money. By shopping smarter, you will have fewer garments to alter, fewer garments ruined by stains or wrong care labels, and fewer garments that sit in your closet, unworn.

Frustration: You will spend less time retracing your steps, and you will have fewer surprises. A large percentage of your wardrobe is made up of dryclean-only garments. Surprises are for gifts and parties, not for your visit to the drycleaner. Make this part of your life more predictable, in a good way.

◆ Before Shopping

The idea behind this section is to condition you to specific alerts. For example, when you feel a fused material, I want you to think of possible bubbles. When you see a pleated skirt, think about the extra expense of hand ironing; the same is true of silk, linen, and specialty fabrics. These clues will help you quickly sum up the "true cost" of a proposed purchase. At minimum, you will know, with few surprises, what to expect from the fabric in terms of wear and care.

Fashion Issues

Let your eyes guide you. Sometimes the exact detail that draws you to a garment can be the one thing that requires the most care. Any clothing that has unusual design aspects may have high-maintenance requirements—uneven or sculpted lapels; stand-up collars; snaps or hardware that cannot be removed; fragile lace and overlayers; fur, suede, or leather next to fabric; "bones" in the bodice; beads and sequins—all of these should make you think twice and prompt you to ask yourself questions: Am I buying a reputable label? Is this the best store from which to buy this garment? Am I prepared to care for it the way it is intended? Also, always read the care label before buying.

Fusible Construction

Fusing may use interfacing, bonding materials (adhesive), and fabric. This fused construction gives jackets a clean, smooth line. The problem with fusing is that sometimes the adhesive breaks down, the layers separate, and small bubbles form. Currently, there is a debate over whether the bubbles are a result of poor fusible adhesives and faulty processing in manufacturing, or a result of drycleaners using too much heat and steam.

When you see jackets made of acetate, triacetate, gabardine (recognizable by the twill weave), and other shiny wool fabrics, think about the fusible dilemma.

This dilemma should be a consideration when buying a jacket made in this manner, and price does not necessarily make the jacket immune to fusible bubbles. Ask before you buy, "Is this fusible construction?"

> **The Fusible Truth**
> As a rule, women's jackets have fewer problems with fusible bubbles than men's do.

Unfortunately, not many salespeople at mainstream stores know the difference between sewn and fused construction or have the knowledge to recognize it on sight, so be persistent.

Hems

It is painful to see how many hems on new garments are poorly sewn. Blind-stitched hems, which represent a growing number of sewn hems, can fall apart when one errant high-heel touches them. Many finer garments have hems that are sewn by hand but, nonetheless, have stitches that come loose while the item is still in the store.

Holes, Seams, Snags, Pads, and Buttons

Take the time to thoroughly inspect a garment before you get to the cash register. Check all seams for separated fabric, check for holes and tears, for loose stitching in the shoulder pads, and for loose buttons. Look very closely for snags; if you see snags on the garment before it has even been sold, then you know there will be long-term problems. Your lightbulb should illuminate.

Poor quality control on the part of the manufacturer, consumer abuse, and carelessness in the clothing stores contribute to many minute problems and needless return trips.

> **Smart Shopping**
> Other people may have tried on clothing before you. They may have caught a hem or pulled a seam. Check the clothing carefully before purchasing and save yourself a return trip and extra expense.

Knitted Fabrics

Depending on the fabric and the designer, some knits may have to be blocked back to shape after cleaning. Most knits are "shaped" during finishing and should only need minor adjustments. If more extensive reblocking is needed, then you may be required to try on the garment more than once while the finisher reblocks it to the proper fit. Each time this process is necessary, it costs you time. Be sure to ask the salesperson about shape retention when you purchase a knitted garment.

Kick Pleats, Vents, and Zippers

Back vents and side vents can be a constant bother if clothing is too tight. The stitches at the top of the vents give way to pressure, which causes the seam to tear or separate with regularity. The same is true of zipper seams, especially with invisible zippers and nylon zippers, which often require replacement.

Make sure that the garment fits well in these areas, or you will be spending time and money repairing them.

Pleats

Pleated clothing is attractive and often complements your figure. It is also expensive to maintain. Pleated skirts and dresses usually require re-pressing after every wearing. Pleats in the bodice and sleeves may only require ironing every *other* time. Pleats are usually ironed by hand, which can be expensive, so you should consider this maintenance expense in your clothing purchase. The more pleats, the more it will cost each time the garment is cleaned and pressed. (See Chapter 5 for different types of pleating.)

> **Extra Expense**
> If pleats are not sewn in and look like an accordion when they spread apart, then the skirt will be very expensive to iron.

Two-Toned Fabrics (Color-Blocked)

Any clothing made of silk or acetate that has a dark dye next to a light dye may have a dye-bleed problem (most prevalent with less expensive clothing). This is also true with less expensive rayon and triacetate fabrics. If the dye does bleed, then it may cause the white area to turn dingy, or gray. This is especially true on a black garment with white cuffs.

▸ Dark clothing should generally be cleaned with other dark clothing. If a dark dress has white cuffs, then does it stand to reason that it would be treated as a dark garment? Doing so is just one of the ways that white trims can become "less than white." If white cuffs cannot be removed, then how will they stay white? Read on.

▸ Such color contrast does not usually pose a problem in professional cleaning, except when the lighter areas need stronger stain removers to keep them clean or to remove specific stains. The chemicals, though generally safe on the fabric, are sometimes not safe for the darker dyes. The spotting can cause the darker dyes—such as black, navy, red, and purple—to leach out onto the white trims.

> **The Real Dirt**
> Studies have shown that dark clothing is worn two to three times more than lighter clothing before it is cleaned. What happens to white cuffs and trims during this period?

▸ Remember to pay special attention to your cuffs, collars, and trims and have the garment cleaned at the first sign of stains or soil. This preventive care will extend the life of your outfit.

◆ Let's Go Shopping

You should now know enough to make your shopping experience a more grati-
fying and profitable one. This next section will continue to sharpen your focus.

Buttons

You undoubtedly read about buttons in Chapter 3, but just a reminder: Be aware
of fragile buttons and unusual shapes, and always ask for an extra button or two
at the time of purchase.

Fabrics

Remember the role your eyes and hands play. They can distinguish a blended
fabric and natural fibers from synthetics. Think about the fundamentals; which
fabrics breathe, which will shine easily through wear or pressing, which will hold
onto odors, which will snag or pill easily, which will lose their shape, which will
wrinkle? Think about comfort and temperature swings. Is the clothing for work
or for travel?

Remember These Observations from Chapter 2?

> ▸ **Acetate** — Thick texture, but it can shine when press-
> ed, and it can snag easily.
>
> ▸ **Silk** — Beautiful drape, but maintenance is high, and
> underarms can discolor in one wearing.
>
> ▸ **Linen** — Rich looking, but must be re-ironed every
> time it's worn.
>
> ▸ **Wool** — Usually soft and thick; most wool won't have
> to be pressed after each wearing. It is good for travel.
>
> ▸ **Rayon** — Great textures, but water sensitive; it can
> become spotted from raindrops.

> **Wrinkle Warning**
> Wrinkled clothing
> should not be re-
> ironed or pressed
> if soiled. The heat
> that accompanies
> pressing may
> "set" stains and
> soil, making
> future removal
> difficult.

Customer Service

If you choose to shop in a store where the customer service representatives are
capable only of organizing and shelving merchandise, then recognize that you
may be the only expert on the sales floor. This predicament is one of the reasons
why I wrote this book. Your fabric training will now pay off. Obviously, the better
clothing stores usually offer better customer service. For another option in customer service, see Chapter 1 on shopping by appointment.

Care Labels

Most "basic" wool suits have dependable care labels. You don't need to read every label as you shop, but most certainly before you buy. For garments such as designer clothing, most outerwear, ski outfits, blended fabrics, and specialty pieces, I suggest that you do not make a purchase without first reading and understanding the care label instructions.

> **This Is True**
> Some care labels have the words, "Do not dry-clean," yet they also have a *symbol* that states dry-cleaning is the preferred method.

Content Labels

Content labels, which are sometimes a different tag than the care label, are worth reading if you are unsure of the fabric content. It will sharpen your fabric identification skills and alert you immediately to fabrics that may be on your "do not buy" list. As a game, I try to identify the fabric first, then check the label to see if I'm right. This game will quickly improve your shopping skills.

An Extra Word about Care Labels

If you find a garment that you really like, but the care label is unclear or contradictory, think about the repercussions before you buy. There is always a way to clean the garment, but some sacrifices may be necessary. Sometimes the garment can only be spot-cleaned, which is much more effective on water-based stains than on oily stains. This limitation means that you could be forced to wear a dress or formal gown with small (or large) oily spots on the front.

> **This Is Also True**
> Some care labels say, "Do not dry-clean. Do not wash. Spot clean only."

I have had customers call me before purchasing such expensive items. I openly encourage this communication. Use your drycleaner's knowledge; that's one reason the drycleaner is there.

Travel

Travel can challenge fabric selection. Obviously, nonwrinkle fabrics, readily available these days, would travel the best, but many are not very flattering. Many synthetics, especially polyester, are wrinkle resistant. Wool, long considered the best fabric for traveling, still remains an excellent choice. Selecting the proper weight garment for the appropriate weather will increase your satisfaction. If the clothing has been folded or placed in a wardrobe bag, then hanging it as soon as possible will help remove creases and relax wrinkles. Packing the clothing in stuffing tissue, available at stores and shipping services, can be an excellent deterrent to wrinkles and creases.

If you attempt to iron your clothing in the hotel room, then be careful of shine; iron the garment on the reverse side when possible and consider using a "pressing cloth" to protect the garment from shining. (See Chapter 25 about ironing.)

What Does Well-Pressed Clothing Look Like?

Upper-Body Wear

Lapels should be softly rolled, rather than creased, with no shine along the edges. Sleeves should also be rolled, with no crease and, when appropriate, stuffed with tissue to provide a rounded, full look. Buttons and pocket flaps should have no impressions underneath them. Sashes, scarves, overlayers, and bows should be soft pressed and steamed with rounded edges whenever possible. Blouses should have the natural drape and texture they had when they were new.

Jackets made of fine wools, such as camel, cashmere, and blends, should always be soft pressed and lightly brushed to give the jacket back its soft feel. That luxuriant look will be restored only by brushing and steaming. Too many drycleaners do not respect this nuance and they press the fabric too hard, which gives it a flat, rather than a luxuriant look. Mention this when you have the jacket cleaned. If the clerk is not aware of this problem, then ask if a manager can attend to it.

Rarely Considered
If you carry a backpack, briefcase, or wardrobe bag across your shoulder, then you are putting tremendous pressure on the shoulder pads of your jacket. This weight and friction can distort the shoulder-pad area and may cause the fabric to shine.

Lower-Body Wear

If slacks are creased, then they should have one straight crease (no double creases). The crease should be sharp on soft wools with a nap, and softer on the fabrics that have a natural sheen, such as gabardine and summer-weight wool. The crotch area should be wrinkle free; there should be no impressions down the side seams—inside or outside the thigh.

Pleats should be sharp, straight, and free of shine. The iron impressions, or imprints, from one pleat onto the next pleat, should be minor, if evident at all. Hems should be rolled whenever possible, rather than flat pressed. The fabric should have body and drape.

◆ At the Cleaners

You have made an investment in your clothing; now make it pay.

When you're dropping off clothing at the cleaners, take the opportunity to inspect your clothing for stains, needed repairs, and pilling. This is also the time to convey finishing details for any unusual or designer clothing. The clerk should be receptive and helpful. If this is not the case, then you may want to think about finding a new cleaner. Voice your concerns and your expectations.

Buttons

If certain buttons need to be removed or protected, now is the time to tell the cleaners. If you want the buttons replaced, they may have new sets there or, in some cases, they may be willing to buy new ones at the fabric store when they go to buy supplies.

Inspecting Your Clothing

Stains

Check each garment for stains. If you know the origin of the stain, then tell the clerk. If you remember any "invisible" spots, then point them out (perfume stains, white wine, fruit spray). If you perspired in the underarms but the stain does not show, then be sure to draw the clerk's attention to that area. If there is serious staining, a large spill, or a special stain such as ink, then ask what the cleaner's expectation is for removal and if there will be an extra charge.

> **Help if You Can**
> When you have a printed scarf drycleaned, you should point out any stains that you remember. The "wild" designs often make stains difficult to locate.

Minor Repairs

Check the most common areas for minor repairs: inside the linings, underarms and pockets for holes; buttons for reinforcing; seams, hems, vents, and kick pleats for resewing; shoulder pads that need basting; zippers and the fabric around them for stress. All these areas tend to need care eventually. These aspects can be hassle free if you permit your drycleaner to do minor repairs of up to $15 without calling you. Try to form that sort of relationship with your cleaner.

Inspection for Holes

If you see any holes in your wool clothing, then try to discern if they are the result of insect damage or a tear. If you believe they are from insects, then check the whole outfit closely for more holes and weakened, thinned areas. The thinned areas could be partially eaten fibers. If you find more holes, then mark them with safety pins and have the clothing cleaned before repairing. If after cleaning you find additional holes, then the expense to repair or reweave all the holes may eclipse the cost of the suit. (See Chapter 27 on "Reweaving: A True Savior.")

If you are going to repair any holes, then ask about the quality of the sewing or reweaving, as well as the outcome, especially if the holes are in an obvious location.

Alterations

If your drycleaner has a good seamstress or tailor, then consider using his or her services. The alterations area is usually located in the front of the store so that you can see if he or she seems friendly and helpful. You can ask to see some of his or her work; he or she should be proud to show it to you. If convenience is an important aspect, then you couldn't ask for more than this arrangement. A good seamstress or tailor can restore older clothing, take in, let out, cut down, replace unflattering shoulder pads, and much more.

Inspecting your clothing at the counter, prior to cleaning, will enable you to discover necessary repairs. If you need alterations, then walk over to the sewing area, try on the garment, and be fitted. You can use these services for new clothing as well.

Finishing Details to Convey

Most people come into the cleaners and drop their clothing onto the counter; or if the cleaner offers a delivery service, then the driver is handed the clothing in a bag. There's nothing wrong with these scenarios, but unless the clerk is going to take a few minutes to inspect the clothing, or unless a note accompanies the driver, certain details may be missed.

Details

▸ If a blouse has a "crinkle-wrinkle" look, or the pleats are supposed to be rolled at the top and ironed the rest of the way, then note this detail.

▸ If a collar should be pressed "up," then make a note.

▸ If slacks are supposed to have a soft crease, or if they should be hung from the waist, then tell the clerk.

> **Small Stuff**
> If you have cuff links, jewelry, removable shoulder pads, or detachable bows or belts, then remove them and leave them at home.

Maintaining a wardrobe and all of the accessories requires time and energy. Sometimes garments that are stored in another closet or drawer, and have not been worn for a season or two, may be forgotten. Check your clothing each season, assess sizes and interest, and rotate clothing from the top of the stack to the bottom. Also, consider using "stuffing tissue" when folding fragile garments such as beaded clothing and cashmere or silk-knit sweaters.

Story Time ...

The wife of a well-known politician invited me to her home to consult with her about the care and maintenance of her considerable wardrobe. She dedicated a complete room to her clothing and accessory collection. Each ensemble, containing the outfit, accessories, and shoes, were hanging together. Each "group" had an index card attached to the hanger, which explained in detail the last time the ensemble was worn, including the date, the event, and other specifics.

Finding a system that works for you to organize and catalogue your wardrobe, be it mentally or in writing, can be beneficial and will help you effectively maintain your clothing investment.

Chapter 12

Party Dresses

Delicate Fabrics and Weaves

Velvet, chiffon, organza, and taffeta are fabrics and weaves that require special respect when wearing and may need special care when drycleaning. These are concerns for you, but sometimes even more so for your daughters. I will address both situations. Don't think that just because you are "grown-up" you are immune to the problems; they are almost universal.

◆ Velvet

If there is one glaring problem that I should scream out to you, it would be that velvet is very water sensitive. Velvet is manufactured in rayon, silk, acetate, or cotton (which is the lowest and least luxurious grade, and the least water sensitive).

Most velvet party dresses and gowns are made from silk or acetate, though many children's dresses are made from rayon velvet. For velvet, consider moisture of any kind to be an enemy. Rain, perspiration, and drink spills can permanently damage the fabric.

Moisture can "crush" the pile fabric and, more often than not, the nap cannot be lifted evenly or restored to the same sheen.

> **How Neat Is She?**
> When you purchase a party dress for your young daughter, always read the care label. If it says, "Dry Clean Only," then keeping it clean may be a challenge.

What Upsets Velvets

▶ When the pile or nap of velvet is exposed to moisture, the "pores" of the fabric are defenseless and the imperfections stand out like a ripple on a calm sea.

▶ This moisture is then aggravated by any pressure or friction on the surface of the pile.

99

▶ Dancing usually starts the moisture ball rolling; the most affected areas are the underarms, inside the crease at the elbows, between the legs of slacks, and the seat area. Once these areas are wet with perspiration, the pile can mat easily.

▶ Drink or food spills have a damaging effect on the surface of the pile. Spills are absorbed and food stains "crust" on the surface.

Sometimes a drycleaner can lift the velvet pile by steaming and brushing, silk velvet being the most responsive. It is imperative that you *do not try to save it yourself* when a problem occurs.

It is almost inevitable that a child will spill food or drink over a large-enough area that only hand washing can help. Only cotton velvet can be washed without changing the direction of the pile.

If you have worn velvet, then you know it is best to be realistic and to approach velvet philosophically. Recognize the limitations of this beautiful fabric and accept the crushed areas as character traits, and try not to be too self-conscious about them.

> **Velvet Challenge**
> Special tools are available to drycleaners that aid them in lifting crushed velvet pile. Velvet is difficult enough to treat for stains, but it is further complicated by cleaners who do not have the right training.

◆ Chiffon

Silk chiffon is the most common type of chiffon, followed by poly-chiffon and fine rayon crepe. You see silk chiffon in most ballet and dance productions because it flows like a feather in a soft breeze. It is also the fabric of choice for many couture and high-fashion garments. Chiffon, because of its drape, is often used to accentuate a design or as an overlayer. Many evening gowns and skirts are made from silk chiffon because it projects a soft, ethereal look. Spills and food stains are reasonably manageable, but silk chiffon snags and tears easily.

> **Good Habits**
> If you use hair spray or perfume, then always put it on *before* you dress. All the fabrics mentioned in this chapter can be permanently stained by the mist or drops from these products.

Concerns When Wearing Chiffon

▶ Because the fabric flows, it catches on edges and handbag hardware. In the case of formal gowns, it is often torn at the hem by high-heels while someone is dressing or dancing.

▸ If the hem is torn and, depending on the location and size of the tear, then it is often best to consider shortening the hem to hide it rather than repairing it.

▸ Snags can cause individual threads to "stand up," and they cannot be easily disguised. A single snag can "run" the material for inches, and there is no easy remedy for this dilemma.

▸ Chiffon is also routinely cut on the bias, which can make simple repairs and redesigning a challenge.

Silk chiffon tends to become distorted more easily when wet. It is imperative that you do not wipe stains with a towel or napkin when chiffon is wet. The yarns can separate, and there is no remedy for yarn slippage.

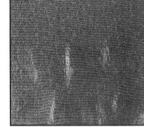

Yarn slippage—often occurs when fabric is wet

◆ Organza

Is there a more pristine weave than organza, with its crisp formality and "debutante-like" aura? If this fabric—and all the lovely dresses that are made of it—could rest gently on brides, mannequins, and Audrey Hepburn, then it would last forever.

Organza is a very brittle fiber with a sheen as perfect as glass. It is commonly used for wedding gowns, evening gowns, and children's formals. Because the fiber is so brittle and has no stretch or give, it is very important that it fits properly. If it is too tight, then the seams may pull and separate. Never rub the material or attempt stain removal yourself. The surface sheen can change with the slightest abrasion, and yarn slippage, or separation, is always possible.

"Wearability" Issues

▸ If you are wearing a gown that has a specific cut or design at the waistline that restricts movement, and if you need to reach or bend, then the fabric will not "give." It generally remains stationary, so, instead of stretching, the fibers separate. This is called yarn separation.

▸ Yarn separation is most evident under the arms, at the waist, and along the hip area.

▸ When organza is altered, especially if it is "let out," the stitch holes will show quite clearly.

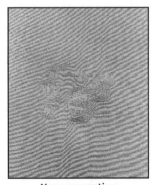

Yarn separation

▶ When organza becomes "bent" or creased, a white line often appears where the crease is. This white line is akin to taking a piece of paper, folding it with a sharp crease, and then unfolding it only to find that there is still a residual line that cannot be smoothed. Ironing organza fabric once it has been hard-creased does not remove the white line.

These "breaks" are permanent and should not be considered "life-threatening" to your gown. Try to think of them as character traits.

◆ Taffeta

Taffeta is a beautiful material; is available in deep, vibrant colors; and is used in very fashionable styles. Whether you have a formal gown, a dressy blouse, a crisp two-piece suit, or an updated version of Mary Tyler Moore's capri slacks, taffeta must have "body" and should never be limp or tired looking.

▶ Although this step should *not* be your responsibility, it is very important to remind your drycleaner to add additional sizing to give the taffeta the proper drape when it is being pressed.

▶ Creases and hard wrinkles that occur from wear, especially at the waist, can usually be improved during pressing. The "white lines," so prominent with organza, are not as severe with taffeta.

▶ Although taffeta needs a crisp pressing, the drycleaner needs to be aware of the seams and double-thick areas. If those areas are not "steamed out" after pressing, then there will be deep impressions and pock marks on the surface of the fabric. Be firm about your expectations.

> **For Longevity**
> After wearing taffeta and organza, inspect the seams at stress areas for yarn slippage. If you see evidence of this condition, then you may be able to alter the garment before additional damage occurs.

Color Change from Perspiration

As mentioned in our chapter on silk and its color changes caused by perspiration, silk taffeta suffers from the same malady. When you perspire, especially under the arms and at the waist, the acids turn alkaline and can cause a color change after the fabric dries. Time, even a few days, can contribute to a permanent color change. You have, no doubt, seen it under the arms of your silk blouses, and this situation is no different.

When an expensive gown experiences a color change under the arms, it compromises the longevity of your investment. If you perspired to the extent that the area has become very wet, you may have a problem.

First, try to remember that it occurred. The next day you should take your dress to the drycleaners, tell the clerk the what and where, and request that the perspiration in those areas be treated with steam. This promptness may be soon enough to allay the color change and head it off. If you perspired and you inadvertently put the dress away for the "next time," you will almost certainly have a permanent color change. You have too much invested in your clothing to be so irresponsible (smile), so think about that.

> **Say It Ain't So**
> Color change can occur after one wearing, so be aware and be proactive.

◆ Let's Go Shopping

All the fabrics I have discussed in this chapter should be considered fragile. These fabrics do not stretch, so they must fit properly or the seams will pull and yarn slippage may occur. Long hems can drag and may get caught on the heels of your shoes—especially chiffon. Take a pair of heels with you when you try on floor-length gowns; don't approximate.

When shopping, check buttons, beads, belts, and clips for sharp edges that may cause snags. The settings around stones are sometimes the worst offenders. Always inspect the condition of the gown; check for snags, pulls, open seams, yarn slippage, and crushed areas on velvet and, lastly, check inside the neckline for makeup stains deposited by other customers.

> **Lightbulb On?**
> Darker colors in organza and taffeta fabrics will show the "white line" more prominently. Think about this aspect when shopping.

◆ At the Cleaners

Inspect your clothing carefully for stains and minor repairs. Check the hems of your gowns for soil from the street. If you have bows, belts, or sashes, then check their condition. If they do not need cleaning or pressing, then take them home.

Check your velvet clothing carefully for crushed areas. If there *are* stains or crushed areas, then talk to the manager or a key person to get an opinion about the chances for restoration. If there are breaks or yarn slippage on the organza or chiffon fabrics, then point them out to the cleaner to ensure care is taken. Take a moment to check the underarms to see if the texture is stiff or if a color change has occurred. This is an important step, so be focused and convey your concerns.

Yarn slippage and yarn separation can sometimes be improved by carefully re-aligning the threads one at a time with a sharp pin. This type of restoration can be time-consuming, but it may offer some improvement.

◆ Special Care for Couture Clothing

Many truly exquisite garments, often referred to as "couture creations," are as fragile as they are beautiful. The fabrics may be as delicate as the construction of the garment. The weight and drape of the fabric is often unparalleled. The hand sewing and use of silk thread further distinguish the creation.

A draped bodice, with its gentle folds of fabric held by well-placed hand stitches, represent the subtle and focused intention of the designer. A perfect bias-cut over-layer, a scallop-edged lapel, or delicately placed feathers, all require an experienced drycleaner who has an awareness of the fragility and value of these creations.

If a few stitches are broken or removed, and if the bodice shifts ever-so-slightly, then it is the seamstress or tailor who will return the creation back to the "original" condition and vision of the designer. If the lapel or overlayer is slightly askew, then it is the finisher who will restore the lay of the fabric.

> **Delicacy in Action**
> Silk chiffon is one of the most delicate fabrics used in the design of couture clothing. Spend a few minutes to examine the sewing in these garments the next time you have a couture creation cleaned.

You know what motivated you to buy a couture creation—it requires equal attention when cleaning and caring for it. Be careful with spills and food stains, with jewelry and other sharp objects; be cognizant of the damage that deodorants and perspiration can do, and be aware of the often delicate construction.

Money, time, and passion are often equal ingredients in the purchase of expensive clothing—make it a worthy investment—help make it last.

Chapter 13

Bridal Gowns
Selecting, Altering, Cleaning, and Preserving

Selecting a bridal gown can be almost as fulfilling as the wedding itself if you have someone to help guide you through the experience. You may ask, "Where do I start? What concerns do I have? And why must I have a guide?" I have some answers to these questions.

There are complete books on the subject, which has become so involved that it has spawned its own "cottage industry." I will just address some practical aspects that are usually glossed over, especially the caring of your gown during alteration, restyling, cleaning, and preservation.

◆ Selecting a Gown

Selecting a bridal gown is a freewheeling experience. There are no rules. You can shop at bridal boutiques, specialty shops, couture dress shops that offer designer gowns, and secondhand stores. If you want to wear a gown that has been in your family for one, two, or three generations, you can do so. Or perhaps you would like to wear a friend's gown. All of these are good avenues to explore.

If you choose a new gown, then you will have fewer issues to consider and your "support group" will likely be the people at the bridal boutique or possibly an outside dressmaker. If you wish to wear an older gown, then you will most likely need some outside assistance from a dressmaker and a restoration specialist such as your drycleaner or a drycleaner who specializes in bridal gowns. This issue is worth thinking about because it is often a very personal one.

> **Looking Ahead**
> A very small percentage of brides think about the cleaning of their wedding gown, especially while on their honeymoon. But if they don't, who will? Mom?

Although I am introducing the subject of cleaning and preservation earlier than you would think necessary, please give it the proper attention now. It is a very important part of the process, and though it comes at the end of the event, it is best to address this matter *before* the event. Here is why:

After the wedding, everyone is worn out. The bride is on her honeymoon, the mother of the bride is completely drained, the father is—well, we'll leave him out of *this*—and the gown, which has been such a large part of your preparation, often sits with stains, and no one is caring for it! Please make a genuine effort to move forward to the section titled "After the Wedding" on page 110 *before* you start shopping for your wedding gown. Read the whole section—I guarantee that you will be thankful you did.

◆ A New Wedding Gown

A new gown will have a care label sewn inside that will give a preferred method of cleaning. The care is generally the furthest thing from your mind because you have not even worn the gown or been married yet. However, it is important to read the care label as you shop—certainly before you buy. Do not be flippant about this aspect because it can jump up and bite you later, which is a hassle you do not need!

Shopping

▸ Some labels state that the gown must be sent to a post office box in another state for cleaning, or they say that it should be cleaned by only one establishment.

▸ Some labels state that the gown can only be wet cleaned, and others actually say, "Do not dryclean. Do not wash." All of these directions are worth a minute of thought. I suggest that you consult with the boutique owner or department manager and, if necessary, also make a quick call to the owner of your drycleaners before you buy.

> **Label Fundamental**
> Care labels are required by law, but that doesn't mean that they are correct or accurate.

Details and Nuances

▸ Some items are *glued* on the gown, such as pearls, sequins, and trims. (See Chapter 3 on trims.)

▸ Sometimes small "knife" pleats may not withstand cleaning, steaming, or ironing. They can break down and lose their crispness or structure.

▸ Many of the glued-on trims can be safely wet cleaned, but that process brings with it other concerns. Do not assume that a gown is easily serviceable just because it is being offered by a reputable store or is being sold for a high price.

Many proprietors are not even aware of the processing problems. In most cases they are—but my voice of experience is begging you to think about long-term care before you buy.

◆ Secondhand Gowns

Second-generation and secondhand gowns can offer oodles of options with regard to fabrics and styles and can offer a special slant at a reasonable price. Your typical concerns include the following:

▸ Color inconsistencies, possible stubborn or unremovable stains

▸ Alteration and repair requirements

▸ Possible restyling issues, costs, and options

▸ Fabric fragility

Restoration Issues

I will address all of these issues, but first … In all my years of involvement with soon-to-be brides, my typically optimistic and good nature has been tested by many women who have chosen to wear older gowns. Certain truths are not negotiable and should be accepted when choosing secondhand gowns.

The beauty and personality that accompany an older gown should be appreciated and accepted, yet so often the bride tries to make it into a "new gown," which is not only contrary but also a waste of time.

▸ If the gown has yellowed, then it can generally be lightened by careful wet cleaning and possible bleaching.

▸ If the style needs a bit of "sprucing up," a patient and experienced dressmaker or tailor can do wonders.

▸ If a bustle needs to be made, it can be done. If there is deterioration to the lace or other areas, then it can be replaced. If there are unsightly stains that cannot be removed by wet cleaning, then consider applying lace or appliqué.

> **Help "To Go"**
> Take this book to help you shop. Sit down, relax, and think about these key questions.

There are many options for interested and open-minded brides. The key is that an open-minded and relaxed attitude will make the experience much more invigorating and rewarding.

Wet Cleaning as a Form of Restoration

▸ First, consider the options that your knowledgeable drycleaner should suggest. Ask questions and push the cleaner to think "outside the box." Can he or she show you a sample of other gowns that had similar issues?

▸ Suggest that the buttons be removed before wet cleaning, and possibly replaced if they are frayed or badly yellowed and cannot be restored.

▸ Decide just how much brighter you want the gown to be. Although restoration is not an exact science, the gown can be monitored during the process. Remember, sometimes the trims will brighten at a different rate than the fabric of the dress will.

▸ You should also consider the slight possibility of further deterioration in wet cleaning and ask if it is advisable to baste some fabric behind the fragile areas before the cleaning process.

▸ Consider the possibility of shrinkage resulting from wet cleaning.

> **Think Ahead**
> This whole process can be very exhilarating, but it is best to treat it like a project. Be organized and allow four to six weeks for preparation.

Note: I suggest that you take this type of restoration one step at time. Up to this point your investment should be minimal, so you still have choices.

After Wet Cleaning

▸ Inspect the gown closely for loose trim, weakened areas, discoloration, and overall improvement.

▸ Slip the gown on to assess and discuss any fitting issues. If there is shrinkage, then can the gown be let out without leaving seam marks and stitching holes? Is the color different in the area that was let out?

▸ Consider any stains that may remain. Are they part of the natural "second-generation" beauty, or are they a deterrent? If you wish to disguise them, think about final redesign issues and let the dressmaker help you envision the end result. Then relax—the hardest part is over.

Very Important: If all these steps have been performed and you are still not satisfied, then it is not too late to choose another gown. It's just like putting a bid on your "dream house" and losing it. You may think that there is no other house that will please you, and you'll never be happy without it, but you usually find one that you like even more. So be relaxed through this process and step back occasionally for a breather.

If you *are* happy with the restoration, then read the next step.

▶ The dressmaker may baste certain areas, have a fitting, design the bustle, have another fitting, and so forth.

▶ Remember that the dressmaker has a personal stake in this process and that he or she is a sensitive person, too. I have seen too many stressed-out brides and mothers who make the dressmaker's life miserable.

▶ The dressmaker is an artist and an integral part of this blessed event, especially if the gown has needed a lot of reworking. He or she may have some excellent ideas. Be cognizant of this and be thankful this person cares so much.

▶ The last few weeks of work will go by quickly. Try on the gown as often as you need, and check the accessories and your list to be sure that all the pieces of the puzzle are accounted for.

◆ Last Details Before the Wedding

A week or so before your wedding day, you may want to have the gown steamed or pressed professionally. Whether you have purchased it locally or it has been shipped to you from out of town, you can make arrangements to have it pressed a day or two before the event. I suggest that you speak to your drycleaner to see if you can set up this type of arrangement.

▶ Review the final details and ask for the gown to be ready on Thursday or Friday if the wedding is on a Saturday.

▶ Your dress can be freshly steamed and pressed, preferably hand ironed, stuffed with tissue and a bodice form, packaged in an oversized poly bag (clear or opaque, as you see fit), and possibly delivered by the drycleaner as well.

▶ We have made many brides very happy by arranging direct contact with the concierge at their hotel or with a designated person at the church or synagogue, and by delivering the gown in its pristine state a day before the wedding.

This concept allows the bride to dress at the specified location without worrying about wrinkling or crushing the gown during the ride there. This approach isn't always convenient for every bride, but most of the time it seems the final touch at the end of a long road.

◆ After the Wedding

Why Clean Your Gown?

Whether you keep your gown to restyle or to hand down, or you intend to sell it to a secondhand store, it will need to be cleaned. A gown that sits uncleaned for weeks or months may not be of use to anyone.

Cleaning

Drycleaning is not a magical process, and it does not remove all the stains encountered at weddings. But it is especially effective on oils, makeup, lipstick, wax, some grass stains, and light hem soil. (See Chapter 8 for the complete story on stains.)

▸ If the weather was wet or the event was held outside, then there could be some very stubborn grass and mud stains on the train and hem. If this is the case, then you must be painfully aware that there may be only limited removal in drycleaning.

▸ Wet cleaning may also be an option. Although not all gowns can be wet cleaned, the process generally removes a greater amount of hem soil and grass stains. It also removes "invisible" spills from champagne and white wine.

▸ Water-based stains such as wine, champagne, soda, certain foods with dyes, and food coloring are improved or removed only by careful hand spotting or wet cleaning. It is very important that you try to recall the source of large spills and convey that information to your drycleaner, for the most thorough restoration possible, before the gown is preserved in a box.

Some of the common spills listed above are typically clear in nature and contain dangerous sugars that can caramelize (turn yellow) but may not be visible until the garment has been cleaned. (See Chapter 8 for more on stains.)

Not only are clear stains, which are most often spills from champagne and white wine, sometimes not removed in drycleaning, but also they are often left in the fabric and preserved that way. If the gown is preserved in that condition, then you cannot fault the drycleaner, who has no way of knowing what occurred unless there is color to the stain, or unless the bride helps in locating these "invisible" stains.

The invisible stains may come back to haunt you years down the road in the form of a yellow or brownish tint, or they may have been so diluted by the cleaning that they will not be a concern at all. Either way, you get my drift.

Note: While at the drycleaners, inquire about preservation practices. Not all cleaners offer "in-house" preservation service, which is often the best method. If you are happy with your cleaner, then you can accomplish both tasks at the same time.

Sewing and Repairs

Make a conscious decision about whether you are going to do repairs now or whether you will leave that to the next generation, should someone choose to wear your gown. It may be more prudent to do only the repairs needed to clean the gown safely and to worry about the other repairs in twenty years. That decision is personal.

Preservation: What and Why

After cleaning and proper inspection, the next step is to store your gown and any accessories in acid-free tissue inside an acid-free box. This process will slow aging and offer the best environment in which to preserve your gown. Allowing any clothing to sit in a closet or drawer for years on end can affect the fabric in many ways. Preservation is important and, without proper attention, you may not have a gown to pass down to your daughter or future daughter-in-law.

▶ Proper long-term storage will eliminate or diminish yellowing, help control moisture, and reduce premature discoloration. Improper storage is the primary reason that drycleaners must do so much recoloring and wet cleaning of older gowns.

▶ Poor storage, or no storage at all, can render a once-priceless or cherished gown to rags, literally.

▶ Long-term storage in an attic, in a drawer, inside a trunk, in a plastic bag, or on a hanger in a closet can dramatically change the pH of the fabric, and possibly discolor it, sometimes beyond restoration. Results can vary depending on the type of fabric and its condition at the time of storage.

▶ The wrong storage location can attract moisture, insects, and stains, and it may cause the fabric to rot and become too brittle to restore. The stains encountered by this type of neglect are very stubborn and often cannot be removed by any process. In one fell swoop, you can ruin your investment or heirloom.

I recommend that you choose a drycleaner that you have a relationship with already. Ask the owner, point blank, if the cleaners specializes in bridal cleaning and preservation. If they don't, then politely move on. Don't be soft on this issue.

As a rule, do not use a service that asks you to ship your gown to them. There are exceptions to this rule, but be specific in your questioning if you choose this type of service. If you live in a rural area and have no choice but to send it out, then you can do research on the Internet, inquire at the store that sold you the gown, or consult a bridal magazine but, again, ask a lot of questions and choose wisely.

The Actual "Boxing" Process

Some drycleaners will offer you the opportunity to "view" your gown (assuming that you are not shipping your gown away) before it is boxed and preserved. In most cases, there is no need to view the gown before it is preserved, but if you want to check specific details, such as stains or sewing, then ask them to contact you before they actually box it.

A TV show was aired in 1998 that made an issue of a drycleaner who had once boxed a woman's gown in someone else's box, and the mistake was not discovered until it was too late. I am sure that anything can happen in any situation, but this is a very unusual occurrence.

You may want to address the issue of "misboxing" with your cleaner, but be respectful about it and just pose the question. The drycleaner will answer you, and then you can move on.

▸ Make sure that the drycleaner uses a pH-neutral, acid-free box, with acid-free tissue, and that the box allows the gown to breathe.

▸ There should be different-sized boxes available for fuller dresses.

▸ In the best situation, you should be told that it is not only ok, but it is also suggested that you open the box every year to "check it out." If the cleaner suggests otherwise or says that you will "void the warranty" by opening the box, then you should find another drycleaner. Be sure to inquire about this matter if you ship the gown away for service.

When you do open the box, make sure that your hands are clean and free of oils (you could wear latex gloves). You may not need to remove the gown because generally a cursory glance will give you the answers you seek. Is it yellowing; is it dry; does it have an odor?

Note: Prior to boxing the gown, ask the cleaners what their policy is if the gown should yellow or develop stains. Much of this situation does depend on the storage environment in your home and how well you were able to identify the "invisible" stains before cleaning.

30 Minutes to Save Your Gown

If you can get 30 minutes to yourself after the reception to look over your gown, then it will save you money, frustration, and possible disappointment. At the same time, you will make your mother or "designated" helper very happy. Just fill in the inspection sheet that is printed in the back of the book, give it to your designated person—and bon voyage!

Your Designated Helper

Who is going to take your gown in for cleaning and, perhaps, preservation after the wedding?

After the wedding, the bride is usually on her honeymoon, the mother and mother-in-law are mentally and physically drained, and the father usually can't even conceive of helping. The gown sometimes sits even after the bride's return, when she is busy adjusting to her new life. And in some cases, the gown is simply forgotten in the whirlwind and may not be cleaned for a year or more.

> **Designated Form**
> By filling in the two inspection forms after your wedding, you will make the designated helper much more comfortable. Your helper need only convey your words, ask a few questions, and pay the deposit.

▸ Discuss this issue *before* the wedding and designate a helper to take your gown in for cleaning and preservation. Many mothers walk into the drycleaners with their daughter's gown after the wedding, feeling unprepared and unsure about the answers to all their questions.

▸ You should also decide which items besides your bridal gown you would like inside the preservation box. You can include the veil, the headpiece, your shoes and gloves, and any other personal items. You may want to think twice about the crinoline if you have a box size restriction.

Set a time to give your gown and accessories to your designated helper. Included at the end of this chapter are two sample forms, "Wedding Gown Inspection Sheet" and "Stain Diagram for Gown, Veil, and Headpiece." Give these forms to your designated helper before you leave town. (Buy her lunch when you return!)

When the Designated Helper Drops Off Your Gown

Let's assume that you are reading this before the wedding, as I suggested in the section "Selecting a Gown."

As you are doing your research and choosing a drycleaner, either to press your new gown for the wedding or to do the restoration on a second-generation gown, start gathering the information you'll need for cleaning and preservation after the wedding. You may find that one drycleaner can do it all for you.

When your designated helper drops off your bridal gown for cleaning and preservation, the following points should be considered:

▸ First, make sure you have all the pieces of the ensemble.

▸ Give the clerk the "Wedding Gown Inspection Sheet" with the "Stain Diagram" on the back. (You could also make a copy of these forms for your files.)

▸ Have the clerk refer to the forms as he or she inspects your gown. Ask the clerk to check closely for dangling or missing pearls, sequins, and trims, and to look for snags and missing buttons.

▸ If there are stains, then ask the cleaner to predict the outcome, especially in the hem, neck, and underarm area.

▸ The cleaner should also inspect the headpiece for makeup and decide if it should be hand spotted before the preservation process.

> **Can You Be Called?**
> If there are stain issues that are important enough to discuss with you while on your honeymoon—although there rarely are—will that be ok?

The drycleaner should then make a list of your concerns. He or she may ask for a 50% deposit, or for payment in full, and may ask if you would like to "view" the gown before it is boxed and preserved.

Note: If there are bad stains that require wet cleaning, then ask the cleaner to wait a few days while the helper talks to the bride about cleaning options.

> That sums up the pearls of wisdom I have to share on the subject of bridal gowns. Have a great experience, a happy event, and a marriage filled with love and respect—and don't forget to be mellow... and to breathe!

The Ultimate Helper is in the back section of this book. That section has removable worksheets for *bridal gowns*, christening gowns, leather and suede, and shopping guides. Tear one out for your trip to the cleaners when you or your designated person drops off your bridal gown.

Stain Diagram for Gown, Veil, and Headpiece

Do not remove this sample page — see the copy in the back of the book.

Front of gown   Back of gown

Veil and headpiece   Slip or crinoline

Put an "X" wherever the stains are and a "Y" wherever sewing is needed.

Wedding Gown Inspection Sheet
* Do not remove this sample page—see the copy in the back of the book.

Any Invisible Stains? (white wine, champagne, clear soda, spills) _____

_____

_____

_____

Any Unusual Food Stains? _____

_____

_____

_____

Heavy Soil on Hem, Neck, or Other Area _____

_____

_____

_____

Tears, Loose Seams, Dangling Beads on Gown or Veil _____

_____

_____

_____

Specific Wishes to Convey to Cleaner _____

_____

_____

_____

Inventory all pieces: Gown ___Veil ___ Headpiece ___ Gloves___ Slip ___ Other _____

A Few Last Words:

After their weddings, brides brought us their shoes to clean. Many were satin, some were cloth, but most had stains such as tar, grass stains, spills, and shoe polish from dancing partners. Many of the stains were spot-cleaned, and the improvement was often very good. This may be a better option than a shoe-repair shop.

Sometimes photos have to be taken or re-taken after the wedding. If your gown has *not yet been cleaned*, then some spot-cleaning and light pressing or steaming may be just enough to prep it for the photos.

If photos need to be retaken and your gown *has already been cleaned* and is ready for preservation, but you want to avoid recleaning and the extra expense that comes with it, then consider these issues: make sure the room is very cool (to minimize perspiration), dress right before the pictures are taken, wear as little makeup as possible and have it applied *after* you put on the dress (use a towel to protect the dress), stay as far from the hot lights as possible, and keep your hands clean and free of oils.

If you get new stains on the gown during the photo session, then it may be possible to spot-clean them before the preservation process. It is best to clean the dress again after the pictures, but there may be an extra expense. Share this information with your cleaner and, under the circumstances, he or she may offer you a discount for the second cleaning.

If you intend to sell your dress rather than preserve it, then make sure your dry-cleaner knows about this, and ask to have it pressed for the store that will re-sell it.

Chapter 14

The Christening Outfit
Representing a Family for Generations

I address the christening outfit, an integral part of family history, at this point, because it mirrors so closely the second- and third-generation bridal gowns that are handed down. The older christening gowns have so much character that saving them for future children perpetuates a great legacy.

Maybe you remember pictures from family albums of your parents, grandparents, or even great-grandparents wearing this exact christening outfit. Images such as these remind me of how special christening outfits can be.

Many families have made it a tradition to share these christening outfits with siblings, cousins, children, and grandchildren. Each generation has received these outfits as gifts from heaven. Why not make every effort to preserve them?

◆ Mistakes with Older Outfits

One of the common mistakes that parents make in the wake of a christening, and the chaos that often accompanies such an event, is not remembering to clean the outfit and properly preserve it for the next child. The next child may come in one year or in twenty years. Drool, formula, breast milk … all of these things seem so very mundane but, nonetheless, are a reality. Many of these stains are "invisible" at the onset. Sometimes a parent or relative looks at the christening outfit—which may consist of gloves, booties, slip, bonnet, gown, and coat—sees no stains, and casually stores it after the blessed event without even washing it. Or the relative may wash it, then "store" it in a box or a drawer, and not think of it again until the next birth. This practice is common and acceptable, but there is a better way.

After the Event, But *Before* the Next Child

If spills and drool are not removed, then they will weaken and discolor the fabric. Because many of these outfits are already generations old, the stains further complicate restoration and holes begin to form. You can bet with some assurance that somewhere along the way these outfits have been abused or disregarded.

119

It is never too late to begin a practice that will benefit generations to come. If you cannot restore your current family heirloom, though most are restorable, and if you must have a new outfit made, then remember that the new outfit will some-day be as old as the outfit you wore when you were a baby.

A Great Idea

Through the years I have watched families pass along their christening outfits. A family member occasionally forgets who had the outfit last and whether it was cleaned after the last ceremony. Of course, each one wanted it cleaned before his or her baby wore it, but no one could be sure if it had been.

▶ Buy a sturdy diary or docket to pass down through the years.

▶ Make a section for births. Title it and record the first family event in which the outfit will be worn.

▶ List the newborn's name, parents, grandparents, perhaps siblings, and the date, time, and circumstances of the christening.

▶ Record the pieces of the outfit, perhaps add a picture, and make sure that this diary accompanies the christening outfit through every birth from this point forward. You can predate the diary, as well, by enter-ing the history of the original outfit prior to these entries. (See a template at the end of this chapter.)

▶ Allow space for a date, name, where the outfit is to be cleaned after the event, what preservation box was used, and to whom it was handed down.

▶ I also suggest that you copy what this book has to say (you have my permission to photocopy this part) on the *care and preservation* of christening outfits, and tuck it in the front of the diary for your family to refer-ence for the years to come.

▶ Ask that this diary follow your family through the generations. The whole extended family will have a great time with it, and it will bring many laughs and tears.

> **A Lovely Image**
> Imagine the joy of pulling out a fresh christening outfit from the archival box for this year's "gift from heaven." The child is new, and the outfit will echo that sentiment.

When the event is over, hand the diary to the next family member, along with the outfit and preservation box, and ask that person to follow the suggestions in the next section, "Cleaning, Care, and Preservation." Have that family member con-tinue the tradition, and your family will have this christening outfit for many generations to come!

◆Cleaning, Care, and Preservation

My first goal is to convey to you the importance of cleaning the outfit *directly after the event*. Putting the gown away and neglecting to care for it in a timely fashion is the main reason for deterioration and poor stain removal later. I know I have introduced a "diary" to facilitate the process but, please, hear my words and respect them. You can have many years of enjoyment in which to experience the sentiment this concept will bring.

Let's assume that most outfits have been disregarded and are in need of special care. If yours is new and has only been worn once, these directions still apply. Most outfits are made of cotton, a few are silk or wool, and an occasional one is made of organza. Many outfits were brought to our attention that had yellow stains from drool and milk, particularly in the upper area. Some had brown stains, usually the result of a water leak or poor storage. Many had weakened areas, dry rot, and holes. It is always our goal to restore the outfit to its original condition.

Stain Removal

Stain removal for these items usually is accomplished by wet cleaning, and usually by hand. Specific stains often can be improved by a targeted approach, spot by spot, but overall restoration will come in the form of bathing in a neutral solution, occasionally with a mild non-chlorine bleach. With this procedure, most christening gowns can be greatly improved with minimal additional deterioration.

If your christening gown has been subjected to one or more of the above problems and is now too fragile to attempt cleaning and restoration before repairs are done, then listen up!

Deterioration

▶ Most deterioration comes in the form of isolated weakened areas with perhaps some small holes the size of a pinhead.

▶ Many of these holes are often within silver dollar-sized areas, which are generally the result of staining matter or poor storage.

▶ If you're a "purist" and you will be happy only with the outfit in its original condition, then ask for a prognosis. The outfit might withstand a gentle wet cleaning, but you should be prepared for some further low-grade deterioration. If your goal is to save the original outfit, and repairs *are* permissible, then I offer the advice on the following page.

Repairs

Repairs and alterations can save many outfits, but you can't be too rigid in your outlook. Small pinholes, dry-rotted areas, and stubborn stains can be disguised by sewing a dart or perhaps adding appliqué or lace. Many of these vintage outfits were made with cotton, which through the years has thinned and softened to have a beautiful feel and drape. The outfits are not easily duplicated, so it's worth restoring the christening gown in its current state. Even if the outfit needs extensive restyling or repairs, this process perpetuates the heirloom, and that is what it's all about.

Preservation

Preserving the outfit is the next step. I will reiterate the section from "preserving bridal gowns" because the basics still apply and contribute to careful long-term storage. Most bridal gowns are preserved in a "keepsake" box, but, for textiles and christening outfits, I recommend a smaller "archival" box. These boxes are typically gray, are acid-free, and have bracketed supports at all four corners. A company in Virginia manufacturers them: Hollinger Corporation 800-634-0491.

The Actual Boxing Process

▸ Make sure that the drycleaner uses a pH-neutral, acid-free box with acid-free tissue, and that the box allows the outfit to breathe.

▸ You will need only a small archival box, perhaps 24"x15"x 4", for these tiny christening outfits.

▸ In the best situation, you should find that it is not only all right, but also suggested, that you open the box every year to check it out. When you do open it, make sure that your hands are clean and free of oils. You may not need to remove the outfit because generally a cursory glance will give you the answers you seek. Is it yellowing; is it dry; does it have an odor?

Now that your christening outfit has been cleaned, perhaps repaired and preserved, it is time to complete the package so that it can sit in waiting for the next blessed event. Take the boxed outfit, attach the "diary" to the outside of the box with a ribbon, store the box in a dry area—and you're finished! You've done the right thing and you should be proud. You can now pass the outfit along to the next family member.

> **A Secure Place**
> Store the archival box on a closet shelf or under the bed. Keep it away from moist basements and attics where humidity and temperature swings could affect long-term storage.

◆ Christening Day

* Do not remove this sample page—see the copy in the back of the book.

The _____ Family Diary

`

Date _____ Time _____ Day _____

Name of Newborn_____

Siblings _____

Parents _____

Grandparents_____

Other Family/Guests _____

_____

Family Thoughts _____

_____

_____

_____

_____

_____

◆Christening Outfit Diary
Cleaning, Care, and Preservation
* Do not remove this sample page—see the copy in the back of the book.

Date _____ Time _____

◆ Cleaning and Repairs

Date of Ceremony _____

Name of Newborn _____

Who Took Outfit for Cleaning _____

Where It Is to Be Cleaned _____

Drycleaned _____ Wet Cleaned _____

Remarks/Condition _____

Repairs Needed _____

◆ Boxing and Preservation

Inventory: Gown _____ Slip _____ Bonnet _____ Gloves _____

Booties _____ Other _____

Any New Clothing Added _____

Reboxed with Acid-Free Tissue _____

Diary Included with Box _____

Other _____

> **The Ultimate Helper** is in the back section of the book. That section has removable worksheets for *christening gowns*, bridal gowns, leather and suede, and shopping guides. There is a perforated copy for each christening diary. Tear one out to take to the cleaners when you drop off the outfit.

Christening outfits can truly bring a family together. We've had whole families—siblings, spouses, and grandparents—collectively bring in the outfits after their family's christening events.

Mark on your calendar to pull out the christening "diary" (located in the back of the book) and archival box one month before the proposed due date for the next child, so as to make sure that everything is in order.

Chapter 15

Men's Clothing
Jackets, Suits, and Casuals

I'm going out on a limb here, but I would say that many men find shopping for clothing to be a chore. I also believe that they prefer to shop in blocks, making larger purchases, rather than shopping regularly for fewer things. I would also venture to say that once the spree begins, it can be quite fun. This is all conjecture, mind you, so you decide where you fit.

This chapter provides men with knowledge, perspective and, ultimately, the control to make their outing organized and focused. A well-prepared shopper will reap greater rewards in less time. Be sure to read about shopping by appointment in Chapter 1. This approach may be the convenience you've been waiting for.

◆ Before Shopping: Sport Jackets and Suit Jackets

Lapel Roll

The length and drape of a rolled lapel is one of the most hotly contested aspects of all jackets, sport and suit alike. Lapels should be rolled, not pressed with a crease. All jackets are designed to have the lapel roll to about one inch above the top button. The larger the jacket size, the more difficult it is to maintain the roll to the right position above the button. Some fabrics such as gabardine and very soft wool, especially in larger sizes, are difficult to roll properly. If the jacket is worn open the majority of the time, instead of buttoned, then the lapel tends to roll past the first button. When this happens, the fabric gains a new memory, and it becomes very difficult for certain fabrics to regain the "top-button memory" without the drycleaner re-training the lapel.

Back Collar Felt

The back collar of the jacket should always cover the felt below it. When you shop, check this condition. It is usually fine while the jacket is hanging on the rack in the store, but once you try it on, it may change. It can also change after altering, so check it closely.

Felt Problems

If the felt has been cut or fitted poorly, then it can protrude below the collar fabric. A person's posture has much to do with the problem as well. If you are slightly round-shouldered or hunched over, then the felt will show along the back edges. Ask the fitter or tailor to cut back the felt before you take your jacket home. If you see progressive shrinkage with drycleaning, then ask your cleaner to steam, stretch, and reblock the collar to cover the felt.

Fusible versus Sewn Construction

Sport jackets and suit jackets are manufactured using either fusible construction or sewn construction. This process applies to panels and lapels.

Fused

The fusing process may use interfacing, bonding materials (adhesive), and fabric. Fusing gives the jacket a clean, smooth line. The process is commonly used with gabardine and tropical-weight fabrics. The problem with fusing is that sometimes the adhesive breaks down, the layers separate, and small bubbles form. There is a debate over whether the bubbles are a result of poor fusible adhesives and faulty processing in manufacturing, or a result of drycleaners using too much heat and steam (both parties may be right). At a minimum, if you buy a fused jacket, then remind your drycleaner to use light steam.

Price does not necessarily dictate the quality of fused construction. Ask before you buy. Unfortunately, not many salespeople at mainstream stores are aware of the difference or have the knowledge to recognize it on sight, so be persistent.

> **About Fusing**
> Perspiration can become trapped in the layers of fusible construction, and any moisture can contribute to eventual bubbling. If you perspire heavily, consider hand-sewn construction.

Sewn

Sewn construction is very popular with more expensive clothing. Some jackets are machine sewn; some are hand sewn. If you look down the edge of the lapel and see stitching, it is probably hand sewn. I have seen some sewn suits develop separation on the front panels and along the lapel, but that occurrence is rare. In these cases, ripples usually form because the lining and the fabric are cut to different sizes. Sometimes, after the jacket is drycleaned several times, the fabric shrinks or stretches, but the lining, being synthetic, remains the same size; hence, ripples form. A tailor or seamstress can usually correct this problem.

Two-Button Jackets

Two-button jackets have longer lapels and traditionally have been the most popular design for men. (Three-button jackets are on their way to becoming a mainstay.) The lapels should have a full roll as opposed to being pressed with a crease.

The proper roll is roughly one inch above the top button and should be maintained. If the fabric is limp or the jacket is worn unbuttoned, then the roll may be affected and might need special attention during pressing to re-train the roll.

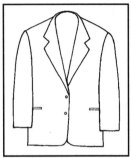

A two-button rolled lapel

Three-Button Style

Traditional

The traditional three-button jacket, originally made famous by Brooks Brothers, presents another concern. The lapels on these jackets are usually rolled like a two-button, relegating the top button to a position behind the lapel. (See picture to right.)

The button behind the lapel is usually brass or dome-shaped. When this area of the lapel is *machine* pressed instead of hand ironed, an impression often forms, making the fabric lighter in this area.

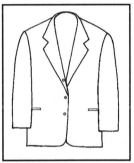

The top button is exposed here for illustration.

Because many drycleaners machine press these jackets, I humbly suggest that you remove the top button. If the button is hidden (and doesn't show anyway), and you think your cleaners may have a problem avoiding an impression, then why not just remove it?

When you have a moment, look at the lapels on your three-button jackets to see if there is an impression from the button.

Button Effects
The impression caused by the top button can affect the fabric color and in some cases may actually turn shades of white in that area.

Note: If you intend to wear a three-button *as* a three-button, where the top button shows, I recommend that you try a designer jacket, or one that is designed to be worn as a three-button.

Designer

Most designers, from casual to formal, are making three-button jackets that are intended to be worn as a three-button and naturally roll to a three-button without the help of the drycleaner.

When you try on a style like this, you will know immediately, because the lapel is cut perfectly to suit the roll. This designer version of the three-button jacket, different from the "classic" three-button, is very fashionable. These jackets are available in a wide variety of colors, fabrics, and textures.

A three-button rolled lapel

Single-Breasted and Double-Breasted

Single-breasted jackets are easy to wear and have less material than a double-breasted jacket. A single-breasted jacket can be worn unbuttoned and still look neat.

Double-breasted jackets look good on all men, but may not be as complimentary on shorter men with a full build. Double-breasted jackets are designed to be worn buttoned. When these jackets are worn open, they look heavy, tend to lose their roll and memory, and may look a bit unfinished flapping in the wind.

◆ Let's Go Shopping

Perhaps a review of Chapter 1, on shopping tips and shopping by appointment, and Chapter 2, on fabric basics, will refresh your focus. A brief recap ...

Natural fibers, such as wool, silk, and cotton, breathe better than synthetics, which make them more comfortable to wear in all weather. If the buttons are unique, then remember to ask for a few extras. If your weight tends to fluctuate, then have the clothing fit comfortably.

Most jackets and suits have care labels that are predictable, but some casual slacks and shirts may have some unusual care instructions. Many men feel they cannot have enough sport jackets. Because sport jackets can be mixed and matched, casual to formal, they are a great alternative to a two-piece suit.

> **The Total Picture**
> I mention drycleaning often because it is a reality with finer clothing. You need to be aware of the added expense with certain fabrics.

Sport jackets are also available (off the rack) in a wider variety of fabrics than suits. When you shop for style, seriously consider the nature of the fabric and its characteristics. Certain fabrics fit your needs and life-style better than others, so be sure to give this some thought.

If you wear your clothing hard, then stay away from high-maintenance fabrics. If you have only a few sport jackets or suits, then buy sturdier materials that will withstand repeated wearing. (Students and young exec-utives should focus on these considerations.) Some fabrics will pill, shine, wrinkle, or show wear faster than others. If you travel often, then consider which fabrics will wrinkle the least and "hang out" the best. (See the table "Fabrics at a Glance" in Chapter 2.)

> **Button Sense**
> Most gold and silver buttons are hollow and will withstand cleaning. If they are solid (you can tell by the weight or by gently tapping on your tooth), then they will need pro-tection during cleaning. See Chapter 3 on but-tons.

◆ Jacket and Suit Fabrics

Low Maintenance
One hundred percent wool clothing will wear longer than blended wools and are easier to press than blends. Flannel, tweed, herring-bone, and other similarly textured fabrics, which are fall and winter weights, are the easiest to maintain. They are generally 100% wool, are wrinkle resistant, and respond to brushing after wearing. (See Chapter 26 on "Good Habits.")

Blended fabrics, which usually contain some polyester, are wrinkle resistant but tend to shine faster. Fabrics with a nap or texture show less soil and tend to press well. Many tropical-weight fabrics are also very man-ageable.

Of the cotton fabrics, seersucker is the most durable and least labor-intensive. Some seersucker can be washed as well as drycleaned, although drycleaning is still more gentle.

High Maintenance
This section addresses labor-intensive natural fibers, synthetics, and some special materials. Many of these fabrics will wear well, but require drycleaning and

> **Rarely Considered**
> If you carry a back-pack, briefcase, or wardrobe bag across your shoulder, then you are putting tremen-dous pressure on the shoulder pads of your jacket. This weight and friction can distort the shoulder-pad area and also cause the fabric to shine.

pressing. Most of the fabrics mentioned here are perfectly suited for business wear, but wardrobe rotation is important.

Cotton

Thin, summer-weight cotton is comfortable to wear but wrinkles very easily. You will need to have cotton jackets and suits pressed after each wearing. Ironing and pressing are time-consuming and require skill. Polished cotton, if poorly ironed, will show imperfections along seams, around pockets, and on the lapels.

> **Wrinkle Warning**
> Wrinkled clothing should not be re-ironed or pressed if it is soiled. The heat that accompanies pressing may "set" stains and soil, making future removal difficult.

Cotton breathes, but you still perspire. Perspiration stains tend to show quite prominently on cotton fabric: under the arms, on the collar, and behind the knees. Stain removal is difficult and often hampered on these dryclean-only garments and will require more care. If you perspire heavily, then think twice before buying a cotton suit for everyday wear.

Linen

Linen is lightweight and cool in the summer, but it wrinkles very easily. Linen and cotton-linen blends require ironing after every wearing. These fabrics are best worn "soft" without additional sizing. The sizing does make the fabric look uniform and smooth, until you put it on your body, and then it causes large breaks in the fabric. It is my personal preference, but I think linen is best worn "soft." Linen garments are most appropriate for social events and for play.

> **Cost of Starching**
> White and off-white linen can be starched, but the texture may change permanently. Spray starch or spray sizing should *never* be applied to dark linen fabrics.

Dark colors fade quickly, are difficult to remove stains from without affecting the color, and should never be starched.

Gabardine

Gabardine can have a soft and handsome look. A lightweight gabardine weave is considered a year-round material. Heavyweight twill, in comparison, should not be considered an "everyday" fabric because of its tendency to shine. If you have only a few jackets, it is best to buy flannel for cooler weather and tropical-weight fabrics for warmer weather. When buying a fabric with a "sheen," keep in mind that these fabrics can become shiny if overworn or overpressed. The back of the jacket can easily shine from the friction that occurs when sliding in and out of the car, and the elbows become shined from the top of a desk. Heavyweight gabardine twill may also have problems with fusible bubbles, so check it closely and always ask the drycleaner to use light steam.

Superfine Wool

Superfine wools, often referred to as Super 100's and Super 120's, are very soft, typically thin, dressy, and often expensive. They can develop some subtle shine on the thighs and elbows, but they generally wear well and dryclean well.

Super 150's are thin, lightweight, and luxurious. Super 180's are very high-maintenance and are not recommended for everyday business suits. The fabric is so thin and delicate that it does not hold a pressing well and may pucker when altered. Super 150's and 180's should be soft-pressed to avoid shine.

Camel, Cashmere, and Silk Blends

Camel, cashmere, and silk blends are soft and comfortable, but should not be considered for everyday wear. Stain removal is relatively easy, but drycleaning for these fabrics can be expensive. These fabrics should always be "hand cleaned" (short cycle). To maintain the luxurious feel and drape, camel and cashmere should be lightly steamed and brushed and *never* hard pressed.

Raw "Nubby" Silk

Raw silk jackets are identified by the "nubby" nature of the yarns and are often blended with a soft wool; they are generally made in salt-and-pepper-type designs (but not always), and are very high maintenance. Of all the fabrics mentioned for occasional wear, raw silk is the most sensitive. I hesitate to take up space with this, but my conscience will not permit me to omit this information. If you must buy a jacket like this, then read on.

▶ Raw silk pills very easily (causing little balls from friction) and can look like a cheap product in one cleaning.

▶ Raw silk is difficult to clean and should be cleaned by only an experienced cleaner. This fabric can easily be affected by overcleaning and overagitating in the cleaning machine.

▶ Stain removal is hampered because of the nature of the fabric. Be careful never to apply water or to rub the stained area. The "pepper" part of the yarn (the darker yarns) is very often water soluble, and in many cases the dyes can bleed from drink spills, especially if they contain alcohol.

> **Fabric De-Pilling**
> To de-pill, you can use a single-edge, disposable-type razor to shave the pill balls off. This process will thin the fabric a bit, but it does help to contain the problem.

Note: Raw silk, silk-wool blends, and cashmere jackets are all sensitive to pilling problems. Remember to remove your jacket before you slide into a car or into an overcoat. All friction contributes to premature fabric pilling.

◆ Suit and Dress Slacks

Suit slacks take a bit more abuse than the jacket does, so when selecting a suit fabric, you should consider the effects of long-term wear on slacks. Slacks are typically drycleaned more often than the jacket is, with a three-to-one cleaning ratio.

Good Idea

Depending on the cost of the suit and your individual habits, you may want to purchase an extra pair of slacks at the same time that you buy the suit. Too many men are forced to retire a perfectly good suit jacket when the slacks wear out. Six months later is usually too late to order a second pair.

Slacks, depending on how they fit and how often they are worn, tend to thin in the crotch and seat area, fray at the pockets and cuffs, and become shiny from sliding in and out of desks and cars. They also snag on objects and tear in obvious places.

Another Good Idea

Having suit slacks half lined (lined just to the thigh area) will prolong their life. If the suit slacks are not lined, then have a half lining added at the time of purchase. Lined slacks are more comfortable to wear. The lining reduces friction that causes thinning in the crotch area.

High-quality casual slacks made of gabardine and other fine wools are often already half-lined by the manufacturer. If you haven't worn a pair of lined slacks before, they are sleek, cool, and comfortable.

◆ At the Cleaners

Since most of this clothing will require drycleaning, you should begin thinking in those terms. You have made an investment in your wardrobe; make it pay. This is the time to convey your concerns about the more fragile pieces of your wardrobe.

When you're at the cleaners, take the opportunity to inspect your suits for stains. If you remember any "invisible" spots, then point them out. Check the hot spots for minor repairs: the inside jacket lining at the vent, underarms, and pockets. See if any buttons need reinforcing. Check the slacks for frays along the pocket edges (from your watchband or jewelry), the cuff hems for loose stitches, the seat for open seams, and the inside of the waistband—all these areas will need care eventually.

These aspects can be hassle free if you permit your drycleaner to do minor repairs of up to $15 without calling you. Try to form that sort of relationship with your cleaner.

Inspection for Holes

If you see any holes in your wool clothing, try to discern if they are the result of insect damage or the result of a tear. (Tears are generally more jagged.) If you believe the holes are from insects, then check the whole outfit closely for more holes and weakened or thinned areas, which could be the result of partially eaten fibers. If you find more holes, mark them with safety pins and have the clothing cleaned before repairing. If you find additional holes after cleaning, the expense to repair or reweave all of them may eclipse the cost of the suit. (See Chapter 27 on "Reweaving: A True Savior.")

What Does a Well-Pressed Suit Look Like?

Jacket

The lapels should be softly rolled with no shine along the edges. The collar should be pressed down in back to cover the felt. The jacket sleeves should be rolled with no creases and hopefully stuffed with tissue to provide a rounded, full look. The buttons and pocket flaps should have no impressions underneath.

Jackets made of camel, cashmere, and fine blends should always be soft pressed and brushed to give the jacket back its soft feel. That luxuriant look will be restored only by brushing and steaming. Too many drycleaners do not respect this nuance and press too hard, which gives these fabrics a flat rather than luxuriant look. If the clerk is not aware of this problem, then ask if a manager can attend to it.

Slacks

If the slacks are creased, they should have one straight crease (no double creases); the crease should be sharp on soft wools with a nap, and softer on fabrics that have a natural sheen, such as gabardine and summer-weight wool. The crotch area should be wrinkle free. There should be no impressions down the side seams—inside or outside the thigh.

◆ Casual Clothing

The casual part of your wardrobe represents a contrast to the suit and tie that work often requires. Casual wear often represents leisure and relaxation. If you have casual Fridays or if you do dress down regularly for work, then this section has some good insights and ideas.

Jeans

The issue with jeans is not whether they are blue or black, but how to keep them looking good and fitting right. Some people "live" in blue jeans—they are part of our national dress code. They are comfortable, like an old shirt or old pair of shoes. Traditionally, they are worn to knock around in, and when it's time, they are thrown in the washing machine, and that's about all it takes to care for them.

Designer and Dressier Jeans

When "designer" jeans became the rage, they were no longer just blue jeans. Designer jeans created a somewhat discriminating market. Once this occurred, and jeans became part of our wardrobe rather than just a casual adjunct, we started thinking, "Now we're not so sure that we should throw them in the washer because we don't want them to fade!" Even shrinkage and fraying have become taboo in some cases.

Ah, the advent of drycleaning jeans—a novel idea. Drycleaning jeans, sometimes with a soft crease, can preserve the color, size, and texture. It keeps them soft and they do not thin as quickly. Every month or two, or if there is a stain that can't be removed in drycleaning, you could consider washing the jeans, but they are never the same again.

Black jeans have also found their way into the mainstream, though it is difficult to keep them black. Fading is fine, if that's your goal, but keeping a pair of jeans true to color also has its place. I have "dress" jeans that I still never wash because I can't afford for them to shrink and I want them to remain rich in color and smooth in texture. I never wear them to clean the yard or to play sports.

If you do wish to keep black jeans black and blue jeans blue, then dryclean them. Do not rub stains with a napkin or towel, for fear of "pulling" the color, and do not crease the jeans because a white line will eventually form in the crease area.

> **Good-bye, Crease**
> Washing and starching jeans with a sharp crease was once the rage. It still has its place, but I think it has given way to a softer look.

If you are going to wear jeans and always wash and fold them, that is fine, too, but at least you know there's another option. Washing jeans "inside out" will help reduce fading.

Khakis

Khaki pants are clearly a mainstay for casual work and play. They are worn for warm nights out and to casual social events with a sport jacket. They are also worn to work, to garden, to play golf, or to walk a construction site—they are very versatile. It may be best to have "casual" khakis and "dress" khakis.

Fabrics

Several new fabrics are being used in the design of khakis. I think that 100% cotton khakis are more comfortable and softer looking than polyester blends, but they require more ironing. Manufacturers have made great strides in "wrinkle-free" khakis, which now look more natural and not as stiff.

The addition of microfiber, rayon blends, linen, and other new fabrics has made a big difference in the marketplace. The image that the word "khaki" elicited—tan cotton slacks—has been shattered. These fabrics have brought different colors, shades, and textures so that khakis can now look casual or dressy.

These new fabrics have also introduced a new set of problems with regard to stain removal. Common stains from food, grass, raindrops, and spills that were somewhat routine to remove from cotton have been compromised because of the sizing used in these fabrics and because many are not washable. Many of these fabrics now require more time and greater skill to process. Some of the fabrics shine prematurely and, if creased improperly, are nearly impossible to correct without it showing.

> **Read Care Labels**
> Did you know that some microfiber and rayon slacks have a dryclean-only instruction, and many can be ruined by washing? Read the care labels closely.

Note: When you read the guidelines for the care of khakis, remember to adjust your approach to account for the "new" fabrics. Some are rather expensive and require more attention.

Casual Khakis

▸ Many khakis have dryclean-only labels, but tend to be washed at home. *Casual* khakis are part of the wardrobe that can be laundered and ironed at home. When they are washed at home, remember that oily-type stains usually do not come out in the wash. If you know that you spilled something oily, try to have the khakis drycleaned before washing.

▸ Ironing at home can also present a challenge. For some reason, many khakis come into the cleaners with more than one crease. Perhaps it's a non-issue for you, but try to be aware of that problem at home. Single, sharp creases are a concept that drycleaners take for granted and removing extra creases without leaving a remnant can be very difficult.

Dress Khakis

▸ If you choose to separate your casual khakis from your dress khakis, the dress khakis will remain part of your wardrobe for a long time. Try not to wear them in the yard, to play sports, or for other nonsocial events. Once they become grass stained or mud stained, they usually need to be washed. Once they are washed, they can fade, fray, and look worn.

▸ Dress khakis belong in the category of finer fabrics. They are available in higher thread counts (microfiber being a perfect example) and in polished cotton and rayon—all of which will make them feel better and look dressier. Armani, Brioni, and other high-end designers make beautiful khakis.

▸ If you dryclean dress khakis, they should retain their depth of color and body as well as their single creases.

Corduroy

"Cords" typically start out casual-dressy, especially the wide-ribbed variety. There are a few basic reasons that they lose their quality over time.

▸ As with khakis and jeans, washing corduroy will fade the color and fray the fabric. Washing can also affect the body and drape.

▸ Corduroy is a "pile" fabric and should not be ironed like other casual pants because the pile can become crushed. Stains that sit on the surface of the pile, such as ketchup, cake icing, and pizza sauce, may cause the pile to crush if left for too long.

▸ If you hang corduroy pants instead of folding them, then be sure to use a padded or protected hanger. If you allow the pants to be draped over a wire hanger for prolonged periods, the wire can permanently "dent" the raised pile.

▸ If you choose to crease your corduroy slacks, then make it a soft crease. A hard crease will eventually form a white line that cannot be removed.

Casual Shirts

I consider a shirt to be casual if it has a playful print, is made of an unusual fabric, or is usually worn without a necktie. A dress shirt is a different species. Dress shirts are typically sent to the laundry to be pressed—in most cases by a shirt machine—and possibly starched.

Rayon, Microfiber, and Lyocell

Most of the time, shirts made of rayon, microfiber, or lyocell are better dry-cleaned rather than washed, regardless of what the care label recommends. All of these shirt fabrics have good body and a soft drape that would be compromised by washing and hard pressing with a hot-head press, like the type used in a commercial laundry. If the shirts are washed, it is better to hand iron them rather than have them pressed by a shirt machine.

Though I did see a small contingent of casual shirts being pressed and sometimes starched in our laundry along with dress shirts, I feel strongly that this is not the best approach for such fabrics. These fabrics require less heat and less pressure, both of which are part of the pressing process for dress shirts.

When a shirt is pressed in the laundry, whether it is cotton or one of the fabrics from this group, the machines impart a very stiff texture. Some men prefer this look, and for them it works. The price for a laundered shirt is considerably less than the price for drycleaning, but if you're looking for a soft finish that will allow the fabric to flow, taking full advantage of the drape of the material, then drycleaning is the best choice.

If you are forced to have these shirts washed in order to remove stubborn stains—sometimes despite the care label instruction—then be sure to have the shirt soft pressed or hand ironed to restore the natural drape.

> **Excellent Drape**
> Lyocell, rayon, and microfiber can all be a viable substitute for silk. They can all look dressy, and none are as sensitive to perspiration as is silk.

Wool

Wool shirts, which are on the upswing, should always be drycleaned. I know that many Europeans still wash their woolens, but drycleaning will reduce shrinkage and pilling and will maintain softness. Although many new wools are soft, many "itchy" wool shirts are still out there, and drycleaning will not soften the wool or make it less itchy. Soft wool shirts (very popular in the button-down "polo" style) are thin and wrinkle resistant, which make them great for travel. They are also warm.

Silk

Men do not wear silk shirts often—certainly not as often as women wear silk blouses—so they are not accustomed to the level of care this fabric requires. Spills, food stains, and perspiration are among the components that shorten the life of most silk shirts—with perspiration being the most damaging. You should be cognizant of this and be sure to allow your deodorant to dry before dressing. (See Chapter 7 on silk and perspiration.) Try to have the shirt cleaned within 24 hours of wearing, and always point out any stains to your drycleaner.

Care for Silk Shirts

Most silk is best drycleaned because that process will control the size and texture and will reduce fading. There are silk shirts on the market that actually recommend washing, called "washable" silk. Experience has proven, however, that most of the shirts fade, sometimes unevenly. Though washing is better for most stain removal, the texture changes enough to make the shirt that comes out of the washer look different than the one you put in. If the faded look is your goal, then washing may work for you. Washing does one thing well: it is an effective tool for the removal of perspiration.

◆ Travel Ideas

Travel can challenge fabric selection. Obviously, nonwrinkle fabrics, readily available these days, would travel the best, but many are not very flattering. Many synthetics, especially polyester, are wrinkle resistant. Wool, long considered the best fabric for traveling, still remains an excellent choice. Selecting the proper weight garment for the appropriate weather will increase your satisfaction. If the clothing has been folded or placed in a wardrobe bag, then hanging it as soon as possible will help remove creases and relax wrinkles. Packing the clothing in stuffing tissue, available at stores and shipping services, can be an excellent deterrent to wrinkles and creases.

If you attempt to iron your clothing in the hotel room, then be careful of shine; iron the garment on the reverse side when possible; and consider using a "pressing cloth" to protect the garment from shining. (See Chapter 25 on ironing.)

> **Travel Advice**
> If you are forced to use an unfamiliar drycleaner when you travel, then be certain to clearly voice your concerns. When you use a hotel concierge, you do relinquish most control.

Chapter 16

Neckties
Basics, Care, Stain Emergencies, and Shopping

Ties are a necessary evil—one that men have come to accept and even take pride in wearing. I know you buy them for color and style and to complete an outfit, but they are also part of your wardrobe investment. If ties always remained clean, then you wouldn't need drycleaners. Because they don't, I have structured this chapter as a survival guide for men.

Every man should recognize the need to keep his ties clean, remember to move them from the line of fire during meals, *gently* remove them at night to reduce rippling, and have them cleaned as soon as there is a stain. Some men have made great strides in this area, but many more have yet to see the value of preventive care.

◆ Basics

Would you be surprised to know that when you purchase a necktie, you should be just as concerned with construction as you are with color, design, and fabric?

Construction

Ties can be broken down into three sections: the small end, called the "tail"; the part that wraps around the back of your neck, called the "gusset" (which usually has extra "diagonal" seams or visible stitches that reinforce this area for durability); and the large end that sits down near your belt, commonly called the "apron."

The inside of the tie usually has three parts: the "shell," which is usually silk, either printed or woven; the inside "interlining," which is usually made of wool or a wool blend, and runs the length of the tie, and is usually tucked into the bottom of the "V" of the tie; and the "tipping," which is on the back of the apron and covers the interlining on the backside of the tie.

Bar tack at tail and apron

141

The back also has two "bar tacks" and a "slip stitch"; the larger bar tack is about five inches from the bottom and looks like a loop, which holds the two folds together, and the other bar tack is very small and is located at the tail end of the tie. The slip stitch is a thread that runs *inside* the tie from bar tack to bar tack, and it can be considered the "life thread" or spine of the necktie.

All of these parts are integral to the tie, and though interesting in regard to construction, only one part should concern you, fully, and that is the "slip stitch." More about this soon!

More about Construction

The shell, interlining, and tipping should all be cut on the bias at *exactly* a 45-degree angle. If all three of these pieces are cut at this angle, the tie should last a long time without it rippling, becoming misshapen, or having the tips become uneven.

If the bias cut on any of these parts is off by even a degree or two, the symmetry of the tie and its longevity are severely compromised. If you are gentle with your tie, but it still has been poorly constructed, then the tie will eventually have shape problems. There is no way for you to know for sure if the 45-degree bias has been adhered to, and this is where quality and trust in your retailer come into play.

> **Bias Cut**
> Bias cut means that the fabric has been cut on a diagonal, which enhances the drape and body.

Note: A new necktie should lie flat with no ripples or waves and should have rounded edges (not flat as though they've been creased), symmetrical tips (even on both sides), and absolutely no snags in sight.

Interlining

The interlining is usually made of wool or a wool blend. The interlining should have been preshrunk before it was cut for use inside the tie. It extends from the tip of the bar tack at the tail and, in most ties, into the large V-shaped apron at the bottom of the tie. The interlining, which should fit snugly inside the tie shell, is then lightly stitched up the back center seam of the tie, from bar tack to bar tack, making the interlining and the shell "one piece." (You can see the stitches by flipping over the tie.) You should understand how integral this interlining is to the drape of the tie.

> **Drape and Body**
> The quality of the silk is important, but it is the thickness and the quality of the interlining and how it is positioned in the tie that will determine the drape of the tie.

If the interlining has *not* been preshrunk, then it could shrink during drycleaning. If the tie retains moisture from perspiration or humidity in the air, then there is even a greater chance of shrinkage in cleaning. When the inter-lining shrinks, but the silk shell does not, rippling and distortion can occur.

Rippling or bowing can also occur if the interlining has not been properly sewn, if it has been cut too small or too large for the shell, or if it has not been cut on a true 45-degree angle.

Exposed mesh interlining

Note: Even if the tie has been perfectly made, ripples and uneven tips can still occur as a result of consumer abuse.

The Tipping
The tipping is the small piece of material that sits inside the back of the apron and covers the interlining. It is mostly cos-metic and is a finishing touch. On some less-expensive ties, on which tipping has not been sewn to the shell, you can lift the tipping up to expose the off-white mesh interlining un-derneath. More expensive ties may have tipping made from better fabric or from the same fabric as the shell of the tie.

Open-style tipping

About Uneven Tips
Every time that you "tug" on a tie to remove it, the tie can dis-tort. This distortion affects the way the tie lies and causes the fabric to become crooked, which can lead to uneven tips and rippling. The thicker the tie, the fewer problems with uneven tips and eventual rippling. I know many men are upset about this problem because I have heard complaints regularly at my drycleaners and at seminars. When a tie ripples or becomes uneven, it looks cheap and unkempt.

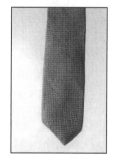

Uneven tips

Fabrics
Most ties are made of silk. There are, however, still some wool and cotton ties floating around, as well as some new fabrics such as microfiber—but silk is still the main player. For ease, consider silk to be the fabric we are addressing. What differ-

entiates one silk necktie from the next are the varying qualities of silk and whether the tie is woven or printed.

Woven Fabrics

The most thick and lustrous neckties are usually made of woven silk. The woven category applies to many styles of silk fabrics but, for our purpose, we will call them textured. The ties may be satin, like the lapel of a tuxedo jacket; faille (pronounced "file") with a flat twill rib; grosgrain (pronounced "gro-grain") with a raised twill rib; brocade-like with raised designs; or looped.

Woven ties usually keep their shape well, have fewer problems with rippling and uneven tips, and are available in an infinite assortment of colors and designs. They are rich looking, have great depth of color, and have a beautiful drape. Though for all their beauty, they are not the best choice for all men.

▶ The woven surface can be snagged by watchbands, jewelry, cuff links, belt buckles, and assorted edges or textures at your place of work.

▶ If you have a heavy beard, it may be coarse enough to catch surface fibers and cause snags. It might be severe enough to actually fray the material or cause pilling.

▶ If your hands are rough or have calluses, they, too, can actually snag the material. You will have to assess these issues when you shop.

▶ Satin and other woven ties are more prone to deluster and color loss if rubbed with a napkin or a towel.

If you are tough on your clothing, then you may want to reserve woven ties for special occasions and consider a printed silk tie for everyday wear.

Raised design

Printed Fabrics

"Plain" silk, often referred to as crepe de chine, is a lightweight fabric typically used for printed neckties. The price and quality will vary, but this weave is very popular and does not snag as easily as woven silk does. It does, however, have its own idiosyncrasies. Quality silk and quality dyes are a key component to longevity.

▶ Printed ties are generally not as weighted as woven ties, and they tend to lose their drape quicker if they are not treated gently.

▶ Depending on the quality, they may ripple or bow faster than woven ties.

▸ Printed ties can also deluster, and the dyes are more susceptible to bleeding. Higher-quality ties respond much better to spills and stain removal and have fewer dye-bleed problems.

▸ Printed ties can still snag from sharp objects and fray from a heavy beard, but they are more resistant than woven ties.

> **Preventive Care**
> Do not tuck a tie into a waistband because it can break fibers and cause snags.

Color and Design

Color plays an important role in a tie's longevity. Background colors and prints, lining colors, and color contrasts are important elements of design.

Best Colors and Prints

Ties with a print or design, light or dark, hide more stains than solid ties. A tie with the same color as the lining provides the easiest care. This is true of light and dark colors. Light-color ties can last a long time, providing the wearer is disciplined about drycleaning them when stains occur. A dark tie may hide more stains initially, but when the stains age and become darker, the tie will look much worse. Dark-print ties show fewer stains than solid ties do, but both show damage from rubbing if you try to remove a stain.

Worst Colors and Prints

Light colors with dark prints are the worst combination. A yellow tie with navy, burgundy, or any shade of red can be problematic. It is not guaranteed to bleed when it gets wet from spills or during stain removal, but these ties are the most likely to bleed. A dark lining can occasionally bleed through to the light shell during stain removal.

In both cases, stain removal is severely hampered by heavily contrasting colors. You should be aware of this condition if you are buying a less-expensive tie or a brand that is unfamiliar to you.

> **A True Story** … A customer was caught in a rainstorm while running for the train. His yellow tie with navy print (not a cheap tie) got wet and bled on to his shirt and his olive Armani suit. During restoration, the shirt was stripped of the loose dye from the tie and the Armani suit was saved by a skilled spotter, but the tie was ruined by the rain. All this trouble from a poorly made tie!

"Salt-and-pepper" silk ties have dots or lines of black interspersed with white, and they look gray from a distance. The dyes on these neckties almost always bleed from water-based spills or during subsequent stain-removal attempts, particularly from drinks containing alcohol. When the dyes bleed, the salt-and-pepper prints turn a muddled gray.

Not all high-contrast ties suffer from dye bleed, but be aware of this problem when you shop.

◆ Taking Off Your Tie at Night

When you remove your tie at the end of the day, do you gently untie it and remove it from your collar, or—like most men—do you pull on it like a "tug of war?" This factor can make a big difference in the longevity of the tie.

Proper Care and Awareness

▶ First, wash your hands. Loosen your tie enough to slip it over your head. Do not pull it through a button-down collar or around an open collar. Untie the knot gently while you can see what you are doing.

▶ Each time that you pull your tie around your shirt collar, it stresses the material, pulls on the bias cut, and contributes to the distortion that eventually causes it to become uneven or rippled.

▶ Pulling also causes the interlining to separate from the silk shell, which contributes to additional ripples on the front of the tie.

▶ Lay the tie down flat in good light and inspect it for stains. Turn it at different angles so that the light can pick up the various spots. If you see stains, have the tie cleaned right away. If you wait, the stains can oxidize, which severely limits spot removal. (See Chapter 26 on "Good Habits.")

▶ If your tie has obvious ripples or is twisted at the knotted area, "relax" the tie by adjusting the slip stitch. This process should smooth the tie considerably. (See "Adjustment of the Slip Stitch" on the next page.)

Rippled necktie

▶ If you use a tie rack, then make sure that the tie bar is padded or rounded so that it will not form a crease. The tie edges should not touch a wall or curl up against another tie. Be sure to air out the tie before storing it, to let the moisture evaporate.

▶ Some experts believe that rolling a tie is a good method for storage. Lay the tie flat on a dresser top with the back side up, gently roll the tie from the *tail* to the apron, and store it in the drawer in this condition. This method will relax the wrinkles and restore the smooth texture. For travel, you could roll your ties, or fold them once, and place them between two layers of soft clothing.

A rolled necktie

Adjustment of the Slip Stitch

The slip stitch runs from the bar tack at the apron to the bar tack at the tail. This is the "spine" of your tie; it is resilient and will help the tie rebound to its proper shape.

Place the tie on a flat surface with the back stitching facing up; lightly grip the lower bar tack between your thumb and forefinger; open the first two fingers on your other hand like a scissors, place the tie between the two fingers, and then *gently* slide your two fingers along the length of the tie from the lower bar tack at the wide end to the bar tack at the tail. This process will smooth out the necktie, restore the length, and remove most ripples. Do not pull loose threads because it may snag the tie or affect the slip stich.

Slide fingers to end of tie

On the Bright Side: If you continue to tug on your tie while removing, there is still hope for you. For a fee, a seamstress or tailor can open the necktie, reposition the interlining, "re-square" the tips, and re-close the tie. If you abuse your ties, then no designer will be able to help you. If the corners of the tie begin to wear thin or fray and if the tie begins to show a white area, then you may be able to save the tie by having it narrowed or shortened.

◆ Stain Emergencies and Faux Pas

If you are in a social situation, eating or having drinks, on an airplane, or at a party or formal event, and if you have a spill, then do not rub your tie with a napkin or cloth, wet or dry. I know it's your first thought, but please refrain. Do not let a host, steward, or friend convince you otherwise.

▶ Never rub a tie with a napkin or towel to remove a stain. You can blot gently with a dry white cloth to absorb the spill, but never rub.

- Never apply water or liquid to the stain. If the stain is oily, you may help set it. If the stain is water-based, you may spread the stain or cause the dye to bleed.

- Rubbing the stain can break microscopic yarns, which causes the surface to deluster. If you rub the stain and deluster the fabric, then you will regret it later. Just blot the tie with a dry, white cloth or napkin and send it to the drycleaner—soon.

Loss of Sheen
Deluster is a loss of sheen on the surface of the fabric. Rubbing causes a "wake" upon a smooth sea, and it is usually permanent.

Bottom Line: I am a trained spotter, and I would not attempt to remove a stain from a tie with a napkin. Without the proper tools I, too, would cause permanent damage. The shinier the tie, the more the damage will show.

Delustered silk (magnified)

◆ Let's Go Shopping

As I stated earlier, selecting a necktie is a personal decision, but if you can remember the basics you will make a wiser investment. Buy the fabric that best suits your taste, but stay away from known problems. Most ties are well made and do not have the following maladies—most, but not all. Here's the list:

- Light colors with dark or vibrant prints can limit stain removal and may bleed from water and spills.

- Dark lining behind light colors, solid or printed, may bleed through during stain removal. Try to buy ties with light linings or at least with the same color lining as the shell.

- Salt-and-pepper designs (black-and-white threads), which appear as a gray color, have a history of bleeding from water, spills, and stain removal.

- Check the tips to make sure that they are even. If they are the least bit uneven when you buy the tie, then they will surely get worse.

- Hold the tie at different angles to check for snags and deluster. Lay the tie flat on the counter to check for ripples. If it is not absolutely flat, then it will get worse with use. Satin ties deluster and snag most easily; check them closely.

- Flip the tie over and look at the lining and the sewing. If the lining is uneven along the "V," then it may contribute to uneven tips. Check the sewing on the back from top to bottom to make sure it is secure.

Be sure to voice any concerns to the salesperson. Ask about the store's return policy if the tie should ripple or bleed. Recognizing that these conditions are mostly within your control, and that your purpose is not to take advantage of the store, you should know the store policy in case the necktie really is faulty or poorly made.

◆ At the Cleaners

When you're at the cleaners, you have a perfect opportunity to inspect your ties. Look at the ties from different angles; check for stains, ripples, uneven tips, frayed areas, and any minor sewing that may be needed. Be firm about your needs and convey them clearly. If you remember any particular stains, especially invisible ones from clear liquids, make sure that you point out the areas. Most ties tend to show stains clearly, but look closely, regardless. Remind the cleaner to softly roll the edges of the tie during finishing.

If you do notice that the tips have become uneven, then ask the cleaner to try reblocking them to shape. If the condition is too severe and cannot be corrected by steaming, now is the time to show it to the seamstress or tailor.

Do not discard a tie because it has frayed corners; ask the seamstress or tailor for his or her thoughts on this, as well.

Lastly, if you think the tie is too far gone to restore because of stains, then ask the clerk at the counter what the outcome of cleaning might be. If the tie can't be restored to meet your comfort level, then put the cost of cleaning toward a new tie.

Wash Your Hands
Every time you tighten the knot of your tie, you deposit soil and oils from your hands onto the knotted area. Be sure to alert your drycleaner to any spot in that area.

Note: If your drycleaner does not offer more extensive repair services such as replacing interlining, making new tipping, or shortening or narrowing ties, Tiecrafters in New York City can "reconstruct" your tie for you. When you call Tiecrafters and mention this book, they will send you a free tie box that can be used for shipping or traveling: 212-629-5800.

Neat Trick
In a pinch, you can use a color marker to cover frayed corners. This remedy is not scientific, but it can work.

There are a number of restaurants and bars in Arizona and Texas that cater specifically to their patrons that wear neckties. If you walk into these establishments wearing a tie, then they will cut it off and either hang it from the ceiling or use it to decorate the walls. This is a good way to get a laugh out of your kids, as well as to thin out your necktie collection at the same time!

Chapter 17

Men's Shirts
Fabrics, Shopping, Construction, Custom, and Care

Are you completely satisfied with your shirts—the design, the fit, the starch, and the pressing? If you're not, why not? And how can you get there? Let's examine this issue.

◆ What a Well-Pressed Shirt Looks Like

A well-pressed shirt should have a smooth collar, smooth cuffs, smooth pockets, and only mild wrinkles, if any, on the body of the shirt. The sleeves, which look best without creases down the side, are usually covered by a jacket and are not a major concern. Special attention, however, should be paid to the wrinkles in the sleeve vent area near the cuffs. (This area is elusive, is often missed by the shirt press, and requires touch-up with a hand iron.)

The shirt should be starched to your satisfaction. The collar stays should be replaced inside the collars, and the broken or missing buttons should be replaced with *matching* buttons. The collar and cuffs should be free of soil. A size 15 collar should still be a size 15 and not a 14½ after laundering. Are you getting this quality from the shirt laundry at your drycleaners?

For twenty years, I have listened closely to customer complaints. I wish to dispel rumors, set the record straight, and build a forum so that you may learn to convey your preferences.

◆ Before You Buy

Cotton Fabric: The Purebred

A 100% cotton shirt breathes better than a cotton-polyester blend. Cotton shirts cost more, wrinkle more easily, and are more difficult to iron. They are available in a wide range of prices depending on the designer and the quality of the cotton. Broadcloth fabric has a higher thread count than oxford cloth. The softer the cotton, the higher the thread count; the higher the thread count, the more expensive the shirt will be. A thin, white cotton dress shirt of average quality, depending on the amount of starch used, will show a fair amount of wrinkles when it is finished. The thinner the cotton, the more difficult the shirt is to press. Thinner shirts, though more luxurious, will require more touch-up with a hand iron.

Unless you enjoy ironing at home, you should plan to use a commercial laundry to give your shirts a crisp and professional look. If you prefer a heavily starched shirt, 100% cotton will get you there better than a polyester blend will. A 100% oxford cloth shirt with heavy starch will probably offer you the stiffest shirt you can get. The higher the thread count, the more starch you will need to achieve the same stiffness.

Cotton-Polyester Blends: The Economical Alternative

The higher the percentage of cotton, the better the shirt will breathe. If you perspire heavily, then a cotton-poly blend may not be your best choice. However, the higher the poly content, the less the shirt will cost. If you're a college student or young professional and you wish to save money by ironing at home, poly blends are easier to iron, making them a smart use of your money. If you choose to use a commercial laundry, there is no discount for blended shirts. Poly blends do not absorb starch at the same rate as 100% cotton shirts, so you should expect a softer finish regardless of the amount of starch used.

Polyester Shirts

The least-expensive shirts are 100% polyester. Poly shirts need little ironing and rarely require commercial laundering, which makes them inexpensive to maintain. They do not breathe well and they do not absorb starch. Though they require the least maintenance, they also tend to look the least formal. High-fashion designers are making polyester shirts, but they are usually for casual wear as opposed to dress wear.

Silk Shirts: High Maintenance

Silk shirts are a specialty item. They are worn in the workplace, but more often are worn as a casual shirt without a necktie. Like cotton, silk is a natural fiber and it breathes well. Food stains, collar and cuff soil, and perspiration are difficult to remove. Silk should be cleaned the day after it is worn to minimize prolonged exposure to soil and perspiration. (See Chapter 7 on silk and perspiration.)

Textured Shirts: Ironing Made Easier

Dress shirts with a texture, regardless of how fine, will press better and faster than will shirts with no texture. Muted colors and fine prints will press better and show fewer wrinkles and imperfections than will a plain white shirt. A fabric with a texture—be it a fine twill, piqué, seersucker, oxford cloth, window-pane, or any other "texturized" finish—will be easier to press and will wrinkle less. Consider this factor seriously if you are ironing at home. Many textured shirts do not look as formal as a plain white broadcloth, so there is a trade-off.

◆ More Basics Before Shopping

Collar and Cuff Construction

Most shirts are single-ply material on the front, back, and sleeves. The collar, cuffs, and front placket (button strip) are constructed with two layers: the outer layer and the back layer. The outer layer is the "showcase," what the public sees; the back layer does not show. But if the back layer has too much material it can show through to the outer layer after pressing.

The collar and cuffs, which are the showcase of every shirt, can suffer from two major flaws: they can have unsightly wrinkles after pressing, and soil removal can be limited. Collars and cuffs are constructed in two ways: sewn or fused. The two layers of material must be sewn or fused together so that they appear as one smooth outer layer. Sewn collars and cuffs usually provide a soft, natural look. Fused collars and cuffs have a flat, hard appearance, which may have a slight sheen. A properly made shirt with sewn collar and cuffs should give you the same smooth result as a properly made fused counterpart. There is no right or wrong decision regarding which to wear; it is a personal preference.

The goal is to purchase a shirt that will withstand the heat and pressure of a shirt press without causing the collar and cuffs to wrinkle, shine, pucker, or show collar-stay impressions after pressing. Any wrinkles or imperfections (usually a result of poor construction) on the back layer of the collar and cuffs will show prominently through to the outer showcase side.

> **Pressing Facts**
> For many shirts, manipulating the front and back layers into one smooth piece during pressing is "part of the process."

Sewn Construction

▸ The two layers of the collar and cuffs are sewn together to make one smooth surface.

▸ If the two fabrics have not been preshrunk or stabilized before becoming collars and cuffs, then they may shift or shrink in washing. This condition can occur in the first washing or at anytime in the future.

▸ If the two layers do shift in washing, then it is the shirt presser's job to realign them into one smooth piece during the pressing process.

▸ If the layers are not perfectly realigned during the pressing process, then wrinkles will appear.

▸ Most shirt pressers are skilled enough to realign the layers during pressing. Many laundry supervisors push the operator to speed up, which may not allow the time it takes to do a quality job. If the operator is capable, then it is your right as a customer to have the job done properly—stand firm.

Fused Construction

Fused collars and cuffs can be constructed in a variety of ways, but there is one similarity: all fused collars and cuffs contain an outer layer (the showcase side that you see in the mirror) and an interfacing on the backside. These two layers are "glued" together to give the collar and cuffs a firm finish. They are *not* sewn.

▸ If the outer layer (showcase side) is bonded to the interfacing properly, then it should form one smooth layer, and there should be no obvious wrinkles on the outerlayer after the shirt is pressed.

▸ The two layers appear as one because they literally have been glued together.

▸ If the fusible process is not done properly or if the materials are inferior, then the layers can separate and shift.

▸ If too much material is on the backside, then wrinkles or creases will form and, after a pressing, they will show through to the outer layer. When this happens, unsightly lines and impressions mar the clean appearance of a fused collar or cuff.

> **Added Awareness**
> The front placket where the button holes are sewn can also be a problem area. The fabric can wrinkle and shine just like the collar and cuffs.

▸ Fused collars and cuffs have a higher incidence of soil retention. Body oils, perspiration, and oxidation from metal watchbands react with the resins in the adhesives and form a bond. This soil is considerably more difficult to remove from fused collars and cuffs than it is from the sewn counterpart. Pre-treating the soil at home before sending the shirt to the laundry will help "suspend" some of the soil until the shirt is professionally laundered. (See "How Much Care to Get Clean" on page 158.)

Collar Hardware: Problems with Snaps and Tabs

Snap-Down Collars

The machine that presses the collars and cuffs is capable of flattening a set of snaps as easily as it can crack a button. When you choose a snap-down collar instead of a button-down collar, you should expect, over time, that the snaps will be damaged. The laundry should replace the snaps *if* the damage is noticed during its inspection. It is an inconvenience if the shirt is returned to you not ready to wear.

More troubling is the impression that shows on the collar after pressing. The snaps are sewn onto the backside of the collar, and the pressure of the shirt press accentuates all the imperfections from the backside of the collar. These snap impressions are more apparent if the collar is fused because the sheen amplifies the imperfection. Snap-down collars offer a clean look, but be aware of these conditions.

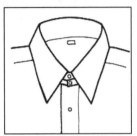

Tab with snap or button

Tab Collars

Tab collars are usually worn with neckties. A "tab" is a small strip of material that sits behind the knotted area of the necktie and is used to pull the collar closer together. A small button or a snap is attached at the center of the tab to keep it closed.

Both snap and button tabs are high maintenance. The shirt press will eventually break the button or flatten the small snap, just like the snaps on the collars. The broken button is routine and should be replaced, but the snap is rarely replaced by the laundry because the condition is not easily noticeable. A button-down collar or a tie bar accomplish the same goal as the tab. Think about the options before you decide on a tab-style collar.

◆ Let's Go Shopping: Custom Made & Designer Shirts

Now you know about different fabrics and textures, sewn or fused collars and cuffs, wrinkles and extra material, and collar hardware. You are ready to shop with the knowledge to make your best buy. As the saying goes, knowledge can be a dangerous commodity, but it is still your prerogative to buy a shirt because you like the style, even if the technical aspects of care may be problematic.

Spread collar   Point collar   Button-down collar

When you shop, focus on the pros and cons of style, design, and custom-made versus off-the-shelf. Try to apply your knowledge to every purchase. If you know that you will be ironing your shirts at home, then remember the advantage of textures.

Hints When Purchasing

Custom-made, designer, and off-the-shelf shirts all have idiosyncrasies. Detail work can make ironing at home difficult and time-consuming. At mainstream commercial laundries, detail work usually does not get much attention. Here's a list of points to consider:

▸ Sleeves with pleats running down the sides require extra time and are rarely ironed properly.

▸ All pocket flaps, especially if they are thick, require hand ironing to avoid wrinkling and shine.

▸ Permanent collar stays cannot be removed before pressing. These stays may leave an impression on the outside of the collar.

▸ When pressed commercially, raised embroidery or painted designs can leave "pockmarks," the threads can bleed, and the painted areas can melt. Check the care label closely before sending these types of shirts to the laundry.

▸ Epaulets on the shoulders, especially if buttons are attached, will require hand ironing. Again, laundries often overlook these details.

Custom-Made Shirts: An Affordable Alternative

A custom shirt can be everything you want it to be. If you are tall, short, robust, or thin—or in any way "hard to fit"—custom shirts may be an answer for you. The word "custom" implies perfection, but it should not be confused with the image it invokes. Custom means that you design your own shirt; you select the fabric, the style of the collar and cuffs, and sewn or fused construction. The only remaining detail is making the shirt fit your body. All of these aspects are pluses, but *you* must make the final decisions, and there are no guarantees.

A few tips when considering a custom shirt:

▸ Be patient and do not make snap judgments.

▸ Because you may be required to order six at a time, ask for a prototype first. Be certain that the prototype is everything that you want it to be.

> **A Pressing Fact**
> Most shirt-pressing machines are designed for *average* body types in average sizes. Custom shirts are designed to fit *individual* bodies. For this reason, many custom shirts require more touch-up with a hand iron.

▸ Do not be timid about your wishes. This investment of your time and money may produce many great shirts in the future. This is the time to speak up.

▸ Ask to see the shirtmaker's samples of sewn, as well as fused, collars and cuffs.

▸ Ask if collars are preshrunk before the shirt is constructed. Many custom-made shirt collars have progressive shrinkage, so you may want to order the collar a half inch larger to account for that problem.

▸ Remember the value of fabric textures and subtle prints.

▸ Remember that the more unique the buttons, the more mismatched buttons you will have down the road. Ask the shirtmaker for a bag of extra buttons. A high-end laundry may offer to keep them for you.

▸ Many off-the-shelf shirts can be replicated for you by a custom shirtmaker. If you like the fit of one of your shirts, then take it to the custom maker to replicate it in your choice of fabric and style.

> **Ultimate Comfort**
> Fine cotton is often sheer. This type of fabric requires more care in pressing and more touch-up with a hand iron.

Designer Shirts

Purchasing a shirt made by a well-known designer does not guarantee that it is well made. The fabric, construction, and texture will determine the way a shirt will press, but the style and fit are personal barometers. Most shirts made by established designers such as Armani, Valentino, and Hugo Boss are very dependable, especially the styles with textured fabrics.

Perhaps lesser-known but dependable designers such as Burberry of London, Tom James, Lorenzini, and Canali make very serviceable shirts as well. On the very high end, Brioni, Borelli, Charvet, Turnbull and Asser, and Zegna make exceptionally fine shirts. Many of the high-end shirts have unique buttons, so get lots of extras.

Department stores very often sell their own name brands. Many of these shirts are of high quality and are competitively priced with other designer brands. Saks Fifth Avenue, Neiman Marcus, Bergdorf Goodman, and Nordstrom, to name a few, have good selections at various prices.

> **Test It Yourself**
> You can detect a sewn collar by rubbing the fabric between your thumb and forefinger. If the outer layer feels soft and the two layers separate easily, then the collar is probably sewn. If there appears to be a lot of extra material on the backside, then wrinkling may get worse with washing.

Many less-expensive shirts, especially cotton-poly blends, by companies such as Van Heusen, Izod, and Geoffrey Beene, tend to press very well. They are simply constructed without too many bells and whistles. They use easy-to-match buttons, and their fit is geared toward mainstream body types.

Note: If you are hard to fit, or somewhat particular, then I suggest that you unwrap the shirt and try it on before you buy it. You may be hesitant to do this, but don't be. At minimum, this practice will save you a trip back to the store—and it may keep you from adding another shirt to your closet that you don't wear.

Casual Shirts

Casual shirts already have a presence in the workplace, but are more evident now with the advent of casual Fridays. Most casual shirts are sent to the shirt laundry, but few are best pressed that way. Many of the fabrics and darker colors in these shirts need special attention to avoid shine. The other concern is the texture. Shirt presses impart a firm finish, but I think that casual shirts look better and typically feel better when they are softer. (For more information about casual shirts, see Chapter 15, "Men's Clothing.")

It is also important, when deciding on the proper method of cleaning, to check the fabric content labels. The shirt may be a rayon, silk, or linen blend, and these fabrics are best drycleaned rather than hard pressed in a laundry. If these shirts are drycleaned, then the fabric will remain soft and the colors will not fade as quickly.

> **Preventive Care**
> Take the time to evaluate your casual shirts to decide what service would be best. It will prolong the life of your shirts.

◆ Decisions about Cleaning

How Much Care to Get Clean

You can identify your individual "soil quotient" by grading how much care it takes to treat and remove the soil from your collars and cuffs, and perspiration from the underarms of your shirts. If you still see graying in your collar or cuffs or yellowing under the arms when the shirt is returned from the laundry, there could be many reasons. Assuming that the laundry is using the optimum washing temperature of 140 degrees and is scrubbing the collar and cuffs before washing, consider these issues:

▸ Is your work environment contributing to the soil buildup? Stress can cause the body to exude heavier body oil and perspiration.

- ▸ Is your work area or desk area contributing to the soil?
- ▸ Do you wear your shirts more than once before you clean them?
- ▸ Do you wear shirts with a fused collar and cuffs? They do not release soil easily, even with prespotting.

Suggestion: Consider pretreating the affected areas with a bar of soap, water, and an old toothbrush. It will take you only five minutes each night. It may seem like a significant amount of work, but it beats replacing the shirt.

> **It's a Male Thing?** Studies show that a surprising amount of men wear their shirts more than once between washings. This practice severely limits soil removal.

Pressing Dark Shirts and Thick Fabrics

- ▸ Dark colors are likely to shine. Black, navy, and burgundy are the most susceptible colors, especially if they are part polyester. Pure cotton fabrics are less sensitive to heat and pressure but are not immune to shining.
- ▸ If the collar and cuffs on these darker shirts have been fused, the press can cause the adhesives to melt. The glues often show through to the outer layer as tiny, dark dots. These dots can usually be removed by rewashing, but they will probably reappear unless the shirt is hand ironed at a lower temperature.
- ▸ Double-thick areas (collar, cuffs, and front placket) tend to shine first. Pocket flaps and epaulets may be similarly affected. Look at your shirts closely, and you will see that they are more faded in *these* areas than they are on the body of the shirt.
- ▸ A twill-woven fabric has fine, raised ridges. The raised surfaces are the first layer to touch the hot press. The fabric becomes matted down and starts to shine. Twill button-down shirts are very popular. Vibrant colors typically fade on the double-thick areas—pastels and dark colors alike.

Twill shirt at double-thick area

Collars with collar stays, both removable and permanent, can also have shine problems. The "pockets" on the back layer of the collar that hold the stay can shine and show through to the showcase area. If the stay is removable, then be sure to remove it before you drop off your shirts. If the stay is permanent, you may want to have the shirt hand ironed to avoid the impression.

Note: There is a "drycleaning side" and a "laundry side" in most drycleaners. The drycleaning side has presses and steam irons that impart a softer finish. This is the equipment used to press silk and woolen fabrics.

> **Test the Shine**
> Try the taste test yourself: have one dark shirt hand ironed and the other pressed by a shirt machine. The difference should be clear.

To Prevent Shine

All the problems listed about dark shirts can be diminished by hand ironing or soft pressing. These same shirts could be washed or drycleaned and then *hand ironed*. This process will slow the eventual shining; reduce fading and color loss on the collars, cuffs, and front plackets; and extend the life of your shirts. I mentioned earlier that there is an extra expense, so you should weigh the cost against the investment. Sometimes keeping a favorite shirt looking good overrides the monetary issue.

Helpful Hint: Examine your pile of shirts for the laundry before you automatically say to the clerk at the drycleaner, "Six shirts for the laundry." White, light blue, and pastel colors in broadcloth and oxford fabric are the least likely to be shined by a shirt press.

To Starch or Not to Starch

Starching a shirt is a purely personal decision. Statistics show that most men prefer no starch on their shirts, which guarantees the softest look and the softest feel. Laundries, almost universally, use chrome-faced pressing machinery that imparts a firm finish on most cotton fabrics. The collar, cuffs, and placket of a shirt are designed with a double-thick material, or an interfacing, making these three parts feel considerably stiffer than the body of the shirt. This stiffness is the reason men believe that their shirts have been starched when they haven't been.

The Real Story

▶ Starch is added in the washing machine. In this process, the whole shirt is starched, not just the collar, cuffs, and placket.

▶ If you still complain about the collar and cuffs being too stiff while the rest of the shirt feels "soft," then seriously consider changing shirt brands or changing to a completely hand-ironed shirt. Remember, sewn collars and cuffs will be softer than fused collars and cuffs.

▸ Dress shirts and formal shirts do look more crisp with a medium amount of starch.

▸ Starched shirts can be uncomfortable in warmer weather. On the plus side, starched shirts hold their body and shape longer than shirts without starch.

▸ Medium to heavy starch can cause a cotton fabric to turn brittle and can shorten the life of the shirt. As a result, you may see some pin-sized holes or premature tearing at stress areas such as the elbows and across the back. Oxford cloth shirts are particularly sensitive to prolonged exposure from heavy starch.

▸ If you are dissatisfied with the amount of starch on your shirts, then do not hesitate to ask for advice from the manager.

> **Longer Life**
> If you routinely starch your shirts, then I suggest that you allow a two-to-three week period when you request no starch. This practice will help your shirts last longer.

Note: Custom shirtmaker Ascot Chang openly recommends that their shirts not be starched. "Starch will shorten the life of a cotton shirt."—Fred Anderson, Tom James Shirts.

◆ Button Philosophy

Most shirts are washed in hot water. After the wash cycle, they cool down. Then they are pressed at roughly 300 degrees on a high-pressure machine. The plastic buttons on the shirts expand and contract and can easily break or chip during this process. I have little positive advice this time, only explanations.

Broken Buttons

▸ Plastic buttons are the most durable. Some plastic buttons will withstand twenty visits to the laundry without breaking.

▸ If the buttons don't *break* during pressing, they often chip or suffer hairline cracks. These cracks can be significant enough to weaken the button just shy of the point of breakage. The breakage usually occurs when you button the shirt. The collar and cuff buttons tend to break first because the button must slide through a double-thick fabric.

> **Problematic**
> Plastic buttons that have raised ridges around the edge, crack and chip regularly during pressing.

▸ Shell buttons are less common than plastic and are more fragile. They break easily and are expensive to replace. They are followed in fragility and expense by metal, brass, and then glass.

▸ If the buttons are brass, glass, or unusual in any manner, then you should have them removed before cleaning and then resewn rather than take the chance of their breaking.

Missing and Mismatched Buttons

There is no excuse for a shirt to be returned to you from the laundry with missing buttons. If buttons are missing, then it is because of poor inspection during the quality-control phase.

▸ Most broken or missing buttons are replaced with generic-looking buttons. A laundry must stock a minimum of twenty button styles in two sizes to have a near-complete collection that will satisfy most shirt styles.

▸ Shell buttons are almost prohibitively expensive, so many laundries do not stock even one style. This factor is why I stress ordering an extra bag of buttons for your custom-made shirts.

▸ The ultra-thick buttons on Brioni and Borelli shirts are nearly impossible for laundries to purchase. Even high-end laundries struggle to replace them.

◆ At the Cleaners

You should know how best to use the laundry services at the drycleaners, how to convey your wishes, and how to resolve problems you may encounter. At the drycleaner's counter, or as a delivery customer, you will have to make choices about the care of your shirts. You should be firm when you convey your wishes to the counter clerk or the delivery driver. You are in this together, you are protecting your investment, and you should not hesitate to express your preferences.

Inspect your shirts for broken or missing buttons, and check for missing collar stays. If you are dissatisfied with the amount of starch you have been using, then make the adjustment now. If you have any specific stains or heavy soil on the collars, cuffs, or underarms, then point them out to the counter clerk.

Note: Read Chapter 18 for more on shirt machines, hand ironing, and on collar and cuff wrinkles.

Shirt Machines
Beyond the Basics

If you have further interest in the mechanics of shirt pressing and if you want to know why some shirts do not press well, read this chapter. It's short and concise.

◆ Shirt Presses

Most shirt operations consist of three shirt presses: one for the sleeves, one for the collar and cuffs, and one for the body. The machines are somewhat automated, but they all need to be "dressed" by an operator. These machines exert heavy pressure and press shirts at roughly 300 degrees. Machine styles can vary but most are designed in this fashion.

Most shirt-pressing equipment is designed for men's shirt sizes 15/34 to 17/37. Each day, laundries press shirts in sizes that are smaller and larger and, depending on the cut of the shirt, most of the shirts will need to be touched up with a hand iron. I mention this fact for two reasons: first, to help you understand the built-in limitations the drycleaning industry faces while trying to please all its customers, and second, to explain why, if your shirts are either smaller or larger, the pressing may be inconsistent.

Hand Ironed versus Machine Pressed

Most drycleaners offer a hand-ironed shirt as well as a machine-pressed shirt. Hand ironing will impart a softer finish, which is especially evident on the collar and cuffs. Thick fabrics and dark colors, which are prone to shine from the heat of a laundry press, can be virtually perfect if hand ironed. Your casual and more fragile shirts can also be drycleaned and hand ironed to avoid shine. These custom services should be available to you at a higher price. Instead of $1 to $4.50 for a laundered shirt, depending on the market, the cost may be $4.50 to $15 per shirt. The price disparity can be great depending on the level of

> **Hot Flash**
> A hot-head press has a chrome surface that imparts a crisp finish on shirts. This process contributes to the shine on dark shirts and the impressions on the collar caused by permanent stays.

163

quality and the fabric of the shirt. For most dress shirts and formal shirts and for many casual shirts, the shirt press does a fine job at an affordable price. But you do have a choice.

Important: While most shirts are safe on shirt-pressing equipment (besides the deep colors and the thick fabrics), you must remember that these machines are air-operated and steam-heated and they can cause delicate fabrics to wear or tear prematurely. If you have a special shirt that is very expensive or irreplaceable, then you should consider having it hand ironed each time.

◆ Collar and Cuff Wrinkles

You probably have some shirts of good quality that always come back from the laundry with wrinkles on collars and cuffs, while others, which appear to be very similar, press much better with no wrinkles. For many shirts, manipulating the front and back layers into one smooth piece during pressing is "part of the process."

> **First to Shine**
> The collars, cuffs, and front placket of shirts are designed with double-thick fabric (sometimes partly made of inter-facing). These layers are the first to hit the shirt press, and they take the majority of the pressure during pressing.

Is the Shirt-Press Operator to Blame?

Each week shirt pressers see thousands of shirts made by many different designers and manufacturers. Many of the shirts they see have various problems and idiosyncrasies, which they attempt to remedy during pressing. If the shirt presser does the job properly, then he or she can eliminate, through stretching and manipulation, most of the wrinkles on the surface.

The only other method for restoring the smoothness to a poorly made surface that has too much material on the front or back layer, or is poorly sewn or fused, is to hand iron the area. Hand ironing is good for "touching up" an area, but it may impart a different texture than that initially imparted by the shirt press. Nonetheless, the texture-change may be better than a wrinkle.

> **Defining Moment**
> Plenty of shirts press well and have few problems with extra material. When you find a brand that suits you, try to stick with it.

Is the Manufacturer to Blame?

If the shirt presser is adequately skilled and has taken the required time to remedy a problem, but the shirt still has visible wrinkles or impressions, then the manufacturer is probably responsible. If the collar and cuffs have been properly constructed (whether sewn or fused), then there should be very little material on the back layer to manipulate.

If there is extra material, then it should be so minimal that it does not show through to the "showcase" layer of the shirt. This is a fact. The machine that presses the collar and cuffs applies an extreme amount of pressure. This pressure can impart a smooth finish *or* accentuate any wrinkles, imperfections, or collar-stay impressions. Rarely can a machine improve a manufacturer's faulty product. The only alternative is to have the shirt completely hand ironed either at the drycleaners or at home.

Too much material on the outer layer of the collar

The shirt presser's ability to align the layers and manipulate the fabric often relates directly to the philosophy of the business owner and management staff. If the shirt pressers are being rushed to turn out a certain amount of shirts per hour—and most are—then the quality level may be compromised. It takes time to re-align the fabric layers of a poorly constructed shirt. The time allowed is purely a function of management, the owner's vision of quality, and his or her ability to maintain that quality.

If you are dissatisfied with the shirt pressing, then share your feelings with a key person to understand what the cleaner's philosophy is.

A Possible Option
Most wrinkles associated with too much material can be rectified by hand ironing, but how many people can afford to have all of their shirts hand ironed? Consider this approach when there is no other option.

Very few parts of the drycleaning or laundering "process" are as automated as shirt pressing. The presses have timers on them, and the actual "real" time spent pressing the shirt, the collar, cuffs, sleeve, and body, can be as little as sixty seconds.

The touch-up process is an additional step that requires more time and attention.

Chapter 19

Shirt Loss or Damage
Holes, Tears, and Loss

◆ Holes, Tears, and Lost Shirts

Holes "appear" for a multitude of reasons: age, poor tensile strength, drink spills, and chemical damage. Most often, these conditions are the result of consumer use. Holes may become evident *during* the shirt laundering process, making the laundry the unlucky suspect, but they are rarely *caused* by laundering. Here is a list of the most common causes of holes.

Causes of Holes

▸ The age of the shirt is often the reason for the holes. A collar could be totally frayed from wear, but when a hole appears in the body of a shirt, the consumer often looks for the responsible party instead of seeing the signs of age.

▸ Buttons on button-down collars break regularly during the pressing process and must be resewn each time. Each time they are resewn, the fabric is weakened by the needle. Because the needle does not penetrate the fabric in the same exact spot each time, it weakens the area around it. This condition contributes to the eventual holes in the button area.

▸ Fabric strength is an absolute barometer. Tiny holes, occasionally in groups, may be a sign of tensile weakness in the "bolt" of material used to make the shirt. Larger holes in sporadic patterns are very common with oxford cloth shirts. When colored oxford cloth shirts develop holes, they often have tiny white threads, like hairs, around the holes.

▸ If untreated for one week, spills—especially from orange juice, soda, and other sugar-bearing foods and drinks—can weaken cotton fabrics at an alarming rate.

▸ Bleach, usually a mainstay for washing white garments at home, is often used improperly. Sometimes straight bleach is poured into the washer or on a stubborn stain without the person realizing the tremendous toll it takes on the fiber. Other assorted, consumer-oriented products account for a percentage of damage, as well.

▶ Travelers who use hotel laundries and unfamiliar drycleaners have no knowledge of what types or strengths of bleaches are being used by these establishments. These services may be contributing to the damage.

Causes of Tears

Tears are usually the result of a weakened area—be it from age, spills, chemical damage or, on occasion, heavy starch use for prolonged periods. Shirts are usually pressed in a stretched condition. If there are weak or thin areas, then they are the first to tear. A new shirt rarely tears during pressing unless the machine malfunctions (which is rare). If a machine does malfunction, then it is usually obvious because the tear is clean, and as a rule there are no weakened fibers surrounding the torn area.

Lost Shirts

Lost shirts are a fact of life in the world of commercial laundries. From discount to custom, all operations suffer from this inevitable occurrence. Owners have tried every quality control and inventory system known to man, but all systems are still run by humans. In some operations, a computer may assemble the shirts into the original group of six that you dropped off, but humans still have ultimate control. If a loss occurs more than once a year, then talk to the manager or owner for further assurance.

◆ Resolving Damaged or Lost Shirts

Damaged Shirts

If a shirt is damaged, then allow your drycleaner to explain, and try to be open-minded and patient. The cleaner is probably as upset as you are. If you trust your drycleaner with your valuable shirts and suits, then you should trust the cleaner to be honest in the assessment of your damaged shirt. Payment or credit is usually a gentleman's issue. Assess the age of the shirt, the condition, and the initial cost, and then come to a mutual agreement on replacement value.

> **Value Adjustment**
> The government publishes guides that offer adjusted values for age and condition of a garment, but they are rarely needed to reach a resolution.

Lost Shirts

No one enjoys being the bearer of bad news, so you can be certain that if a shirt is lost, the manager has already searched in every possible place. The most common reason for a missing shirt is improper assembly: staff put one of Mr. Smith's shirts with Mr. Jones's order.

The second reason, and a fairly common one, is a miscount. You thought you dropped off six shirts when there were actually five. This scenario works in reverse as well; sometimes there are more shirts than you originally counted. Either way, if the count is wrong and the laundry is aware of it, then you should expect a phone call. (Be sure to provide your drycleaner with your phone number.)

It is common practice for the manager to ask you for the exact size, color, design, brand name, and perhaps the age of "missing" shirts. The drycleaners know that you may have many shirts, but try to be as helpful as you can, for they are on your side. You should allow the cleaners two to three weeks to research the situation, during which time the shirt may find its way back. Another customer may discover it and subsequently return it. If the shirt cannot be found, then the drycleaner may ask you for the original sales receipt.

Assessing the value of a missing shirt requires trust from both parties. The business owner may be skeptical if the claim you submit is for a very expensive shirt when the rest of your shirts are of average quality. You may be upset if the owner questions your word. The situation is a two-way street.

Incidences of lost shirts and other assorted clothing have become immortalized in movies, on television, and in real life. I am often within earshot of someone relating yet another "lost shirt" story. At a party, when people find out that I am a drycleaner, the stories start to pour out. Almost every person has a lost garment story. Loss and damage, percentage-wise, is a rare occurrence, but because it makes for such a captivating story, it seems more commonplace—which just shows how many people use the services of the 27,000 drycleaners in this country!

Chapter 20

Tuxedos and Accessories
Fabrics, Styles, Renting, Shopping, and Cleaning

A tuxedo, depending on your social life or job requirements, may be a necessary part of your wardrobe. If you wear a tux only once or twice a year, then renting may be advisable. If you are socially active, then you may need to own more than one. Having read this far, you will not be surprised when I tell you that the question of a tuxedo purchase can be multifaceted.

Wearing a tuxedo and the associated accoutrements can be fun. Depending on the event and the state of mind it elicits, dressing up for formal occasions provides an air of excitement. If you have a well-fitting, comfortable tuxedo, then you will be more relaxed, more confident, and perhaps more socially energized. For many, however, wearing a tux is not a pleasing experience. Perhaps the general bad rap that formal dressing has received arises from the discomfort many men feel when the tuxedo is ill-fitting or the tuxedo shirt is too stiff.

◆ Before Shopping

Most of the basics reviewed in Chapter 15 on men's clothing are applicable here. Most tuxedos are made of wool or wool blends. Choosing a tuxedo and accessories is more a matter of taste and preference than of substance. Because your tux will not be worn as often as a business suit, it should last many years, assuming that you buy a "classic" design. Because a tux is an ensemble purchase, you will want to make purchasing it a leisurely experience. All of this is easy to accomplish. The lapels, however, which are the crown jewel of a dinner jacket or tuxedo, require a bit more thought.

Lapel Construction
Some lapels are hand sewn to create a soft drape, and some are machine sewn to provide a stiffer look.

Hand Sewn
Hand-sewn lapels tend to have a softer drape and conform to the body more elegantly than do machine-sewn lapels. Depending on the interfacing or backing, the

length of the lapel, and the fabric chosen, lapels may naturally have a wave or a pucker along the edges. Hand stitches can be less consistent than those done by a machine, which may contribute to some minor puckering. The stitches may show slightly along the edge of the lapel, but this fact should not be a deterrent because it really is a matter of preference and style. (Many business suits that are hand sewn also have stitches that show, but perhaps less prominently.)

> **Puckering …**
> Materials that have not been stabilized or preshrunk can contribute to minor puckering.

Machine Sewn

Machine-sewn lapels are generally more firm looking and tend to ripple less, although this appearance, too, can vary according to the material. The stitching usually doesn't show with this type of construction.

Fabric Choices

Lapels are generally made from silk. Silk can be fabricated in a crepe de chine, which has a finish with a flat sheen; in satin, which is very lustrous; or with a gros-grain finish (pronounced gro-grain). The grosgrain lapel has a ribbed design with ridges. This type of lapel offers the firmest body and drape.

Concerns with a Satin Lapel

▶ If you choose a satin lapel and you want it to be firm and flat, then make sure that it is short enough to avoid waving. You will probably want to steer away from the classic "shawl" style lapel unless the interfacing provides enough body. You can view a few different styles, and you will see the difference.

▶ If the satin does not "lie down" naturally, then you should accept and respect this nuance. It is a waste of time to try to change this detail with an iron. If you are fastidious to the extent that you would feel un-kempt or self-conscious because the lapel is not flat, then consider your selection very carefully.

▶ Satin is a fragile material, and it can deluster and snag easily. If deluster occurs, then it can cause "scars" on the surface that will affect the natural sheen of the fabric. These scars are akin to a "wake" on a smooth sea.

> **Home Ironing**
> Do not allow anyone at home to use an iron on your satin or gros-grain lapels. These fabrics can scorch and deluster very easily.

▶ Satin can get very small "hairs" that stand up as a result of friction caused by slipping on your overcoat or by brushing rain off the lapel with gloves on. When you get enough of these hairs, they tend to dull the rich, black satin.

▶ Deluster can occur if you try to rub a stain or a spill off the surface, so try—as hard as it may be—to wait for an experienced drycleaner to attempt removal. The satin can snag on any sharp item: a cuff link, a watchband, or the edge of a hanger. The slightest contact with any of these items may mar the surface of the lapel. Recognize that regardless of these warnings, the majority of satin lapels are fine and last for years. Just be cognizant of their fragility.

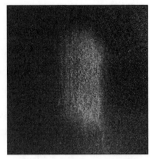
Delustered satin (magnified)

Lapel Styles

The three lapel styles are peaked, notched, and shawl. All three are popular, but peaked lapels, commonly seen in double-breasted tuxedos, have recently become fashionable in a single-breasted jacket. Peaked lapels offer a very formal look.

Peaked

In the peaked style, the top of the lapel has an upward line, which forms a peak. Peaked lapels are the most popular. It's a handsome look for single and double-breasted jackets.

Notched

In the notched style, the top of the lapel has a line that points downward.

Peaked

Shawl

The shawl lapel has soft lines and is longer than the peaked and notched lapels. It looks like a smoking jacket and is a popular design for dinner jackets. These lapels, because of their length and drape, may have a wavy texture.

Notched

Shawl

Jacket Styles

From wearing sport jackets and suits, you probably know whether you prefer a single- or double-breasted style. These days, double-breasted tuxedos are designed with a slimming look. The buttons are set wider as they go up toward the shoulder, which makes the waist look smaller. The only real disadvantage to a double-breasted jacket is that it doesn't look as neat when it is worn unbuttoned.

If the "open" look is more to your liking, then you may prefer a single-breasted jacket. A double-breasted jacket, though, when worn buttoned, is a very sharp look.

◆ Renting a Tux

Before we go shopping, let me offer you a different slant on the rental experience. If you have been satisfied with renting a tuxedo in the past, then by all means continue. The rental industry has made great strides in quality, style options, and convenience. Rentals are, however, not getting any less expensive. The price of the rental, depending on how often you rent, may be enough of an incentive to buy a tux. If you are renting more than once a year, then you should at least consider purchasing as an option. Are you wearing your own shoes, shirt, and tie? The comfort and familiarity of wearing your own outfit may make a difference in the way you feel about formal events. Would the convenience of having a tux you like—hanging in your closet—make a difference?

◆ Let's Go Shopping

First, let's examine the man who wears a tuxedo only once a year but prefers to purchase rather than to rent. When a tuxedo is worn so seldom, you have to consider the inevitable—your physical stature. If you are a man whose weight has not varied more than five pounds in as many years, congratulations. But if you do have a history of sliding up—and perhaps down—the scale, then consider the following points.

> **Relax and Enjoy**
> Don't rush when shopping for a tuxedo; you might consider taking your partner with you for feedback.

Your One and Only Tuxedo

Tailors are available at your beck and call. You can have your tux altered every time your weight vacillates enough to change the fit, but that practice obviously doesn't make good sense.

▶ Each time that you alter a jacket or slacks, you create new stitching holes. These small holes can be "steamed out," which will improve the condition, but they cannot always be hidden. You will also need to re-press new seams, and this procedure costs you time and money.

▶ I heartily recommend that you buy your tux in a size that you can live with for years, according to your own history of weight gain or loss.

▶ Although a tuxedo is a formal item and serves to show a certain sophistication and sense of style, you can have it altered to be fitted more loosely, but professionally. If I were to tell you how many men have had their tuxedos let out through the years, you would be stunned.

▶ When you buy your tuxedo, check your "crystal ball" and take your time to find a style that will stand the test of time. Don't buy anything too trendy that will look out of style in five years. Steer away from unusual lapels, and buy a more conservative tuxedo that you will feel good about for many years to come.

> **Fashionable**
> Short lapels and three-button tux jackets are *currently* hip, but if it's your only tux purchase, then think hard before buying.

Your Second or Additional Tuxedo

If you know that you will eventually own more than one tuxedo, then focus on style more than substance. You may want two very different designs, perhaps one more formal than the other, or one more conservative than the other.

I recommend that you call your favorite salesperson, set up an appointment, and allow enough time to make an educated decision. Consider the scenario outlined above and make sure that you have a clear image of what you want. Prices for formal wear—like other fine clothing—are all over the map. (If you do not have a "favorite" salesperson, see Chapter 1 about shopping by appointment.)

◆ The Cummerbund and Bow Tie

The cummerbund, though perhaps not as fashionable as it once was, deserves a little ink. It is generally made from silk or acetate. There is a method for pressing it to reduce the amount of shine and impressions, so ask about this method specifically before entrusting a cummerbund to your drycleaner. The cleaning is not difficult and need not be done very often.

The bow-tie usually remains tied. Not many men know how to re-tie one if it becomes undone. If your bow-tie needs care, then it can be spot-cleaned and steamed in its tied condition. If it is untied, then it should be soft pressed to minimize shine.

◆ At the Cleaners

Tuxedos must be soft pressed to avoid seam impressions and shine. The silk or satin lapels on a formal jacket can shine very easily from poor pressing. Shine can make a quality tuxedo look cheap, and once it is shined it is very difficult to restore. Be sure to bring this matter to the attention of the clerk. It is improper to hard press a satin lapel with the hope of removing waves and ripples. If you purchased the tux with a wavy lapel, then it will probably remain that way.

Use this opportunity to make sure that the buttons on your tux are secure. If any are frayed, the seamstress or tailor may have replacements.

Check the hot spots for minor repairs: the inside jacket lining at the vent, under-arms, and pockets. Check the slacks for frays along the pocket edges (from your watchband or jewelry), the cuff hems for loose stitches, the seat for open seams, and the inside of the waistband—all these areas will need care eventually.

If you see any holes in your tuxedo, then try to discern if they are the result of insect damage or the result of a tear. (Tears are more jagged than moth holes.) If you believe the holes are from insects, then check the whole tuxedo closely for more holes and weakened or thinned areas, which could be the result of partially eaten fibers. If you find more holes, then mark them with safety pins and have the garment cleaned before repairing. If you find additional holes after cleaning, then the expense to repair or reweave all of them may eclipse the cost of the tuxedo. The lapel fabric usually cannot be rewoven, but in many cases, *can* be replaced. (See Chapter 27 on "Reweaving: A True Savior.")

Chapter 21

Tuxedo Shirts
Styles, Buttons, Fabrics, and Pressing

Many men are unsure about starching tuxedo shirts. Making a shirt too stiff may make it uncomfortable, but make it too soft and it may look unkempt. I have also found that some men are put off by wavy, soft pleats. Some tux shirts develop yellow stains at the collar from cologne and dye bleed under the arms caused by perspiration. Buttons and button strips are also an issue.

Remember all the fundamentals of shirt construction discussed in Chapter 17 when you think about purchasing a tuxedo shirt: fused versus sewn collars and cuffs, collar stays, shrinkage, fabric choices, hand ironing versus machine pressing, starch preference, and custom-made options. I will make a couple of additions to this list for formal shirts: pleat construction and silk fabric.

The fashion industry has put its stamp on the formalwear market by expanding the traditional designs and adding fabrics. You are no longer limited to the typical cotton, pleated-front tux shirt with a spread collar or wing collar.

◆ Before Shopping

Tuxedo shirts can have a traditional spread or point collar, a wing collar, or a banded collar. The shirt can have narrow, medium, or wide pleats, a plain front with no pleats, or perhaps a bib front with a piqué texture.

Collar styles: traditional spread, popular wing, and seldom-seen banded

Body Styles

Pleated

There are three basic pleat styles: the narrow knife pleats, the quarter-inch-wide pleats, and the widest pleats, which are about ¾ inch and have only a few pleats across the front of the shirt. The decision is purely personal.

Plain Front

Tuxedo shirts without pleats are gaining popularity. They offer a breezy sense of style, being both dressy and fashionable. The collar choice is what makes this shirt distinctive. The quality of the fabric and the collar construction are your main considerations.

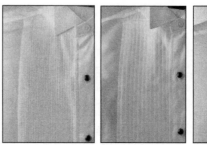

Pleated front: narrow, medium, and wide

Piqué Front

This textured fabric has a pebbly finish on the front bib, although some piqué shirts have the textured finish over a larger area than just the front. These shirts are worn with spread and winged collars, the spread being more popular. The texture is easy to iron, shows less wrinkling, and will have body without heavy starch.

Buttons and Studs

As mentioned in the chapter on buttons and trims, buttons can make an outfit. With tux shirts, the top button, the two on the cuffs, and the studs down the front make a statement. Any raised plastic, brass, or glass buttons will enhance the shirt. However, they may need to be removed when the shirt is laundered to avoid melting, chipping, or breaking. The lower front buttons are usually made of plain, flat plastic or shell, which should be fine in laundering.

Dressy shirt buttons and studs

Note: Button strips (next page) and studs are often misplaced by laundries, so remove them at home and put them with your jewelry for safekeeping.

Button Strips

Button strips can be used in place of individual decorative studs for the three button holes below the collar. The buttons are sewn to a half-inch-wide strip of material. By sewing the buttons to a strip, you are less likely to misplace the buttons, and it is a more efficient way to dress. Both the individual studs and the strips are a handsome touch and a good alternative to plain, flat buttons. You can select from a wide variety of buttons to fit your taste.

Button strip

Fabric Choices

Cotton

Most formal shirts are made of cotton or cotton-poly blends. Sheer cotton fabric (almost transparent) offers a formal look and is lightweight and comfortable. If you prefer a stiffer look and feel, thick 100% cotton fabrics accept starch much better. A cotton tuxedo shirt can be laundered along with your other dress shirts, but it may require more touch-up than a dress shirt does. After wearing the shirt, just decide on the amount of starch you want, and put the shirt in the pile for the cleaners.

Polyester

Formal shirts are available in 100% polyester. They do not look sophisticated, and they do not accept starch, but they are less expensive than cotton is. It is probably best to dryclean this fabric.

Cotton with a Silk Collar

Cotton shirts with a silk collar are usually designed in broadcloth-quality cotton, or a similarly soft equivalent. The collar usually has a black silk band on it. This type of shirt can only be drycleaned because the silk band will bleed in washing. If you want the shirt starched, then ask for starch to be sprayed on the shirt during finishing.

Silk

Silk tuxedo shirts have a soft feel and a beautiful drape, and are available in all three collar styles. They are usually designed without pleats down the front. As I have noted elsewhere, silk is clearly the most high-maintenance fabric you can buy. It has perspiration, dye bleed, and longevity issues. Do not allow silk shirts to be sent to the laundry with your cotton dress shirts; they should only be dry-cleaned. (See Chapter 7 on silk and perspiration.)

◆ Let's Go Shopping

If you are buying your tux shirt at the same time as your tuxedo, then do not let the tux purchase dilute your focus on shirt basics: collar shrinkage, fused versus sewn construction, quality of the cotton, and button choices.

Pleat Construction: Follow Your Fingers

Before you buy a pleated tux shirt, take time to examine the way the pleats are sewn down the front of the shirt. Open the package, lay the shirt flat, choose one pleat, and run your finger down the path from the top of the pleat to the bottom of the pleat. The pleat should follow a straight line.

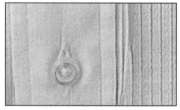

Improperly sewn pleat

If the pleat is sewn unevenly, if it wavers in an obvious way from left to right as your finger follows it down, or if any part of the pleat is sewn off-center, then there may be a problem during pressing. Narrow pleats are more prone to poor construction and require more care in pressing. Invest five minutes to do the finger test.

Shirt Fit

Most men do not take the time to actually try on the shirt at the time of purchase. It is wrapped neatly in the package, and it seems a sacrilege to disturb it—but *do* disturb it. If the sleeves are too long, then the cuffs will fall too far below the jacket sleeves. You will also be able to see how the type of pleat you have chosen looks on you.

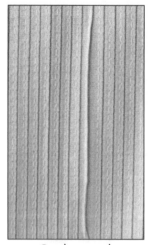

Poorly pressed

◆ Before the Cleaners

It is wise to examine your pressing options, starch preference, and stain removal issues *before* you go to the drycleaner. Knowing the choices and limitations will enable you to express your preferences and, therefore, give you more control.

Hand Ironed versus Machine Pressed

If you choose to have your tux shirt hand ironed, which is a more expensive process than having it pressed in the laundry by machine, then the pleats will always be soft and wavy. Hand ironing is also the least abrasive process—one that may be worth the additional price, and certainly worth the investment if your tux shirt is very thin, very expensive, or custom made. Hand ironing is also more gentle on buttons and will make the shirt soft to the touch. Extra sizing or starch can be added at your request.

Machine pressing always imparts more body and should always be your first choice if you want a stiffer finish. The process is more taxing on the fabric than hand ironing and may shorten the life of the shirt, but most men still prefer this method. It is clearly less expensive.

> **Opinionated**
> Formal events are often warm and stuffy. Why would you want your shirt to be too stiff?

Pleats

A pleated tuxedo shirt can have a soft look, with wavy pleats down the front, or it can have a firm look, with flat pleats. There is no right or wrong way.

Soft and Wavy—No Starch, Please

If you choose no starch, then hand ironing will give you the softest finish. The machine process would be a bit firmer but still soft, compared to a starched shirt.

The pleats on a hand-ironed shirt will be more wavy, and the process will be more gentle on the fabric.

Firm and Flat—Starch It

If you want your tux shirt to have a firm finish with flat pleats, then you will want the shirt pressed by machine with medium starch. Starch is approximated and is specific to each individual laundry, so "medium" will vary at different cleaners. If you want your shirt to be very stiff like a washboard, then you may want heavy starch. It is purely a personal preference. Hand ironing, regardless of the amount of starch added, will never impart as firm a finish as a shirt machine will.

Firm and flat on the left—
soft and wavy on the right

◆ Important Incidentals

A few details need to be shared: care for silk tux shirts and care for special buttons on the collars and cuffs.

Care for Silk Shirts

Your cotton tux shirt can be put in the same pile as your dress shirts while waiting to go to the laundry. Care for a silk shirt is different, though; silk must be treated on a case-by-case basis, with an emphasis on care and the amount of time a stain remains in the fabric.

Formal events can be exciting, often fast-paced, and sometimes intense. There may be dancing, drinking, and sweating, and when this combination occurs, a plethora of issues will come to light.

▶ What appears to be simple collar and cuff soil is never "simple" when it is on silk. Abide by the 24-hour rule.

▶ Perspiration can cause the lining of a tux jacket to bleed, which may deposit dark dye under the arms and occasionally on the back collar of the shirt.

> **Good Habits**
> Silk shirts should be drycleaned within 24 hours.

▶ Dye stains can occur on cotton tux shirts just as easily as on silk, but the dye stains are much more difficult to remove from silk.

▶ If the underarm does not turn purple or some similar shade, but it is still wet with perspiration, then there is a very good chance that the silk has already begun to discolor, even if it is not obvious to you at the time.

▶ Underarm moisture, which may be bone-dry by the end of the night, carries with it chloride salts and other minerals from your body. This condition, coupled with an alkaline color change, can turn the underarms yellow if left untreated. These stains cannot easily be washed out at home after the event.

Note: There is very little water in drycleaning, certainly not enough to remove the discoloration that forms under the arms. Any dye or color-change under the arms or on the collar will have to be hand spotted and dye-stripped. Few drycleaners have the expertise to perform this restoration on silk.

Special Buttons

If you have chosen a formal shirt with fancy or decorative buttons, then think of them as perishable. (See Chapter 3 for more on buttons.) When you take your tux shirt in for laundering or drycleaning, tell the clerk that you would like the buttons to be properly cared for.

▶ Average shell and flat plastic buttons should be fine during pressing and should not need to be removed.

▶ If you have chosen brass or glass buttons, then have them removed before cleaning and resewn afterward.

Jet buttons with fragile shanks

▶ The "jet" black buttons that are made of glass are handsome and formal looking and a popular choice. Typically, the collar and cuff buttons match, so have all three removed before cleaning and then resewn.

▶ Plastic raised buttons with a shank (pictured on the previous page) tend to bend or melt during machine pressing. Be sure to have this type of button removed and resewn.

◆ At the Cleaners

Inspect the collar, cuffs, and underarms of your tux shirt for soil and dye. If you know that you perspired, yet no stains show, then point out the areas to the clerk so that they can be spotted. (Clerks are accustomed to discussing stains like this, so don't be shy.) If the stains are invisible now, they won't be after the heat of cleaning. Once the underarms turn yellow from perspiration, or the collar turns yellow from cologne, the stains are often permanent. If there is dye on the collar or under the arms, then ask specifically for the cleaner's prognosis on stain removal. The clerk may be concerned enough to ask you for approval to dye strip the area.

On the Bright Side: Most stains from dyes that have transferred onto white garments can be improved. If your drycleaner is skilled in stain removal, a dye stripper may be used to improve or remove the fugitive dye.

If you have studs or a button strip and if you have not yet removed these items from the shirt, then do it at the cleaners or before the delivery driver picks up your clothing. Do not expect the laundry to return them to you. The same goes for cuff links. If you have any fragile buttons on the collar and cuffs, then ask that they be removed and resewn.

It's time to make a decision about the type of shirt service that you want. Remember the different pressing options such as hand ironing versus machine pressing. Also describe to the clerk how you want your tux shirt to feel, and ask how much starch will be required to fulfill your needs.

If you are socially active, then you should have at least two tuxedo shirts in your rotation. Between unexpected invisible stains that may surface from oily foods and cologne, style preferences, and travel, having an additional shirt will pay off many times over.

Chapter 22

Sweaters

Sweaters are a very personal item. Depending on where you live, you may buy them for warmth, to complement your fashion wardrobe, or both. The choice of fabrics and blends, weights, and styles makes sweaters possibly the largest investment in your wardrobe. Many people have sweaters for every kind of weather and every mood, but nobody needs another sweater that doesn't get worn. Keeping sweaters in good condition—in fact, just keeping them in "shape"—is a challenge. By addressing the most common problems, I hope to help you manage the challenges while I also help you thin out your selection (but not the thickness of your sweater!).

These are my sweater pet peeves:

▸ Too many sweaters pill after just a few wearings.

▸ They stretch out of shape in the collar, cuffs, and waist.

▸ They occasionally shrink or tighten up in the body especially as they age.

▸ They snag, and the snags can eventually turn to holes.

▸ They sometimes hold odors.

◆ Before Shopping

The basics in this chapter are not about components of sweaters—such as zippers, buttons, beads, and embellishments, although they are mentioned—but are more about fabric knowledge. I discuss which fabrics will be high maintenance, which require drycleaning (regardless of what the care label says), which ones will last, and which you should avoid. Each fabric will be examined for my peeves. Once I establish the basics for sweater fabrics, as I did for general fabrics in Chapter 2, you will find that walking through a store or browsing through a catalog is like a walk in the park.

◆ Fabric Choices

Cashmere

Cashmere generally wears well. It pills at a moderate rate, resulting from the frequency of wear and the amount of friction it experiences, but the shape will remain reasonably consistent. Lower-quality cashmere will have pilling and shape problems to a greater extent. Once you find a brand that you like, try to be true to it. Cashmere can be hand washed, but a "good" drycleaning will be better in the long run.

Cotton Knit

Cotton sweaters can be inconsistent in their quality. They generally never pill, but they do have shape-retention issues. Ramie fabric has more of the same issues.

▶ Tightly knit sweaters hold their shape better than loosely knit sweaters; they tend to snag less and ultimately have fewer holes down the line. Many cotton knits have brittle yarns, which tend to break instead of stretch.

▶ Tightly knit sweaters will not catch on as many things and do not unravel as easily.

▶ The main problem with cotton knits is the texture. They remain relatively soft after drycleaning, but they tend to turn stiffer after washing, especially if a fabric softener is not used. The condition becomes worse when the sweater is air dried, as opposed to being fluffed in the dryer. If it is removed from the dryer slightly damp and allowed to air dry, then it will be softer to the touch.

Mohair and Angora

These sweaters are actually low maintenance, and the only true concern is heat. If they are washed and tumble dried, then they will shrink so much that they will fit only a child. If you can lay the sweater flat after hand washing and adjust it to the approximate correct size, then it should be fine. Drycleaning will generally retain the shape better, but if the drycleaner overdries the sweater, then it will also have problems.

> **To Retain Shape**
> Measure the sweater before you wash it. After you wash it, and while it is damp, lay it on a white terry towel and gently block it back to shape.

Merino

Merino wool is very soft and comfortable to wear. It has short, tightly wound yarns that remain true to size. Merino wool does not pill easily, it keeps its shape, and it comes in beautiful colors. It does snag, so be careful around sharp objects. Even a hangnail or jewelry can snag the fabric.

Basic Wool

We all know that basic wool sweaters—Shetland and such—are not very soft. They pill quickly and tend to stretch out of shape at the collar, cuffs, and waist. We all have sweaters like this in the recesses of our drawers or perhaps tucked away to wear when we clean the attic. This type of sweater can be maintained. If you are not too aggressive when you remove the pills, if the sweater is steamed properly during finishing (to reblock the misshaped areas), and if the sweater is protected from moths, then it will last a long time.

Wool Blends

Wool blends are usually thin, lightweight, and very soft. For women, they provide a feminine look. They do not pill or wrinkle easily. When you buy a wool blend, check the content to see what wools are being used (possibly blended with acrylic). If you find that the sweater is blended with a high-quality wool such as merino, you will be paid back handsomely for your extra effort. Drycleaning is the best care method to retain the texture and size of these sweaters.

Chenille

Chenille sweaters have come a long way, but they still have the most problematic wear and service issues. Chenille is manufactured in many fabrics, but rayon and cotton are the most popular. To date, chenille sweaters still have the most shape-retention problems. The sleeves, waist, and neck gain inches just from wearing. Chenille has very little "memory" to return it back to its original shape after wearing. The condition can sometimes become worse from drycleaning, even if the sweater is properly "netted" to protect it. A few observations:

> **Water Sensitive**
> Be sure to check the care label first, but do not hand or machine wash chenille sweaters without some thought. The nap will change, the sheen will change —and these changes will be permanent.

▸ If you find a particular brand or blend of chenille that works for you, then stick with it.

▸ Chenille is *very water sensitive*. Water-based spills, including plain water, can cause a ring or a deluster to the fabric that is nearly impossible to remove without leaving a trace.

▸ Chenille sweaters can also snag easily. The snags can become holes, and the holes are difficult to reknit.

Note: Chenille scarves and shawls, though still problematic, tend to show fewer shape-retention problems and stain issues than the sweaters.

Silk Knit and Rayon Knit

Silk-knit and rayon-knit sweaters are very popular because they are soft, thin, and stylish. Designers are making them in very attractive colors and distinctive neckline cuts—"V" necks and off-line neck designs—as well as in every sleeve length. These sweaters are becoming more common, and they have serious issues.

Problems

▸ Silk knits and rayon knits snag and pull easily. These snags can sometimes be repaired or "pulled through" by a seamstress or tailor with a deft touch. Because of the weave, the snags often run along a line, so they damage inches at a time. I would think twice before purchasing these types of sweaters.

▸ Silk and rayon knits often have serious problems with underarm and body odor after wearing. The drycleaning process, which uses very little water, does not always improve the problem.

▸ Soap and water can be effective, but some odors cannot be removed even by hand washing.

▸ The resins used in manufacture, which some people say smell like formaldehyde, are often the reason for the odor problem. My wife, being a "drycleaner's wife," noticed the odor soon after the sweaters became fashionable. Coincidentally, after she brought this problem to my attention, I began to hear many more complaints about silk- and rayon-knit sweaters.

▸ Try to choose a good deodorant, let it dry before dressing (as you should with all upper-body clothing), and try not to perspire too much when wearing these sweaters. I know that trying not to perspire sounds ridiculous, but there are certain events that cause you to perspire more than others, so give this matter some thought when dressing.

Fabric Pilling

Most wool sweaters form pill balls because of broken fibers and the long, loosely wound yarns used to make them. Acrylic sweaters tend to pill at a greater speed than wool sweaters, and acrylic produces smaller "nubs" that cannot be easily shaved.

Pilling is exacerbated by friction that occurs when the "nappy" surface of the sweater rubs along other nappy or textured surfaces. Pilling is heavier under the arms and down the sides.

Several things contribute to pilling:

▶ Lying on or under a blanket creates friction, and all friction promotes pilling.

▶ Rubbing against the inside of a coat (especially if unlined) or against uphol-stered furniture with a texture contributes to pilling.

▶ The drycleaning process can also contribute to the condition. During the dry-cleaning process, sweaters touch other sweaters, and the friction during the cycle can cause additional pilling.

Note: In the drycleaning machine, sweaters are agitated as they are cleaned, and this repeated motion can contribute to pilling. Careful drycleaners are putting their sweaters in mesh nets during the cleaning cycle to minimize friction, thus re-ducing the pilling and misshaping of many fabrics.

Story Time ...

A female customer asked me to de-pill her pale-yellow Shetland sweater. After-ward, she said, "Can't you do more? It still has pills." I did as she asked while she watched. When I was finished, she tried it on, and I could see her lace bra beneath the sweater!

You can de-pill these pill balls with tools that are readily available, but be aware of thinning the fabric. Each pill may contain numerous yarns, and when you shave or brush it off, you take a significant amount of yarn with it. You can remove every pill if you are so inclined, but you may have a somewhat "transparent" sweater when you are done. Be sure to de-pill sparingly, and step back to check your work regularly during the process.

> **Home Remedy**
> You can de-pill with a battery-driven shaver designed to re-move pill balls. These shavers work very well, but be sure to practice first and to use a light touch.

◆ Beads, Trims, and Zippers

Sweaters with ornamentation—such as beads, sequins, crystals, painted designs, leather or suede trim, snakeskin, or piping—can play havoc with consumers and drycleaners. Often, care labels are not accurate but even when they are and you follow the instructions, there can still be problems.

Beads, Sequins, and Crystals

Beads, sequins, and crystals are types of ornamentation rarely tested by the manufacturer, so the care label doesn't usually apply to them. Many times the ornamentation is manufactured or attached by a "secondary" maker. The clothing manufacturer who makes the sweater knows that the fabric can be washed or drycleaned, but after the trims are added, the care label may become inaccurate. Sometimes you will see a secondary label or warning that says, "Exclusive of beads and trims."

Consumers and drycleaners are forced to test each bead or crystal. Some of these beads, which may be painted or dyed, can peel and bleed. Sometimes they do not bleed in a test and do so only with prolonged exposure to water or drycleaning solvents. Crystals often have backings that allow liquids into the crystal, which can cause them to fog in washing or cleaning. Painted designs and piping can melt, peel, and bleed under the same conditions.

> **Special Sweaters**
> If you buy a sweater adorned with such embellishments, try to shop at a reputable store. Ask if the store manager has heard good things about that brand.

Trims

Trims and patch designs made from leather or suede can be particularly sensitive. Light-colored sweaters with darker shades of sewn-on materials usually have dye-bleed problems. Snakeskin, leather, and suede are very heat sensitive, so keep the iron away from these parts of the sweater.

Fact: This type of specialty wear is rarely cleaned as often as it should be. People are generally hesitant to have these garments cleaned because they sense the challenge and ultimately end up wearing the sweater many times before cleaning. When the time comes to clean it, the sweater is often badly stained or too soiled to improve satisfactorily. Don't wait!

What Can Be Done?

Spot-cleaning may be the answer. It may be true that the sweater cannot be washed or drycleaned safely without the dye bleeding or some associated problem, but it can almost always be spot-cleaned, providing that you do not wait too long. A thorough inspection after each wearing will help you see the soil and will give you enough time to get the sweater to the cleaners. The neckline, cuffs, underarms, and front may have small stains that require attention. Not all stains can be removed by spot-cleaning, but many can, if caught early.

Washing at Home

If you choose to wash this type of sweater at home, follow the care instructions, test appropriately, and be sure not to leave it in the water for more than a few minutes.

A simple "dip and swish" with light agitation by hand should remove most of the general soil. Certain stains, especially yellow ones, may not come out. A thorough rinse, followed by air drying—usually laid flat on a white terry towel—will be the safest method. Watch the ornamentation and patches during drying to see if the dye bleeds or "leaches" out during drying. If it does, then take the sweater to the cleaners. If the cleaner cannot help you, then you should take it back to the store.

> **Early Detection**
> Inspect your sweaters in bright light. When spot-cleaning is the only option, timeliness is the key to successful stain removal.

Zippers and Buttons

Sweaters with zippers require extra care and preparation because of the zipper pulls. The pulls can bend, break, or peel during the cleaning process and may need to be removed with a pliers before cleaning. These metal pulls are often fragile and cannot withstand too much bending. So whether the sweater is being machine washed or drycleaned, use a gentle touch when removing and re-attaching the zipper pulls.

Unusual buttons (outlined in Chapter 3) often make an outfit and should also be protected or removed before cleaning.

◆ Let's Go Shopping

Remember to read care labels. If you buy a "trendy" or unusual sweater, then ask the salesperson about the designer, the quality of the company, and the return policy of the store. Natural fibers breathe better, acrylic pills easily, silk and rayon knits may have odor problems, and merino wool is a great midpriced investment. If the sweater has shoulder pads, then make sure that they fit properly. (See Chapter 6 for more on shoulder pads.)

Men's sweaters, though still subject to pills, snags, and shrinkage, tend to be more basic in design with fewer service issues. They are occasionally available in "trendy" fabrics, in which case similar concerns should still apply before you buy.

◆ Important Incidentals

Be sure to air out your sweaters before you fold them. Restaurants, bars, and certain work environments often lack air circulation, which contributes to odors. Because sweaters are typically worn more than once before washing or drycleaning, allowing them to breathe will keep them fresher. By airing them overnight, you will allow the perspiration and moisture to evaporate. By reducing moisture, you will reduce wrinkling. For more about clothing preparation and good habits, see Chapter 26.

◆ At the Cleaners

This is the time to closely inspect your sweaters for stains, open seams, small holes, stretched neck, cuffs, and waistband, loose shoulder pads, and snags. If the shoulder pads in the sweater are attached by snaps or Velcro,® remove them before cleaning. If they are sewn in, ask the clerk for suggestions to prevent the pads from shifting or becoming lumpy. Use this opportunity to inquire about the cleaner's method for protecting sweaters from pilling. Also, ask if they de-pill as a service to the customer.

Inspection for Holes

If there are holes in need of repair on your sweaters, try to discern if they are the result of insect damage or from a snag or tear. If they are from an insect, then check the sweater very closely for more holes. Hold it up to the light and look through the surface for more holes or partially eaten and thinned areas. If you see more holes, then mark them with a safety pin and clean the sweater before repairing. If there are additional holes after cleaning, then the cost of repairs may eclipse the cost of the sweater. If you are going to repair the holes, then ask about the quality of the sewing or reknitting and the outcome, especially if the holes are in an obvious location.

> **Insect Protection**
> You might want to consider storing your sweaters for the summer. Inquire about "cold" storage for woolens. (See Chapter 28 on storage.)

Chapter 23

Outerwear

Outerwear, depending on where you live or play, may be an integral part of your lifestyle. It can be fashionable but must also be functional. Simple fabrics, such as wool and cotton, have their idiosyncrasies but are rather straightforward in their care requirements. Synthetic fabrics tip the scales in complexity and care issues. Doesn't it seem odd that some rain gear designed to get wet cannot be washed? Technology has produced some great products for all varieties of weather, but, along the way, manufacturers have made the care for some of these creations a bit challenging.

My pet peeves about sweaters were examined in Chapter 22. Now I have another list for outerwear:

▸ Fabrics that are too fragile to iron or press

▸ Accessories and hardware that break

▸ Raincoats that are not waterproof

▸ Foul-weather gear that cannot be washed

▸ Fabrics sold as outerwear that cannot withstand the elements

◆ Before Shopping

Rather than examining every fabric in the marketplace (and they are constantly changing), I will focus on awareness and fabric construction. Having an eye for "red flags" will serve you much better than attempting to know the quirks about every fabric. As you read these facts and insights, remember to apply them to every purchase, every wearing and, eventually, every cleaning.

Construction Concerns

What do cotton, rayon, microfiber, some wool, and some outer shells have in common? They can all have problems with shine and color-loss down the front placket, along seams and pocket flaps, and on all double-thick areas. I'm sure you have seen this condition on dark or rich colors. It is especially apparent where the button, zipper, or snap pushes against the back of the fabric onto the outer surface. This produces a lighter area or abrasion on the outer shell. The abrasion from wear or pressing breaks the surface fibers, which then creates the light, chalky discoloration. This occurrence is very common with casual jackets, coats, and skiewar. Think about this problem when you buy dark colors. Check the thickness of the zipper and the way the buttons and snaps are attached to the garment.

Color Loss
Once a fabric loses color from abrasion, the color cannot be restored. Once a solid, dark color has become chalky or white, that loss of color compromises the appearance of the garment forever.

Hardware

If you examine outer clothing for hardware, you will see it on most designs. Clothing for skiing and hiking have metal hooks, clasps, buckles, zipper pulls, toggles, and slides. Some of this hardware can be protected or removed before cleaning, but most cannot.

Removal and Protection

Most outerwear is cleaned in a machine that agitates as it goes around. Hardware can hit the edges of the machine during the process, which can cause the hardware to bend, break, or lose its finish. You should think about this eventuality. Many parts can be removed by releasing a few stitches or with needle-nose pliers, and some can be protected by various button protectors, before cleaning. Check closely before you buy, and make an educated decision.

Buckles

Many classic raincoats have buckles on the sleeves and belts. These buckles can be plastic, metal, leather-covered and, occasionally, glass or some other breakable material. Burberry of London and other well-known designers continue to use leather-covered buckles. If they are not protected or removed, then they will fray and lose color—maybe not in the first cleaning, but eventually.

Most plastic and metal buckles are safe in cleaning, but glass and similarly fragile buckles should always be removed before cleaning. If the design of the garment will not allow these fragile accessories to be removed, then consult your drycleaner, your seamstress, or tailor to see if he or she can suggest a safe alternative.

"Sensitive Ware"
Do not assume that the designer has made hardware that can withstand the conditions of machine cleaning.

Belt buckles on skiewar (especially on Bogner jumpsuits and similar brands) should always be removed before cleaning. I recommend that the belts *not* be cleaned unless it is completely necessary, and then only hand cleaned to remove specific stains. These buckles have many moving parts and I have personally replaced more than my share.

Hooks, Toggles, and Slides

Hooks, toggles, and slides are important to outfits, and these rascals can be as functional as they are cosmetic. Many are made of "space-age" plastics that do not break or chip. Hiking gear and ski clothing have many of these parts integrated into their designs, and they are largely dependable. If these pieces are functional, then check them closely and try to mentally picture the abuse they will take during daily activity. Not to beat up on Bogner (I have two Bogner ski suits and I love them), but that company's slide toggles do not withstand cleaning very well. Be sure that your drycleaner removes them. The "zipper pull" on most outerwear should be scrutinized as well. If it appears fragile, then have the ornamental part removed before cleaning.

Note: Bogner has been 100% responsive and timely about sending replacement buckles and assorted parts when drycleaners have failed to remove them before cleaning.

Trims: Different Fabrics

Outerwear that is trimmed with leather, suede, or high-contrast colors may require extra care. These garments should not be cleaned without some thought and concern. I know you probably assume that the care label "protects" you, but don't be fooled.

Leather and Suede

Light-colored fabric that is trimmed with dark leather or suede is an accident waiting to happen. This is true 90% of the time. The most common example is tan outer jackets with brown leather collars, cuffs, or pocket piping. These trims and patches have extra dye, and this dye bleeds through the surface and around the trimmed area during drycleaning or washing. There is no remedy. If the trim doesn't bleed, it usually fades.

Why do designers and manufacturers make garments such as these? Most have not taken the time or the care required to have these items tested before they sell them in the marketplace. Some designers make trims like these that do not bleed in cleaning, but almost all fade. The retailer is often un-informed as well. The stores that do not sell these types of garments may know that they can be trouble.

> **Real Problems**
> Many people encounter "resistance" at the drycleaners when trying to clean trimmed garments that are poorly made because most cleaners have had a negative experience with them already.

If you have purchased such a garment and your drycleaner has refused to clean it, then consider having the leather collar or cuffs removed *before* cleaning, and resewn afterward. It is expensive, but it is a viable alternative.

Note: For garments that have been tested and appear to have faulty dyes, but for which you do not want to invest in removing and resewing the collars and cuffs, spot-cleaning in the troubled areas, rather than drycleaning the entire garment, may be an option. Not all stains can be removed with this approach, and the spot-cleaning must be done at the first sign of soil.

High-Contrast Colors

Light-colored fabrics with dark *fabric* piping can also be suspect in cleaning. Burgundy, navy, and black are the most unstable trim colors. In most cases, these trims are fine, but be aware of the problem, especially when the piping is made of unusual materials.

Water-Repellent versus Waterproof

Raincoats and most foul-weather gear are water-repellent, not waterproof. If you wear a raincoat made of natural fibers, then I'm sure that you have had gripes about it getting wet from rain and snow—maybe even allowing your clothing underneath to get wet. As a drycleaner and as a perfectionist, I have tested no fewer than six different brands of water-repellent products available to the drycleaning industry. All had less than sterling results. None of these "after-market" products have replicated the repellent quality that the manufacturers originally used. Nonetheless, if it's pouring rain, then no trench coat will keep you dry.

There are, however, different qualities of repellent and different ways to apply them. If you're disappointed with the repellency after drycleaning, then let your cleaner know. The cleaner could repel the garment twice and might even be willing to test the treatment for you after it is finished. There are products available to consumers at hiking, ski, and department stores that can be applied for further protection. If you decide to try one on your own, then spray a small, discreet area and let it dry—then spray water on the area to test for repellency. Regardless of the result, when water sits on the surface of a fabric for a period of time, it usually becomes absorbed.

Waterproof clothing is made to be *waterproof*, and it stays that way. It does not require treatments because it is the fabric that is waterproof, not a surface repellent. Ski gear, hiking gear, and foul-weather gear designed to be breathable and waterproof are made of synthetic materials under brand names such as GORE-TEX® and Conduit™.

Care Labels and Cleaning

Care labels are a tricky area. As I have mentioned before, they can be misleading, ambiguous, and sometimes just plain wrong. For outerwear, it is very important to be clear about the care instructions and to follow them properly. Outerwear is meant to be worn in inclement weather, but it does absorb soil, including oil and water-based stains. Unfortunately, many of the care labels restrict either washing or drycleaning.

If a jacket or any outerwear garment becomes badly soiled and requires drycleaning to remove oily grime and grease, but the care label says, "Do not dryclean," then what can you do? Conversely, if a garment becomes very soiled and only soap and water will improve it, but the label prohibits washing (which is common), then the garment will be forever dingy. There are times when it makes good sense—and is necessary—to make an educated decision to disregard the care instruction.

I'm sure that you have owned light-colored outerwear and have seen the soil firsthand, especially at the cuffs. If your wish is to continue wearing a clean garment rather than discarding it, and only a contrary method will help, then do it. But before you do it ...

> **A Simple Truth**
> Light-color outerwear does get dirty from everyday wear and from specific stains. It is often necessary to both wash *and* dryclean the garment to get the best results.

Consider the Most Common Problems

The most prevalent problems associated with washing your dryclean-only outerwear are dye-bleed problems (specifically with the trims) and texture changes, such as shrinkage or excessive wrinkling.

Drycleaning your wash-only outerwear garment may cause stiffening that is so severe, it can ruin the garment.

Note: The care label may be entirely correct—and processing contrary to the instructions may ruin the garment. Don't be cavalier about the cleaning or make any quick decisions. If you are unsure about what to do, then first ask for a professional opinion.

◆ Down-Filled Outerwear

The most important issues for the category of down-filled outerwear address the care and maintenance, the longevity of the garment, and the security of your investment. Reading the care label is important, as is recognizing the limitations of the suggested care instruction.

You would be surprised at the number of down-filled garments that have only one suggested method of care. Knowing what you now know about soil removal should show you the futility of such an instruction. No single process will always keep the garment clean.

Simple Facts about Down Clothing

The feathers and the outer shell of a down garment are coated with protective oils. The oil on the feathers helps provide water resistance and helps the garment breathe. The oil coating on the shell provides further water resistance and keeps the feathers from poking through the outer shell.

Because most drycleaning solvents are oil based, they can dissolve some of these oils during the cleaning process. The coating inside the shell can break down and blister, and the oil from the feathers can dissolve and stain the outer shell. The actual reduction in the insulating value, from the loss of oil on the feathers, however, is imperceptible.

Nonetheless, the dryclean-only care label is still a common one, and the process remains reasonably safe for down clothing.

Washing

Washing is probably the best all-around method of care for down clothing. It is important to choose the right detergent; one that is too mild will not remove enough soil or oily stains, and one that is too strong may remove too many oils—as with drycleaning solution.

Washing has two downsides: washing rarely removes oily stains and may limit the future removal of the stains if the garment is not drycleaned first; down must be tumble dried to remove feather clumps and to fluff the feathers, which requires time, sometimes hours. Proper drying may also require a large-capacity dryer and the ability to "flip" the garment during the cycle. A couple of tennis shoes or a half-dozen tennis balls will help.

> **Preparation**
> Be absolutely certain to inspect all down items for holes, tears, and open seams before washing or cleaning. During the process, feathers can—and will—find their way out of open areas.

Drycleaning

Though washing is often recommended, your drycleaners will still play a role in the care of down clothing and down comforters. Some oily stains will be improved only by drycleaning, and if the cleaners use a hydrocarbon solvent, which is very mild, all the better. Drycleaners usually provide wet cleaning as well, and have the large-capacity equipment for down garments.

Properly drycleaning down garments requires clean solvent, a thorough rinse, minimal soap (so as not to overcoat the feathers), and a long drying cycle. If the charge for this service is expensive, then you will understand why. Be sure to ask your drycleaners if they have specific experience with down products.

◆ Stain Removal for Light-Colored Outerwear

The best way to combat soil when a garment cannot be both drycleaned *and* washed is to clean it more regularly, or at the first sign of a bad stain.

You know that light colors soil much faster than dark colors do. Whether you wash the garment at home or take it to the cleaners, time is your biggest enemy. A soiled area left unattended is compromised considerably by repeated wearing and the addition of more layers of soil. When the garment is finally cleaned and the soil is not completely removed, most people blame the process when they should blame themselves. Avoid this problem; be proactive.

Sometimes a garment is selected for style rather than substance. A purchase is not always driven by function, but here are some thoughts on this issue: Stripes, prints, and graphic designs—common with outerwear—can disguise soil and stains quite effectively. A pure white or light color shows soil and imperfections immediately. Printed designs mask the soil, which is good, but they tend to be worn more times before the garment is finally cleaned, which can be bad. Try to inspect these garments closely, regularly, and in bright light. Regular cleaning will increase the life of the garment.

Note: Many people wrongly believe that if the garment is white, then bleach can save the day. Bleach does not remove stains; it only whitens. The stain or soil needs to be removed before the bleach can do its job properly and to the fullest extent of its capability. Remember, most outerwear cannot be bleached.

◆ Know Your Fabrics

Wool, cotton, rayon, and microfiber have care requirements, but they are usually less stringent than those for specialty fabrics used for activewear. Refer to previous chapters for basic information regarding pressing, stain removal, and cleaning.

Wool

Wool breathes, it's wrinkle resistant, and it's warm, but it can be heavy and cumbersome. After you wear a wool garment, it should be hung and perhaps brushed and aired out so that it will be ready to wear the next time.

Cashmere, angora, mohair, and fine wool blends are soft and lightweight. Stain removal is usually easy compared to cotton, but wool is easily damaged by bleach. Bleach should never be used on any wool material, regardless of color.

It is imperative that wool be cleaned at the end of each season even if the garment was worn only once. Perspiration, body oil, moisture, and food stains invite insects. Wool should never be stored in plastic, including the plastic in which the drycleaner returns your clothing. (See Chapter 28 for the complete story on storage.)

> **Pressing News**
> Gabardine garments must be soft pressed to avoid shining the fabric. Be sure to convey this message to your drycleaner. Unless very skilled, you should not attempt ironing gabardine at home. (See Chapter 25 on ironing.)

Cleaning and pressing are comparatively easy with soft wools, but these wools must be steamed and lightly brushed during finishing to retain the soft feel and lustrous finish.

Polished Cotton

Cotton that is not washable has stain-removal limitations. The deeper the color, the more difficult the stain removal. Home spotting is particularly difficult to do without affecting the dyes. Never rub the fabric with the hope of removing or improving a spot. If you have a stain from colored foods—such as chocolate, red wine, mustard, or soy sauce—then complete removal is unlikely. Drycleaners are challenged as well because the fabric can become easily roughed. Light-colored garments are less challenging, but if the stain is dark, the same issues apply.

Like gabardine, polished cotton must be soft pressed to avoid shine on the seams and double-thick areas. (See Chapter 9 on finishing.) Cotton raincoats can become very wrinkled inside the elbows and on the seat and will require a firm pressing to improve the condition. The garment will be much easier to maintain if it is blended with polyester or some other synthetic fabric.

Rayon

I find it interesting that rayon has made it into the outerwear market. It is water sensitive and becomes badly water spotted from rain, it shines relatively easily, and stain removal is often difficult. I would think twice before choosing this fabric for everyday outerwear.

Microfiber

Microfiber is lightweight, soft, and has good drape. I have seen microfiber ski jackets that can be washed or drycleaned, which makes this fabric a very good choice.

Read the care instructions carefully on these fabrics. Many of the garments—which can be made with rayon, polyester, nylon, or acrylic microfibers—are very serviceable.

Other Fabrics

If a fabric feels different or foreign to your touch, then it may be one of the new and ever-growing fabric options. I would not discard an unfamiliar fabric as a choice for outerwear without first reading the care label and doing a little research—microfiber was once in this category. The fabric may be a blend of familiar materials that have a good track record. If you are unsure, then you can call your drycleaner for some inside information before you buy.

◆ Linings

The linings in raincoats and overcoats take a lot of abuse. They become thin from friction and they tear from stress, especially under the arms and at the vent.

It is common to see the lining in the sleeves protruding past the cuff hem. I call it cuff droop, and it makes the coat look unkempt and worn. The cuff material along the edge tends to fray and, once the fabric frays, small holes may begin to form. Watch for these conditions and repair them along the way. The frayed area at the cuffs can be re-edged with the same or a contrasting fabric.

◆ Let's Go Shopping

I have some practical observations for purchasing outerwear for sports and other physical activities. These observations come from both personal opinion and practical experience.

Activewear: Jackets, Pants, and Jumpsuits

When you're buying a jacket for active sports, a key to your satisfaction is comfort. Along with function, always think about the ease of design.

A jacket should fit your body in an easy manner. If it's too tight, too big, too bulky, too stiff, too long, or too short while you are in the store, then it's not going to change when you are outdoors. When a jacket is too short and it rides up and exposes your back, it can be very uncomfortable. Does the jacket have a two-way zipper? Will it be too warm or not warm enough? If you plan to wear layers, bring the underlayers with you when you shop. If you can't bend with comfort or move freely, you will never be happy when you're in action. Put yourself in the moment of truth—on the ski slopes or a ski lift, on the trail, in the rain or snow, or in the lodge. This planning also applies to accessories such as pockets and hoods.

Note: Care labels are very important with these jackets. If you hope to maintain your garment at home, and if water repellency is important to you, then read the label before you buy.

Pockets

Pockets are not given the proper respect and attention during shopping. Because the store does not simulate reality, sometimes our minds go blank. Consider the following questions about pockets:

▸ Are there enough pockets for your needs, and are they in convenient locations?

▸ Are they deep enough to hold all your possessions, but not too bulky once filled?

▸ Are they easy to zip and unzip?

▸ Are the snaps well made and easy to close?

▸ Can all these things be done while wearing gloves?

> **Tailor Them**
> Pockets can be added, shortened, or lengthened. If you like the garment but the pockets lack what you need, then change them!

A seamstress or tailor can do wonders with a poor design. Keep that option in mind when shopping, and don't let small details derail your purchase.

Attached Hoods

When looking at hoods on activewear, consider the following:

▸ Is the hood streamlined and easily tucked or folded into a pouch?

▸ Does it feel comfortable along the back of the neck when stored?

▶ When used, does the hood contour to your head properly so that air or the elements cannot get onto your neck and ears?

▶ Do the drawstrings close efficiently and fully? Are they easy to manipulate?

▶ Can all these things be done while wearing gloves?

Detached Hoods

▶ Does the hood attach easily?

▶ Will you wear it regularly?

▶ Is it too bulky to store in your jacket if you choose not to use it?

▶ Will you have it cleaned each time the jacket is cleaned?

Note: Activewear jackets become soiled quickly. Darker colors and prints show less soil and are cleaned less frequently. Light colors show every stain and need cleaning regularly to maintain your investment. If you do buy lighter colors, then read the care label to see if you can wash the jacket at home.

One-Piece Jumpsuits

A few words about jumpsuits for skiing. It's important to check the water-repellent ability of most of these fabrics. Many are not waterproof, which makes them a poor choice in wet weather. Few have GORE-TEX or similar treatments, so be sure to read the label before you buy.

For those of you who have not worn a jumpsuit before, the weight of the suit is also important. There are shells, which are thin and intended to be worn with layers, and there are lined, insulated suits. The insulated ones are very cozy in cold weather but can be suffocating in warmer conditions, making them less versatile than a separate jacket and pants. Consider this fact when shopping if you are going to commit to just one outfit for the season.

The fit is another issue worth examining. Jumpsuit designs are not as varied as our body shapes. I have found that most brands have a specific cut from the crotch to the shoulder, often making the jumpsuit ill-fitting, which can restrict movement. When you try on a jumpsuit, wear your normal layers and spend time moving as you would on the ski slope. Try bending, stretching, and jumping—even falling. If you feel any constraint of movement in the store, then the ski slope will be much worse. While you are in the store, tighten the waist belt, fill the pockets with gloves and goggles, and give yourself a fighting chance for comfort.

Overcoats

This section is for people who wear coats to cover business suits and more formal clothing. These coats may be rayon or heavy cotton, occasionally silk or other special fabrics, but most often they are made of wool. Most of these garments have straightforward care labels that will not cause you any problems, but I still recommend that you read them before you buy.

Coat Design

Fashion and style are always in the forefront of any decision with this type of coat, but comfort should ultimately be just as important. Traditional overcoats are heavy, typically bulky, and sometimes cumbersome to wear. Because of the length, the hems tend to pick up soil from cars, subway floors, stairs, puddles, and street splashes. Most of the time you are not even aware that this soiling is happening.

Although you see people wearing this type of coat over T-shirts and blue jeans, it is much more common to see suits and dresses underneath. Underlayers create bulk, bulk restricts movement, and restriction diminishes comfort. Restriction also loosens buttons and weakens the fabric around the buttons. Remember this important aspect when you assess the proper fit of a coat.

> **Fabric Stress**
> An ill-fitting coat puts more stress on the lining and buttons. The vent, underarms, and hem pull and tear more quickly if the coat is too tight.

Specialty Lapels and Trims

Wool coats with lapels made of velvet, velour, silk, or various types of fur require more care. Lapels with contrasting materials enhance the coat and add a look of formality, but they do not come without a price. Stains, rain and snow, and snags from jewelry and other sharp objects can all affect the nap or the sheen. These added designs increase the "care-quotient" and increase the frequency of your trips to the drycleaner.

Trims on the collar, cuffs, and pockets of the coat may require special care as well. Collars can be stained by cologne, perfume, body oil, and perspiration; cuffs become soiled from food and liquid spills.

Pocket trims that protrude from the base fabric can become abraded, scuffed, and soiled. All of these conditions are inevitable, but if treated regularly, they can be maintained.

> **For Extra Care**
> Drycleaners usually send fur-trimmed garments to the furrier for cleaning. You should know this before you buy so that you can allot extra time and money for drycleaning.

Special Wool, Gabardine, Rayon, Silk, and Cotton

Special Wool

Cashmere is soft and luxurious and is a comparatively lightweight alternative to basic "hard" wool. It can be expensive, as well, depending on the quality of wool. Mohair, angora, and blends are in the same genre. Wool resists wrinkling, travels well, and is relatively user-friendly when it comes to stain removal. These fabrics cannot be washed at home and may be more expensive to dryclean.

Wool is also very susceptible to insect damage from improper storage. You will see long-term benefits if you store your wool garment in a temperature-controlled vault during the off season. (See Chapter 28 on "Seasonal Storage.")

Gabardine, Rayon, and Microfiber

Gabardine, rayon, and microfiber provide a lightweight alternative to basic wool overcoats. However, gabardine and rayon are water sensitive, may show raindrop spots, and present a challenge for stain-removal technicians at the drycleaners. These fabrics can shine from wear and poor pressing, and they require soft pressing and steaming to restore and avoid shining. If you are rough on your clothing, then you should stick with more basic fabrics.

Note: At our cleaners, we regularly receive overcoats with large stains down the front: spills from coffee, beer and alcohol, food leaks from "to go" containers, and vomit stains. All of these stains are very difficult to remove from dryclean-only fabrics such as gabardine and rayon. You know your "neatness quotient," so you be the judge.

Silk and Satin

Silk or satin jackets and coats are beautiful, soft, luxurious, expensive, and high maintenance, but they are very lightweight and fashionable. Most stains on these fabrics are noticeable, and many are difficult to remove. For occasional wear, these fabrics make a great choice.

Silk outerwear is closely identified with fragility. Stitching along the pockets, seams, and stress areas has a history of coming loose. These areas also tend to tear from pressure, and repairs may show.

Cotton

Cotton overcoats, most often seen as raincoats, are another lightweight alternative. It would be helpful if more cotton coats were washable, but regular drycleaning can allay most problems. Polished cotton overcoats, like activewear jackets, become very soiled in lighter colors. Large spills are difficult to remove, and stains with food coloring are nearly impossible to remove without damaging the base color. Most cotton fabric wrinkles easily, especially at the elbow and the seat, and hard wrinkles are difficult to remove without shining the fabric. Cotton-poly blends are much more manageable.

◆ At the Cleaners

Use this opportunity to inspect your clothing for stains and minor repairs. If there are light-colored trims that need special spotting, then point them out. Give the care label a second reading, and if there are questionable instructions, then be sure to speak to someone in charge about your concerns. If you have any concerns about water repellency, now is the time to ask.

Talk to the clerk about removing or protecting the buckles, zipper pulls, and toggles for Bogner and other skiwear, and question him or her about the procedure. If you are dropping off a down jacket, then ask about the cleaning process and the use of a clear rinse if that's what the label recommends.

> **Trims Reminder**
> If you have a coat trimmed in fur, satin, or velvet, now is the time to express any concerns: How long will it take? Is there an extra charge?

Minor Repairs

Check the hot spots on outerwear: the lining at the underarms, vent, and hem. Put your hand inside the pockets to check for holes and for open stitches along the seams and outer pockets. Wiggle the buttons to see if they need reinforcing. If there are snaps or Velcro® enclosures, then look them over as well. Look at the sleeve cuffs to see if the lining droops and, if they do, then ask the seamstress or tailor to put in a few stitches. All these areas tend to need care eventually. These aspects can be hassle free if you permit your drycleaner to do minor repairs of up to $15 without calling you. Try to form that sort of relationship with your drycleaner.

Inspection for Holes

If you see any holes in your wool clothing, then try to discern whether they are the result of insect damage or the result of wear. If you believe they are from insects, then check the whole garment closely for more holes and weakened or thinned areas, which may be partially eaten fibers. If you find more holes, then mark them with safety pins and have the coat cleaned before being repaired. If after cleaning you find addi-

> **Holes in Overcoats**
> If the price for re-weaving is prohibitive, then holes can be darned by hand. On wool fabrics with a textured nap, the repair can be almost invisible.

tional holes, the expense to repair or reweave them may eclipse the cost of the coat. (See Chapter 27 on "Reweaving: A True Savior.") If you are going to repair the holes rather than having them rewoven, then ask about the quality of the sewing or reknitting and the outcome, especially if the holes are in an obvious location.

Finishing Details

Many outer coats and raincoats are too fragile to hard press, which would help remove most of the wrinkles. Hard or stubborn wrinkles in the seat, elbows, and waist may not be completely removable on fabrics that have a sheen, and wrinkles should be accepted as part of the nature of the fabric. Double-thick areas on the collar, down the front placket, and along the seams are particularly sensitive to pressing and may shine if pressed too hard. Water repellent can also add body to the fabric and can help give the raincoat a firmer finish.

If there are any special conditions—such as a velvet lapel that has become crushed, snaps that have left a slight impression, sleeve cuffs that you wear rolled up and wish to have pressed that way, hems that should be rolled, or a special wool coat that needs to be gently steamed to lift the nap—now is the time to convey that important information.

During the "off" season, allocate fifteen minutes to inspect your jackets, coats, and activewear for stains, soil, and wear. Many people have one or two pieces that haven't been worn for a year or more that could be donated. This contribution will help less-privileged people, as well as make more room in the closet for your clothing to breathe.

Chapter 24

Suede, Leather, and Fur

This chapter will sharpen your shopping skills and care habits and will educate and enable you to talk to the drycleaner about garments made from skins.

Most people buy suede, leather, and fur for the feel, the warmth, and the style, with little thought for the care it takes to preserve them and keep them clean. And, honestly, this approach is the way it should be. The eventual trip to the drycleaners may not even be a thought at the time of purchase, or is dismissed if the salesperson "candy coats" the care and maintenance required for leather and suede. (In all fairness, *some* salespeople will be knowledgeable enough to convey the real story.)

I'm not going to bore you with technical terms and obscure references; instead, the descriptions and images I provide will be a blend of layman's terms and jargon that will help you convey your points in a language that retailers and drycleaners will understand.

Here are some basic points:

▸ A skin produces leather on one side and suede on the other.

▸ Finished leather used for "bomber" jackets is *low* maintenance.

▸ Suede, shearling, and nubuck are considered to be *medium* maintenance.

▸ Dyed leather is butter-soft and *high* maintenance, particularly in vibrant colors.

▸ Cleaning leather and suede is much more challenging than cleaning fabric.

Throughout the following sections, leather and suede will always be addressed by the above names and descriptions.

> **The Ultimate Helper** is in the back section of this book. That section has removable worksheets for the care of *leather and suede*, bridal gowns, christening gowns, and shopping guides. Tear one out for your trip to the cleaners when you drop off your leather or suede.

◆ About Skins

Most skins have scars and imperfections. These imperfections are covered up with fillers and glues at the tannery before the skins are made into garments. Some of these fillers may fall out during cleaning and cannot be restored. This condition affects both leather *and* suede—but may be more obvious on suede because the marks cannot be disguised by "repainting" after cleaning. Though this condition only affects 10% to 15% of garments, it may account for why you notice imperfections after cleaning. If this change does occur, then try to accept these marks as character traits.

When you're walking through a store, your fingers should definitely be sending you messages: Is the skin stiff? Is it soft? Is it thick or thin? Your eyes will help you make the final assessment.

◆ Finished or Pigmented Leathers

Type of Skin
A finished or pigmented leather is usually thick and looks and feels "painted." Bomber jackets, sport jackets, athletic jackets, and other garments that show little or no grain are usually referred to as finished or pigmented.

Identifying Skins When Shopping
Finished leather is usually identified by a slightly stiff texture and a pronounced shine. If you wet your fingertip and touch the leather, the moisture will not be absorbed and will not leave a mark. This type of leather is durable, it repels stains, and it is harder to get dirty. The stiff skins will soften a bit from wear.

Care and Stain Removal
Finished leather, with its "painted" finish, is by far the easiest to maintain; it repels stains, can be wiped clean of soil and basic stains with a damp sponge, and can take a comparatively enormous amount of abuse without requiring professional cleaning. However, this finish will not help imbedded stains, oil, or ink. When the garment does need cleaning, it can be resprayed afterward to cover any stains that cannot be completely removed. This process, however, will make the skin stiffer.

◆ Dyed Leather

Type of Skin
Dyed leather is usually identified by its rich, deep color and soft texture. The surface feels supple, and the dye appears absorbed rather than painted.

Identifying Skins When Shopping

Dyed leather is easily identified by its butter-soft texture and its rich, supple drape. An easy way to identify a dyed leather is to touch an unexposed area with a wet fingertip. If the leather immediately absorbs the moisture, then it is usually a dyed skin. This test may be indicative of the way soil and stains will be absorbed into the skin during normal wear.

These leathers are often soft because of the treatments they undergo during preparation and because the skins are thin. Thin leather is fragile and can tear more easily. (See the picture on page 217 about repairs.)

Most high-fashion leathers are dyed and are designed in deep, rich colors; they are butter soft and fragile in construction; and they are usually expensive.

Care and Stain Removal

Butter-soft dyed leather is the most difficult to maintain. General soil can be readily removed in cleaning. Spills, food stains, oil stains, and ink are deeply absorbed into the skin. Ink may be impossible to remove. Each time a stain is treated, the area must be touched up and the color must be matched. The base dyes are fragile, making machine cleaning a challenge. Dyed leather is hard to hand clean without causing a blotchy area, which again requires a sensitive touch-up with custom-mixed dyes to match the base color.

◆ Suede

The texture of suede generally will be soft; the better the suede, the softer the skin. Both suede and leather garments can have "mismatched" skins, but mismatches are easier to see on suede. Before buying a suede garment, you should inspect the front and back for mismatched skins.

If the garment is unlined, then you can check the condition of the skin from the back side: Is the skin thinner or scraped in areas? Thin skins make the suede very soft, but if the skin is *very* thin in an area and appears fragile, then it probably is fragile. Although thin skins don't always mean that holes or tears may occur, this condition can affect the longevity of the garment.

> **Mismatched Skins**
> Quality garments have matching skins. Some designers mismatch skins intentionally for effect, but those are exceptions.

Suede is a dyed skin. It has a soft nap, and the sheen changes if you brush along the surface of the skin. Suede needs to have the oils replenished each time it's cleaned to retain its supple feel and depth of color. Apply these thoughts to the following sections on suede.

◆ Pigskin

Type of Skin

Pigskin is usually the least expensive type of suede. It is easily identified; it has very little surface nap, and it has visible small holes in the skin where the bristles have been removed.

Identifying Skins When Shopping

Pigskin is the roughest suede skin with the least nap. It will also have obvious pockmarks and small holes on the surface. Although pigskin can be pricey at times, it is usually the least expensive.

Care and Stain Removal

Pigskin is very porous and it absorbs stains. It has very little nap, which makes "working" the stain, during removal, a challenge. The less expensive the suede, the more difficult the care—and this difficulty usually applies to pigskin. Pigskin does not hold the original oils and dyes well, and requires a skilled cleaner to restore the depth of color after cleaning.

◆ Sheepskin (Sheepsuede) and Shearling

Type of Skin: Sheepskin

Sheepskin is a generic term for garments that are made from the hide of sheep. The skin is softer than most suede. Sheepskin is a dyed skin, and it tends to hold the dyes and oils better than less-expensive skins do.

Type of Skin: Shearling

Shearlings are also made from the hide of sheep. Shearlings have the fleece still attached, which makes these coats very warm. Sheepskin and shearling coats are generally of very high quality and are expensive.

Lambskin coats, both unlined and fleece-lined, are softer and more expensive than sheepskin. Sheepskin and lambskin have very few imperfections, and fillers are rarely used.

Identifying Skins When Shopping

Sheepskin and lambskin should always have *matched* skins. In recent years, great strides have been made in the design of sheepskin and shearling coats: more available colors; softer, thinner skins; and better water repellency. The thinner skins have made these coats lighter and less cumbersome without sacrificing warmth.

Care and Stain Removal

The jury is still out regarding yearly cleaning for these coats. Some experts say that it is better to wait until there is obvious soil or stains, while others maintain that a yearly cleaning will keep the skin supple. But one thing that all factions agree on: these coats should be stored in a temperature-controlled environment to protect the fleece from insect damage. (See Chapter 28 on proper storage.)

◆ Nubuck

Type of Skin

Nubuck is technically a grain leather with a sueded nap. The smooth side of the skin (the outer layer) is dyed and then buffed to look and feel like suede.

Identifying Skins When Shopping

Though nubuck looks more like suede than leather, it also looks more finished or buffed than a suede. The nap will change appearance as you brush it, but it will appear more dense than suede and will have fewer loose "hairs."

Care and Removal of Stains

See the next section for care of all suede.

◆ Care and Stain Removal: For All Suede

Suede is easy to clean for general soil. Oily stains usually come out, and lipstick in many cases can be removed as well. Suede doesn't have to be redyed; usually replenishing the oils will bring back the color and depth. Suede can be hand cleaned if the stains are not too embedded.

The real challenge comes when there is a stain disaster. Large spills, certain protein stains, and most ink stains may be impossible to remove. Raindrops can also be very damaging. The stains that do not come out cannot be camouflaged the way they can on a pigmented leather (and, to a lesser extent, the way dyed leather can). More-expensive suede usually responds better to stain removal procedures.

Story Time...

A female customer of ours went to a movie, ordered popcorn with butter, and sat down for the show. As she was munching, a few kernels dropped on the front of her shirt and down her lap. You usually pick up the pieces, pop them in your mouth, brush off the rest, and get back to the movie.

That approach doesn't work with suede.

Hers was a beautiful $3,000 teal-blue outfit made of thin butter-soft skins. We sent the suit to the leather cleaner. I told him how valuable it was and what our expectations were. The leather cleaner tested it and was honest about his feelings; he wanted to hand clean the suit to maintain the softness and deep color, but there were twenty small oily spots from butter that were absorbed into the skin, and they probably would not come out.

He didn't think he could meet our expectations by hand cleaning and was too nervous to machine clean the suit.

I decided to send the suit to a cleaner in New York that specializes in leather and suede. The process took two weeks and it cost $250, but they did a nice job. They did, however, have to clean the suit three times to get the stains out, and they struggled to match the dyes.

> **Say It Ain't So**
> One strategically placed ink or embedded lipstick stain may compromise the whole garment. Consider color carefully when you shop.

◆ What *You* Can Do: Suede and Leather

▸ Painted leather can be wiped down with a damp cloth to remove surface dirt. However, this approach will not help imbedded stains, oil, or ink.

▸ Water-based stains on leather—such as alcohol, milk, and blood—can be blotted with a damp (*not* wet) cloth. This procedure will reduce the chances of the stain setting. Once you have attempted to remove the stain, it is important that you feather out the area (with the damp cloth) so you do not form a ring where the stain was. Let the area hang dry overnight. Do *not* try to accelerate the drying process by the use of a blow dryer, iron, or any other source of heat.

▸ Oily stains can be blotted with a dry cotton cloth. Sprinkle the skin with a substantial amount of cornstarch, allow it to sit for 24 hours, and then use a specially designed brush (bought from a leather store or via the internet) to remove the surface dust. If the stain remains, then have it cleaned by a specialist. Do not allow the remaining oil stains to sit in the skin and oxidize. Never use household cleaners on leather or suede, even in a pinch.

> **Oil Stain Removal**
> I rarely see cornstarch work without leaving a powder residue. This remedy is recommended by some leathermakers but has not been corroborated by leather cleaners.

▸ If you are caught in a rainstorm or snowstorm and the skin becomes soaked, blot with a clean, white cloth to absorb excess moisture, empty the pockets of heavy or bulky objects, place the garment on a broad sturdy hanger, and allow it to dry at room temperature. Keep the garment clear of any direct heat source, including heat vents. Leather can then be treated with a recommended conditioner, and suede can be brushed.

▸ Regular conditioning is valuable and necessary to keep skins supple. For leather, use only lotions that allow the pores to breathe.

▸ Age sets stains and allows oils to oxidize, which then become very stubborn. It is important to clean leather before it becomes too soiled. It's best to watch the soil level in key areas, such as the collar, cuffs, pockets, front seams, and hems. When soil starts to show, clean the garment.

▸ Skins can fade from prolonged exposure to light and poor storage. Fading can vary, but is more prevalent with vibrant colors.

◆ Leather and Suede: Common Traits

▸ Both leather and suede can be ruined by adhesive name tags. Name tags usually distributed at meetings can leave a permanent glue residue on the garment.

▸ Always remove the plastic bag from both leather and suede before they are stored because the bag does not allow the skin to breathe.

▸ Both can stretch out of shape when wet.

▸ Both are susceptible to shrinkage if machine cleaned. The skins "relax" from their "overstretched" state during tanning and shrink back during cleaning.

Note: Skins are stretched during tanning so that each skin will make as many garments as possible. The skins are then dried in this stretched condition. During cleaning, the skin may "relax" back to its original "pre-stretched" size.

▸ If the garment has mismatched skins, then these mismatched skins may be more pronounced after cleaning.

▸ Two-piece suits and ensembles should have their pieces cleaned together to help ensure that the colors match after cleaning. Even with this approach there may be some color variance or shade difference after cleaning.

▸ Both leather and suede easily absorb stains and body oils. The neck area is especially susceptible, and the only way to remove the oil is by machine cleaning. It is recommended that you wear a scarf around your neck to minimize the problems associated with body oils and lotions. Finished leather is more resistant, but is not immune.

▸ Both leather and suede can tear easily if the skins are thin.

Note: It is common practice for manufacturers to use glue in the production of leather and suede garments. This glue can occasionally break down in cleaning. Most of the time when glue bleeding occurs, it can be corrected. However, there are some cases when glue will leave a darker shade by the seams, pockets, or wherever it was used.

◆ Let's Go Shopping

If you're not concerned with eventually cleaning your leather or suede, then you can buy any style or design you want, regardless of serviceability. You can be as unconventional as you wish. But if you want to retain the garment, then you will eventually have to negotiate the reality of drycleaning or wet cleaning. If the leather or suede cannot be cleaned safely, then you can wear it until it dies. Knowing what *is* a good investment can be the best investment. Here are my shopping tips for suede and leather:

▶ Buy suede and leather items that fit comfortably. They should not fit "perfectly snug," especially if worn with underlayers. Skins can shrink in cleaning, and it is not always possible to stretch them.

▶ Dark colors show less soil. They will also allow longer amounts of time before the garment will need cleaning, and they offer greater longevity.

▶ Many pigskin jackets are so inexpensive that sometimes it does not make financial sense to clean them; at times it is better to wear the jacket "to the end" and then discard it.

▶ Try to avoid complicated decorative trimmings such as sequins, beads, and hardware because they may not withstand normal cleaning procedures.

> **Color Choices**
> Leathers that are made of skins with contrasting colors—such as green next to red—are almost certain to bleed in cleaning. These items can be hand cleaned, but soil and stain removal may be limited.

▶ Multicolored garments also may be limited to hand cleaning, which severely limits soil and stain removal.

▶ Have the garment water repelled *before* you wear it. Assume that it will take most cleaners two weeks, from the date of purchase, to perform this service. A repellent is especially necessary for the protection of suede garments.

Leather and suede items generally fall into two categories: either they are worn occasionally for fun and fashion, or they are worn all the time as a permanent fixture in your wardrobe. If your garment is worn occasionally, then routine cleaning will preserve it very well.

If the garment is a knock-around piece and is fun enough to wear every day, then you should wear it until it dies. Once it is oversoiled or badly stained (especially on the collar and cuffs), cleaning may not be able to remove all the soil. The only exception that seems to work, and that is actually considered a fashion statement, is black or brown leather with the lived-in, abused look, chafed edges, and cracked dye. That distressed look still works.

Note: It is a rare salesperson, indeed, who truly knows about the care of the leather and suede garments that he or she sells. Sometimes it makes sense to go to a leather specialist to buy, but you may find that the leather of your choice is available only at a department store or perhaps at a specialty store that sells leather as a "side dish." If you can't get reasonable care advice from the retail store, then buy the garment because you love it and don't worry about the rest. You can always get additional advice from your drycleaner before you wear the garment.

◆ Repairs, Alterations, and Restyling

The typical problems with leather and suede are nicks and tears in the skin, panel replacement, zipper replacement, and heavy scuffing where the top layer of the skin has come off and the dye has been removed.

Nicks, Tears, and Scuffs

Nicks are very common and can occur easily with softer skins. They are routinely re-glued by the leather cleaner free of charge as part of the process after cleaning. Small tears that leave half-inch "divets" often look V-shaped. The divets are again re-glued but are generally more noticeable, and there is usually a charge for that repair. The repair can look pretty good depending on the skin, the color, and the quality of the work.

Leather with nicks and tears to be reglued

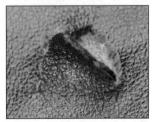

Close-up of half-inch "divet"

The larger tears that commonly occur from brushing up against a sharp item tend to tear large slices of leather and are often too unsightly to re-glue. In these situations, it is not uncommon to replace the panel or section. The leather cleaners probably have an alterations department with plenty of scraps. If they don't have the right piece to match, then it can be ordered. The result can be quite impressive.

Scuffing at the collar, cuffs, pockets, and waist is common. During the cleaning and redyeing process, the underlayer will be recolored by dye, but the surface texture will remain scuffed. There is no real remedy for scuffing.

Zippers

Zippers break. We all know that. Rather than fixing them, we usually replace them. When a zipper breaks on a leather or suede item, especially a jacket or a coat, it is rare to find a drycleaner that can replace it. Some tailoring shops do have access to the correct zipper but may not have the heavy-duty sewing machine needed to replace it. If they can't help you, then your drycleaner can send the garment to the leather cleaner for you. In this case, you should be clear about the type of zipper replacement you expect.

There is a tendency within the industry to replace zippers with whatever is available, so be specific about the weight of the zipper, the type of finish on the zipper (shiny or brushed), and the color (brass, bronze, or silver)—and be sure to ask the price beforehand. Although the zipper must be replaced, sometimes replacement can be rather expensive.

Alterations and Restyling

Leather and suede can be taken in (tapered) without evidence of alteration—but usually cannot be let out (made larger) without noticeable creases or marks.

Alterations such as hems, cuffs, shortening sleeves, and tapering can be tricky. Alterations on fabric garments are sewn, but many leather and suede alterations are done with glues and cements, which may be used in addition to sewing. This is very common with hems. Be sure to address the issue of glue bleeding, which can occur as a result of cleaning, so that there will be no surprises in the future.

If you use a tailoring shop that does work on the premises, then you can be sure that the tailor's fitting will be accurate. Because most drycleaners send out their leather and suede garments for cleaning, most of their leather repairs are also sent out. If the *fitting* is done at the cleaners, but the garment is sent to the

> ### Restyling
> A surprisingly large segment of the population has at least one "funny-looking" or dated leather coat in the closet or basement that hasn't been worn for years because of the style. It can be restyled.

leather cleaner for the actual sewing, then there can be an occasional discrepancy. Ask the person who "pins you up" if there is any reason for concern with the tailor or seamstress reading his or her pin work. Try to make sure that the fitter is qualified and that he or she is "on the same page" as the person who will be doing the sewing.

Restyling as a form of restoration can make old or out-of-date leathers stylish again. This concept may mean cutting down the collar, narrowing lapels, removing belt loops, or cutting a trench coat down to a "hip- or waist-length" jacket. Restyling is a great way to save a good piece of leather or suede and to bring it back into your current wardrobe.

◆ At the Cleaners

Many drycleaners do regular drycleaning on the premises, but very few offer suede and leather cleaning on the premises. Leather cleaning is a specialized part of the business. The majority of the drycleaners in the United States send out their leather and suede to a wholesale leather specialist that may service a two-to three-state area.

Larger cities will have more drycleaners processing their own leathers. Whether your drycleaner processes on the premises or sends leathers out to a wholesaler, I suggest that you make every attempt to speak to a key person to ask his or her learned opinion. I hope that you have garnered enough from this book to ask the right questions and to make a good judgment. (See "Questions for a Key Person at the Cleaners," in the "Ultimate Helper" section in the back of the book, for a perforated copy.)

The term "hand cleaning" may mean different things to different people. So that we understand each other, here is my translation:

Hand cleaning is a process that guarantees the suede or leather will not change color, size, or texture (unless it becomes softer). Stain and soil removal may be limited because of the nature of hand cleaning, and certain embedded stains may not be removable. This type of cleaning may be the only method that will not harm multicolored leathers or those with embellished designs, beads, or hardware.

Machine cleaning is an immersion process that agitates the garment. It can be very aggressive and can change the nap, color, drape, texture, and softness, but its stain-removal potential is excellent. The agitation

> **Cleaning Options**
> Some leather and suede garments are now being cleaned by "Clean and Green," a water-based method for cleaning skins.

may also cause shrinkage. Nonetheless, most garments are machine cleaned and they come out fine.

Questions for a Key Person at the Cleaners

▶ What kind of stain removal should I expect?

▶ Will the leather cleaner be able to properly match the original dye? If it needs to be re-dyed, will the dye look natural?

▶ Do you think that my garment requires hand cleaning in order to maintain the body, texture, and color?

▶ If it is machine cleaned, then will the size, color, or texture change?

▶ Should I expect any shrinkage from cleaning? If there is shrinkage, then can the skin be stretched? If so, how much?

▶ If there are scars, belly wrinkles, or imperfections that have been filled in and covered by the tannery during manufacture, approximately how badly will they show after those fillers and resins fall out during the cleaning process?

▶ If a hem has come down, will the leather cleaner routinely glue it back up?

▶ Will the leather cleaner automatically reglue the nicks and touch-up the scuff marks?

▶ Will the buttons, zipper, and trims be safe in cleaning?

▶ Will the leather cleaner protect heavy buttons and clasps on my shearling coat, if needed?

A Necessary Step: Even with their best and most earnest efforts, cleaners cannot always predict the condition of a skin after cleaning. Most cleaners will ask that you sign an agreement before they accept your leather or suede for cleaning.

Note: Handbags, belts, and accessories have the same concerns in cleaning as garments do, sometimes more. Most of these items can only be hand cleaned, and stain removal is more challenging.

◆ Fur Care and Storage

Preventive care for furs is an ongoing process that involves cleaning and glazing. At the end of each season, consider having your fur cleaned, inspected, and professionally stored in a temperature-controlled fur vault. Furs are "skins," but we tend to forget that fact. Too many fur pelts dry out because they have not been cleaned, conditioned, and properly stored.

Skins that become dry can tear and crack and may be dry-rotted. Dry-rotted skins actually tear as easily as tissue paper. If you have a fur with this type of dry rot, then do not invest any money in cleaning or repairs—retire it and invest in a new fur. Furs often represent a sizeable financial investment and, though many furs have been "passed down" within the family, responsible upkeep will extend their life.

> **Clean and Glaze**
> Cleaning restores oils to the skin. Glazing electrifies the hair, lifts it on end, and restores the sheen. These processes are imperative for the longevity of the fur and should be done every year or two.

◆ At the Cleaners: Fur

Most drycleaners send their furs out to the same company that cleans their leather and suede. These companies usually have temperature-controlled vaults in which to store furs and woolens. Because the cleaner sends the furs out, the clerk may be less informed about fur care than about clothing. Nonetheless, you can ask the clerk to check for stains, to look at the condition of the fur, and to check for repairs.

When you take your fur in for cleaning and storage, make sure that your homeowner's insurance covers storage outside of your home.

Repairs, Alterations, and Restyling

You may already know that your coat has a loose hook, but you should check all the hooks and eyes (look closely under the fur). Also check the lining at the neck, under the arms, in the sleeves, and at the hem.

If you see any breaks or small tears in the skin, then be sure to point them out before they get worse. That tear may be the beginning of dry rot.

> **Storage Options**
> Cleaning and storage may also be provided by the furrier that sold you your coat. The furrier can also be instrumental in helping you restyle your second- or third-generation fur.

Alterations and restyling actually play a big part in the life of a fur. Many furs are handed down through generations and are stored year to year without ever being worn by the current owner, who may not be aware of the benefits of restyling.

Restyling can make the difference between just storing the fur to protect it or actually wearing it with pride. It can be cut down, reshaped, or remade into a jacket, a throw, or a stole. You can even have a monogram sewn on to the lining or change the current one to your own initials.

A monogram is very good for identification purposes at social events. Whether your fur is thrown on the bed at a party at someone's home or left with a coat-check person at a hotel or restaurant, a monogram can help assure that you get back your own fur.

If there is one single aspect of suede and leatherwear that screams out, it would be consumer abuse. The number one thing that shortens the life of a skin is accumulated soil. For some reason, people generally do not see the oils that darken the collar and cuffs or the soil that builds up on the pockets and trim, especially with darker colors. Probably half the suede and leather garments brought in for care have been worn too long before cleaning.

Chapter 25

Ironing at Home
Accessories, Sizing, Irons, Creases

We have all ironed clothing at home at some point, and ironing seems like a "no-brainer." Right? Whether you do the ironing or a helper does, there are some basic concepts that may help preserve your clothing.

◆ Your Turn to Iron

Accessories
Drycleaners have all kinds of "helpers" that they use to finish delicate clothing. Some of these are available to you at retail stores. Stuffed hand pads and stuffed finger-shaped pads are used to shape and stretch fabrics; sleeve boards are used to iron a sleeve without a crease and to reach small areas; and steam puffers (called puff irons)—available to drycleaners in many shapes—are used to restore lumpy shoulder pads, reshape sleeves, and steam slacks with rolled, soft creases. If you iron often, then a hand pad and a sleeve board would be a good addition to your home.

Fabric Sizing
You should be very careful when using spray sizing and starch because they can cause spotting on clothing. These additives can also build up on the iron and can transfer yellow residue onto the fabric. Such stains can be removed in water if the garment can be washed, but if it's a dryclean-only garment, the sizing and starch could deposit permanent spots.

When you use spray sizing, starch, or plain water, it is best to allow the garment to air dry a bit before ironing. This step will reduce the yellowing that often accompanies the use of starch and water when using a hot iron. The wetter the fabric, the more likely it will be stained by the iron.

> **Professional Irons**
> Most drycleaners use steam irons to finish clothing. These irons do not scorch fabrics or leak water.

223

Home Irons

Home irons are usually electric, and electric irons can scorch fabrics. Scorch is nearly impossible to remove. Average-quality home irons that produce "steam" often leak water. With this water often come impurities, which are very hard to remove, especially if the clothing is not washable.

Quality steam irons are readily available and are worth the investment. Gravity-fed irons with heat adjustments for different fabrics make ironing much easier. They are generally heavier than the typical home iron, but they produce a much better finish. An iron like this would require a solid, high-quality ironing board.

Home Ironing Boards

Buy a high-quality ironing board; it's a sound investment. Ironing boards should have a sturdy metal or extra-thick aluminum frame and legs; a broad, flat ironing surface that does not bow under the pressure of an iron; and a quality iron rest. Proper padding is essential for the iron to glide easily over uneven surfaces and to minimize impressions on the garment caused by the iron. Make sure that the padding and cover are easily removable, and keep an extra set of each available so that you can rotate them when a set needs washing or replacement.

Shine Caused by Home Ironing

Irons can cause a fabric to shine. The severity depends on the type of iron, the setting on the iron, the type of fabric, and whether a pressing cloth is used (a piece of white cotton muslin will do). If you shine a gabardine, acetate, or triacetate fabric, then the shine will be very difficult to restore. Drycleaners use steam-operated machines that produce heavier steam than most home irons do, which can improve low-grade shine, but restoration is still a challenge and is not always successful.

Many clothing stores that have alteration departments with high-quality steam irons still have occasional problems with fabric shine. I've even seen new clothing shipped by the manufacturer that already has low-grade shine.

◆ Creases

When you crease a fabric with an electric iron, the crease is usually permanent. You should be very careful when ironing a sleeve, bow, ruffle, cuff vent, or pair of slacks to avoid creasing the wrong areas. If you don't feel comfortable using the iron on certain areas, then buy the proper tools that will help facilitate a safe and proper job. Sometimes steam is needed to correctly finish the garment. Sleeve boards, stuffed hand pads, and stuffed finger-shaped pads are used regularly by drycleaners to steam and shape hard-to-reach areas that irons cannot reach.

Creasing Slacks

When you iron slacks, be careful to line up the crease. If you inadvertently add a second crease or slightly miss the correct line, the mistake can be very difficult to correct. Always be patient and iron in good light. If you are adding a crease where there is none, then be extra careful to line up the seams. Check the crotch area, the hem, and any pleats to ensure a correct line before applying heat.

◆ Ironing Fine Fabrics

Hand ironing fine fabrics and dryclean-only fabrics at home really tests your skills. Be very careful not to shine the fabric (use a pressing cloth when needed), and be especially aware of buttons, hardware, and uneven surfaces. Water, spray sizing, and spray starch can cause spotting on the garment and, in most cases, cannot be removed.

Fabrics such as silk, rayon, acetate, triacetate, moiré, microfiber, chiffon, satin, and taffeta, as well as many trims, are better left to the drycleaner to iron. Velvet and most knits are never ironed; they should only be steamed.

When Out of Your Home

If you attempt to iron your clothing in the hotel room, then be careful of shine; iron the garment on the reverse side when possible and consider using a "pressing cloth" to protect the garment from shining.

I am constantly surprised by the number of men who still prefer to hand iron their own shirts and by how many men still have the time to do it. I have been told that the ironing process is very therapeutic. Few things are as rewarding as wearing a hand-ironed shirt.

Chapter 26

Good Habits—Long Life
True in Life—True of Clothing

This chapter is about finding the time, the energy, and the will to care for your clothing. It is normal for someone to undress, toss the clothing in the proper pile for washing or drycleaning, and then collapse after a long day or night. You probably refold or rehang the clothing that you will wear again.

You have rituals in your life, both daily and long-term; the same should be true of clothing care. Good habits require discipline, and they usually pay off handsomely. Clothing care has immediate and long-term benefits that will save you money from the first day, and for years to come.

You don't have to be obsessive or compulsive to accomplish the tasks I outline in this chapter. In fact, *any* practices that you adopt toward better clothing care will prolong the life of your clothing.

I have covered bits and pieces of this approach throughout the book. I have seen these practices work. They will reduce your drycleaning bill, reduce the daily laundry load at home, reduce the amount of unremovable stains, and reduce the necessity for replacing damaged clothing. All this from better habits? Believe it.

> **Think Ahead**
> Good clothing care is like good oral hygiene; the results can be immediate and long-term.

◆ It's Time to Put Away Your Clothing

When you get home from the day's activity, you are probably tired, perhaps mentally and physically drained, and eager to move on to the relaxation mode—the mode you associate with changing into your "house" clothing.

First Step—Creating Your Space
The optimum environment for putting your clothing away is one that offers a secure hook to place a hanger on, a bright light (perhaps one that rotates), a small table area for a brush, and perhaps a seat for you to relax on while you look more closely at a troubled area.

The goal is for you to air out your clothing for a few hours (more if it is very wrinkled or has an odor). Create an area, if possible, that you can permanently allocate for inspection, as opposed to re-creating a space every day. Routines are healthy: they create an identity, a place to be, and a process to follow. Have hangers available, preferably with a broad frame to avoid pinch marks. Cedar hangers are a good choice because they absorb moisture, emit a "warm" aroma, and offer some protection from insects.

Direct the light so that you can closely inspect your clothing for soil and stains. This important step allows bright light to reveal much more detail. It can make the difference between seeing a minor stain or soil on the collar and cuffs and not seeing a stain, which may turn permanently yellow over time. (The training in this book will help you to develop a discerning eye.)

Inspecting Clothing

In the drycleaning and retail clothing industries, people develop routines for inspecting clothing that are thorough and efficient and that do not repeat movements or waste time. They have hundreds of garments to inspect, so efficiency is paramount.

Upper-Body Clothing

Inspect the sleeves first, down to the tip of the cuff. Flip the cuffs, one at a time, to see both sides. Then start at the top of the collar, go down the front button placket, and then inspect the left front and right front. Next, flip the garment over and do the same thing on the back. If you use the same process every time, then the inspection will be quick and complete.

Lower-Body Clothing

Lay slacks and skirts flat, if possible, or hold them face front. Look from the waist to the hem, check the cuff or hem stitching, flip the garment over, and repeat the process on the back.

Hand Care

Have a soft, light-bristled brush available near the lighted area. Woolens and most sturdy clothing respond well to a *gentle* brushing. Brushing

Inspection diagram

will remove dust particles, pollen, and some crusty food. At the same time, brushing will relax the fabric and ease out wrinkles. The process can be very therapeutic, like gardening or cutting your nails.

Note: If you do not have the energy and the focus to follow the process through, then break it into steps. First, get your clothing hung up and ready to breathe. Then do the more time-consuming inspection and brushing after dinner or at a time when you are more relaxed.

◆ What *Not* to Put Away

You can easily assess which garments should be washed or drycleaned and which can be worn again. You can refer to Chapter 8 on "stains" for the whole story, but here are some quick tips.

Assessing Stains

Generally, I consider food that sits on the surface of a sweater or on a "nappy" material and that can be gently scratched off to be reasonably harmless. This type of stain can typically wait a week or two before cleaning. Although painful for me to say, especially with my training, I want to give you a point of reference so that you don't have to clean each garment every time you wear it.

If you are relaxed when you inspect your clothing, then recalling the type of stain may come more easily to you. Knowing the origin of the stain can give you and your drycleaner a tremendous advantage.

Water-Based Stains

Stains that appear to be absorbed into the fabric should be cleaned within 48 hours. Stains that have an obvious ring or an outline are probably water-based. If the garment is washable, then wash it as soon as possible.

Oil-Based Stains

If the stain has *no clear outline*, but looks as though it has been absorbed into the fabric, then it is probably oil-based. Some oily stains, on close inspection, may be shaped like a cross because oil typically "wicks" out into the fabric along the weave. These oily stains must be drycleaned, instead of washed, within 48 hours in order to give your drycleaner the best chance of removal.

Note: Many stains contain both water *and* oil. If you think a stain contains butter, fat, or other oily ingredients, then drycleaning may be necessary. Lipstick, makeup, paint, chocolate, caviar, icing, and salad dressing, all contain a percentage of oily matter.

Invisible Stains

The best way to "see" invisible stains is to remember the spill and to make a mental note at the time that it occurs. Most invisible stains will surface a week or two later looking slightly opaque or yellow, often making removal very difficult and sometimes impossible. When you take a bite out of a crisp apple and the juice sprays onto your shirt, do you really think, "This will appear as a yellow spot in two weeks?" I think not, but this is a perfect example of an invisible stain. *So are these*: citrus spray, oil splatters, perfume, cologne, and white wine and other alcohol.

> **Yellow Stains**
> Think of an apple with a bite out of it, and how that area turns brown. Citrus, oil, and white wine can do the same thing to your clothing.

Underarm Stains

Underarm stains may be invisible 50% of the time. If you know that you perspired, then inspect the underarms of your garment closely. You may see a ring or some discoloration (possibly perspiration, deodorant, and dye), and the surface may be stiffer than the rest of the fabric. If any of these conditions are present, then *do not put the garment away*, or it will have permanent damage. Have it drycleaned or washed, as instructed by the care label, within 48 hours (sooner if possible). When the garment is drycleaned, ask the clerk to have the technician "steam out" the underarms.

Summary: Most stains should be treated within 24 to 48 hours for the best removal. Be sure to point out the stains to the drycleaner, especially the "invisible" ones. Remember, garments that are taken to the cleaners are rarely cleaned the day they come in, so the sooner you get your clothing there, the better.

◆ Folding versus Hanging

After you have allowed the garment proper breathing time, making the right storage decision is your next move. (See Chapter 28 for a more in-depth look at short- and long-term storage.)

The weave, fabric, and construction of a garment dictates whether it should be folded or hung. Most knits and loosely woven garments should be folded to minimize stretching and distortion. Beaded or sequined clothing, especially if it is heavy, should be folded with tissue. Soft fabrics with a nap can be folded and will not show wrinkles and creases. Generally, garments that are folded have fewer fading and dust problems. If the clothing is rotated regularly within the drawer, that's even better.

Most homes are short on hanging space. Storage habits are often dictated by space restrictions, but I've found that most closets contain too many items that could be folded. If closets are routinely assessed for "dead" clothing, then hanging space would not be at such a premium.

Sheer fabrics and delicate weaves, if cramped, may develop deep wrinkles after a prolonged period, requiring that they be ironed before they can be worn. You can use tissue paper to minimize wrinkling, but garments of this nature may be better off hanging.

Clothing that is left hanging for prolonged periods gathers dust particles on the shoulders and along the folded line of the legs. Fading can occur over the long term but, in most cases, if clothing is rotated seasonally, fading should not be a concern.

> **Don't Do It!**
> Slacks, including blue jeans and khakis, should never be folded over a bare wire hanger.

Selecting the correct hanger for the garment is part of the solution. Too many delicately constructed garments are hung on improper hangers.

Wire Hangers

Wire hangers provide little protection in the shoulder area, often causing the fabric to pinch at the shoulder while placing extra stress on the material. Drycleaners typically use this type of hanger. (Some are caped with paper, but price prohibits the use of better hangers.) These hangers are suitable for lightweight, "hard" constructed garments such as men's cotton or wool shirts and similarly designed women's blouses. Unless the shoulders have been padded by tissue at the cleaners or the blouse has shoulder pads, more delicate fabrics should be moved to a broader hanger.

Silk blouses are also returned from the drycleaners on wire hangers. I firmly believe that if the hanger is not padded, then the blouse should be moved to a more suitable hanger. Over time, the shoulders develop points and become pinched, which affects the soft drape and flow of the fabric. Move your more delicate clothing onto a broader plastic or wooden hanger as soon you hang it in your closet.

Plastic and Wooden Hangers

You rarely see fine clothing sold on a wire hanger. Jackets of all types, better dresses, and overcoats are usually sold on sturdy plastic or broad wooden hangers. (This is one good way to build your hanger collection.) These hangers can be purchased quite inexpensively from stores or catalogs, and they generally last forever.

Check the construction to make sure that the plastic does not bend under the weight of a heavy garment, and check the swivel hook on the top of wooden hangers to make sure that it will not unscrew or strip. If you must pay a bit more for quality, then do it as an investment; it will pay off in the long run.

Sport jackets and suit jackets, because of their weight, must be stored on broad or padded hangers. The shape of the shoulder can become permanently distorted by a wire hanger. Padded hangers are best for clothing made of satin, chiffon, velvet, and organza. Your clothing deserves this better type of protection.

> **Hanger Savvy**
> Once your closet is equipped with better hangers, buy an additional quality hanger each time you purchase a garment that requires one.

Clip Hangers and Struts

Slacks that are returned by the cleaners are usually folded over a hanger. These hangers have a half-round cardboard shield or a round tube over the wire that is called a strut. Both of these hangers contain a mild adhesive on the cardboard surface, intended to keep the slacks from sliding off the hanger. Long-term storage on this type of hanger is usually fine for firm fabrics. Delicate fabrics, however, including gabardine, may show a line or impression after a short period. Most closets are designed to hold two poles, one high and one low, so hanging slacks from the waist is not always an option, but certainly is worth consideration.

> **Delicate Balance**
> If you buy a delicate fabric, such as velvet or satin that is sold on a clip hanger with ridges, then be sure to check the waistband closely for damage and *change* the hanger as soon as you get home.

Clip hangers, which are made in various qualities, should be used for slacks that are hung from the waist. This is the best method for silk or velvet slacks and for all delicate fabrics that could be damaged or wrinkled by folding over a strut-type hanger. Skirts of all types are hung from the waist, but many are hung with straight pins or safety pins. To avoid holes in the waistband, request that your drycleaner return your skirts on a clip hanger.

Which Clips Are Best?

Clip hangers are equipped with various types of clips, but the best designs have a smooth surface with *no ridges*. The drycleaning industry, as a whole, is slowly coming around to this way of thinking, but interestingly enough, retail clothing stores are still using too many ridged hangers. These ridges, once thought to be the best tool for gripping garments, do more damage than good. The impressions caused by such ridges are sometimes permanent.

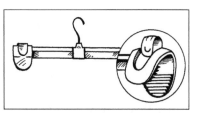

Hanger with ridges

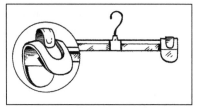

Hanger with smooth, soft grip

Many drycleaners and household supply stores have "hanger caddies," which are used to stack hangers. This method controls most tangling and offers a compact and efficient way to take the hangers back to the drycleaners to be recycled.

When selecting plastic hangers for upper-body garments, check the flexibility of the hanger. If the plastic is too brittle, then it tends to crack under the weight of heavier garments. If the plastic is too flexible, then it will bend forward and may cause the shoulders of the garment to become rounded.

Chapter 27

Reweaving: A True Savior

Old, New, Damaged, and Almost Forgotten

How many times have you retired a skirt, jacket, or a pair of slacks because of a hole, tear, or burn? Reweaving is a well-kept secret, but it can be a great way to save or resurrect your clothing.

This "old-country" skill has been around for many years. Sometimes people refer to it as "invisible mending," and though it can be invisible, the texture and the thickness of the fabric will dictate the result. In 75% of cases, a skilled reweaver should be able to predict the quality and outcome of the reweave *before* beginning, which makes it a sound investment.

◆ What You Need to Know

▸ Reweaving is the art of weaving threads together, one thread at a time, in a warp and weft (crisscross) fashion. These threads are taken from an unseen area within the garment. This process is essential in order to accurately match the color and the texture.

▸ If you look at a rewoven garment from the reverse side, then you can see how many threads it takes to mend a single hole or tear. A hole may require as few as five threads or as many as a hundred, depending on the fabric. (See picture on page 237.)

▸ At its best, reweaving *is* "invisible" and it is a true wonder. At its worst, with difficult fabrics or complex color schemes, it produces a flat but perceptible crosshatching where the hole was.

▸ Reweavers who are good at their craft will openly suggest that you refrain from certain restorations. A good weave is also very strong, but if the weave is in a high-tension area such as the knee, seat, or elbow, then first ask about longevity. Why spend $50 to $100 on a weave just to have it re-open from stress?

> **What, Where?**
> Reweaving is a painstaking and time-consuming form of restoration. If you can find a reweaver locally, it still may take three weeks. Ask your drycleaners for help finding a reweaver.

235

What Types of Tears and Holes Respond the Best?

Tears

The typical request for reweaving may come from a person who has caught his or her jacket or slacks on a sharp edge or a door frame. This type of tear is often "clean" and sometimes L-shaped. If you are fortunate enough to have the tear at least *one inch* from any seam, then you have the best opportunity for an invisible weave. If the tear is too close to a seam to reweave, then I suggest hiding the tear by tapering the garment. Most jagged tears cannot be rewoven.

If the tear is larger than two inches, then it may be prohibitively expensive to restore. The age and condition of the fabric will dictate how large of an area can be rewoven and still retain the strength of the original material.

> **Cannot Weave**
> It's important to note that frayed or weakened areas, typically in the seat and thighs, cannot be rewoven. In this case, it is best to have a patch or gusset sewn in by a skilled seamstress or tailor.

Holes

In many cases, reweaving offers the best alternative to discarding woolens that have been damaged by a cigarette burn, moths, or other insects. For wool suits, dresses, and the like, small holes can be rewoven quite effectively. Depending on the number of holes, the process can be cost-effective as well. If you believe the holes have been caused by insects, consider this money-saving approach:

▸ If you find more than two holes, then you may have an insect problem. Dryclean the garment to expose additional holes before you invest money in reweaving.

▸ Look the garment over very carefully after cleaning, put a safety pin in each hole, count the total holes, and then show the garment to the reweaver for an estimate.

▸ If you see partially thinned or "eaten" areas that are not yet holes, then drycleaning could help to expose *all* the holes before you invest money in reweaving.

> **Save Money**
> You definitely want to identify all the holes before you invest money in reweaving. You waste time and money if you find more holes after one hole has already been rewoven.

I suggest that you place safety pins in the affected areas (providing they won't damage the fabric), clean the garment, and then inspect it again. If you do *not* see any additional holes, then it should be safe to do the reweaving.

What Fabrics Respond the Best?

In most cases, the heavier the nap, the better the reweave. The more texture, the better the reweave. If the fabric is very heavy, then it may be possible to reweave even a three-inch tear.

How much will a rewoven area show? Depending on the condition of the fabric, the type of fabric weave, the color(s), and the sheen, reweaving should be superior to a sewn mend. If you have a question about the outcome, then you will want to talk to the reweaver personally (or through the help of the clerk) to get a professional opinion. As with most artisans, you would hope that the reweaver and the clerk have a discerning eye. At our drycleaners, we have a book of rewoven samples to show the customers, which helps to convey the possibilities and limitations.

> **Matter of Opinion**
> Judging the quality of a weaving job is subjective. For this reason, it is important to believe in the artisan and in his or her representative, which in this case is probably your drycleaner.

Best

Winter-weight wool, tweeds, and heavily textured fabrics hide the weave best. If the threads are available from the seams of the garment, as most are, the reweave can be invisible. A good reweaver can also restore a pinstripe, which can make the difference between wearing an outfit again or retiring it.

Reweave on a challenging wool

Challenging

Reweaving tends to show as a cross or a scar on thin fabrics such as summer-weight wool, rayon, and other similarly constructed fabrics.

Most Challenging

Gabardine fabric, with its flat, twill weave and slight sheen, is one of the most challenging to reweave. It is a popular fabric for all-season wear and represents a large percentage of reweave jobs. Because this type

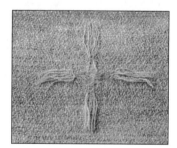

Backside of a reweave

of weave is rarely invisible, the question to consider is whether the tear or hole is located in a prominent place. The reweave can be very good, depending on the color of the fabric, but the woven texture will be different in that area—and it will never be invisible.

Our reweaver would say, "May show heavy, like a scar." If you are particular and if the weave is in an obvious place, then buy a new outfit. If you can accept a mar and wish to save the outfit, then this reweave may work for you. Ninety percent of the reweaves we suggested for gabardine were acceptable to our customers.

Worst

Fabrics with a flat texture are the most difficult and show a reweave more prominently than other fabrics. This category would include most silk and all flat-textured formal fabrics, such as chiffon, taffeta, and organza. Reweaving on these fabrics would show badly—and most reweavers have a good sense for when to say no. Velvet, corduroy, and other pile fabrics cannot be rewoven.

Note: A deft seamstress or tailor can do wonders with moth holes on outer coats and nappy fabrics. When reweaving is not an option, a mend, sewn by hand, can be very effective, and it is typically half the price of a weave.

Sweaters with holes are often best left to a seamstress or tailor with experience at darning and hand mending. The reweaver can check the inside seams to see if the yarns are long enough to use for reweaving—but if they aren't, then it is best to mend the holes with the closest color thread available.

In Summary

Regardless of your predicament, reweaving can be a very affordable solution and can save many expensive or cherished garments. It can be done for as little as $35 for a single hole and as much as $150 or more for large L-shaped tears. Many expensive suits have been put back into rotation with this method of restoration. If you can connect yourself with a quality reweaver, then you will be very pleased with the results.

Chapter 28

Seasonal Storage

Insect Damage, Woolens, Furs, Closet Sense

Have you discovered holes in your clothing that you do not remember being there at the end of the last season? Has any of your clothing had a moldy or wet odor? Have you noticed any color fading on the shoulders or in other areas of your clothing? If you haven't experienced any of these problems, then you are very fortunate. If you have noticed some of these conditions, then you are not alone.

Perhaps you just don't have the room to store every piece of clothing from every season in your immediate closet, yet you have no other "safe" space in your home. Temperature-controlled vaults for fur, suede, leather, and woolens may be necessary for you during seasonal changes.

You can think of storage as either short-term or long-term. Your closet and drawers, used for "in-season" clothing, are generally perceived as short-term, and anywhere outside of them should be considered long-term. Long-term may be possible within your home, depending on the environment.

As a drycleaner, I have seen the toll that poor storage practices can take on perfectly good clothing. Insects do not distinguish between moderate and wildly expensive clothing; they just munch. With proper education and awareness, you can avoid most insect damage.

Together, let's assess the critters and conditions that do the damage, look at your home storage capacity, and then consider preventive care and viable options. Remember, insects are not your only nemesis—sometimes the environment in your home can do as much damage.

> **Insect Bait**
> If you wear a garment only once, even for an hour, and you feel that it is ok to store it away for the season, then you are wrong. Even a remnant of food, oil, or perspiration can attract insects.

◆ What Insects Want

Moths, crickets, silverfish, and carpet beetles are responsible for the majority of the damage to fabrics, tapestries, textiles, and clothing. All four of these insects are attracted to dark areas. Insects are attracted to food, perspiration, perfume, body oil, and food oils, which means that any clothing that is put away for the season and contains any of these components may attract insects.

▸ Moths attack wool and silk and are attracted to dry areas such as closets, chests, and drawers. These are not the same moths that fly around your lights at night.

▸ Crickets are scavengers and they attack wool, silk, cotton, linen, and fur. They are attracted to moist areas and mildew and are commonly found in basements and garages.

▸ Silverfish are scavengers that attack rayon, cotton, and linen but do not like silk or wool. You will usually find them under carpets and inside bulky textiles.

▸ Carpet beetles attack only wool, and though they are not the most damaging insect, they are found in possibly 50% of homes. They are also attracted to bird feathers, which may be present in attics and garages.

Moths still cause the majority of the damage to wool and silk clothing. They will eat any and all clothing, worn or unworn, clean or dirty. Unworn wool sweaters are almost as susceptible to insect damage as dirty sweaters are. It is a fallacy that insects attack only "dirty" clothing. But remember, if you put your clothing away at the end of the season, uncleaned, you are inviting trouble.

The Moth Story ...

"Casemaking moths" fly in the window and lay their eggs on wool or silk. The eggs hatch and become larvae. It is during this stage that they eat clothing and do damage. Then they crawl off the clothing and find a shelf or ceiling corner to hang from so that they can build a vertical cocoon. If you inspect these areas, you may see the cocoons, which are usually less than a quarter inch long and shaped like a sack. If you squeeze the cocoon, then the insides will ooze out!

If you see moths, either flying or lying dead in the bottom of your closet or chest, then it is safe to assume that they have already done the damage that they are going to do.

"Web-making moths" tend to attack folded or rolled-up clothing in dark areas. These moths are very prolific, and they make their cocoons on the fabric they are damaging. They may be somewhat camouflaged because they use the fabric they have attacked in which to make their cocoons. The eggs are the size of the head of a pin, they are white, and they can be seen on the surface of the damaged object.

It is worth mentioning at this point that uncleaned clothing stored for prolonged periods will have problems other than insect damage. Stains can become "set" and sometimes cannot be removed by even the strongest chemicals. Stains can also weaken fabric with time, and the stained area may develop holes. (These problems often become evident after washing, drycleaning, ironing or pressing.)

Note: A dry closet or storage area is the safest environment and the best deterrent to most insect damage. If there is moisture in your carpets or on your floors, walls, or windowsills, then you have a much greater chance of attracting crickets and other insects.

◆What *You* Can Do to Combat Damage

Besides storing clothing in a dry, well-ventilated area, you can try some other preventive practices. You probably already know about the value of cedar chests and cedar closets, but there are also products that you can buy that may help. Mothballs, cedar balls, cedar hangers, and cedar spray offer varying degrees of protection. Mothballs may be the most well-known approach, but the odor they emit can be overpowering and is not always removed by drycleaning. Mothballs are also poisonous to humans and should be kept away from children and animals.

A housewares store, such as the Container Store, sells many products that are intended for insect protection. Some are only marginally effective, and none are as dependable as temperature-controlled storage facilities.

◆ Conditions in Your Home

Some homes have excellent storage areas that give clothing the space to breathe, are well ventilated, have few temperature swings, and are properly lit, but these areas are in the minority. Some homes have very few of these amenities—yet have no insect problems. This inconsistency can affect your decision to store clothing off the premises. No two homes should be considered the same—and each must be judged on the basis of performance.

I have stored my sweaters and suits in my home every year (when I could have stored them professionally at wholesale) merely because I have had none of the problems described above. They are house-specific, and I've been lucky.

Lighting

Direct exposure to sunlight or artificial light is dangerous for fabrics. White clothing can fade to yellow, and all other colors can fade to lighter shades. Recessed lighting is the best, but any prolonged exposure is dangerous. Clothing stores have to rotate window displays regularly to avoid damage. Clothing on racks may develop discoloration on the shoulders if not rotated.

At our drycleaners, we saw clothing that looked fine before cleaning, but had faded areas after the process. Upon further questioning, we learned that many times the garment was actually new and had never been worn. The fading had taken place in the store but was not obvious before cleaning. Some surface soil was "washed away" during the agitation in the cleaning process, exposing the color loss. The same problem occurs with poorly stored clothing that has been exposed directly to light.

Moisture

The humidity in many areas of the world, especially in the warmer months, can actually cause moisture to accumulate in clothing. Temperature swings during storage can cause moisture to form in clothing. Clothing is often stored in basements, in attics, or in spare rooms that have poor air circulation or inconsistent air supply. All these conditions contribute to moisture problems. I'm sure you have seen various insects crawling around wet drains, or in the corners of certain rooms, and certainly in summer vacation homes. Some of these insects make their way into your less climate-controlled storage areas.

Moisture can contribute to mildew in fabrics. Prolonged exposure to moisture can bleed the dyes, develop green and black discoloration in the form of dots and splotches, and cause a terrible odor.

Because mildew (and the colors and odors that come with it) is a water-based mold, drycleaning is only marginally effective in its removal. Mild cases can be improved by drycleaning, but more severe cases require washing and bleaching. Unfortunately, many of the clothes typically affected are not washable and are often delicate, with dryclean-only labels.

> **Moisture Alert**
> I have seen complete wardrobes ruined by mildew. Clothing can absorb moisture without showing any particular signs. Sometimes you have to put your nose close to the source to smell the moisture.

Note: If a storage area smells musty or wet, it may be a sign of the early stages of mildew. If the area is actually wet, mildew may have already begun to grow.

Storage Areas

Many people believe that any extra space in their home becomes an appropriate place for storing clothing and assorted possessions. People rarely analyze these spaces for light exposure, moisture, air ventilation, and heat exchange.

Attics and Basements: Long-Term Storage?

Attics and basements that are used for clothing storage should be surveyed and tested regularly for wet or moist conditions. Attics should also be checked for temperature swings because high humidity and condensation contribute to moisture problems. Some attics are temperature controlled and have air-conditioning vents, which can be a good environment for clothing storage. Some possessions that are stored in basements and attics can survive wet conditions, but most *clothing* cannot.

Basements often have moisture problems, too. Temperature swings can cause floors and walls to sweat, which adds humidity to the air. Closets, even when closed, can still become moist.

It is also worth mentioning that many basements leak and sometimes flood. Too often clothing is stored directly on the floor—in harm's way. We've seen thousands of water-damaged garments through the years from all types of homes, including very expensive ones. No one home is immune.

If you must store clothing in these areas, then do not store it in plastic of any kind. Keep clothing off the floors, use a dehumidifier if necessary, and check the area regularly.

> **Plastic Alert**
> The poly bags that drycleaners use to cover your clothing may, over time, promote moisture and contribute to staining. These bags should be removed as soon as possible. Many cleaners use paper dust covers on the shoulders, which should remain on the clothing.

Closet and Drawer Sense

When your clothing is hanging in a closet for an extended period, the sleeves and shoulders are exposed to dust and any sunlight or artificial light. If certain garments are not worn or rotated through your wardrobe regularly, then they remain in the same position, and they often fade first.

▶ Let your clothing air out overnight before hanging it back in the closet or folding it in the drawer. This practice will minimize the moisture the clothing absorbs, which contributes to wrinkling, promotes mildew, and attracts insects.

▶ Lightly brushing your clothing after wearing will diminish wrinkling, remove dust and food particles, and keep it fresher longer.

▶ For clothing that will not be worn for three months or more, and cannot be moved to another area for long-term storage; put the hanging garments in a line, take an old cotton sheet, and drape it over a three to six-foot section of the closet pole to protect the garments from fading. The cotton allows the fabric to breathe better than a plastic wardrobe bag would.

▶ You probably know that clothing can stretch out of shape by hanging, but pay special attention to knit outfits, heavy fabrics, and long items that may sweep the floor. You can use a second hanger to distribute the weight more evenly.

▶ Lastly, remove all jewelry and stick pins from clothing before storing. These items snag the fabric and may cause discolorations. Oxidation from jewelry is difficult to remove from some fabrics. (See Chapter 26 on "Good Habits—Long Life.")

Cedar Chests and Closets

Do you have cedar closets in your home? Cedar has long been considered the optimum storage environment outside of a temperature-controlled vault. If you store uncleaned clothing, then you are still flirting with danger. Cedar drawers, chests, and closets do offer a deterrent to insect damage, but they offer no guarantees. They must be tightly closed to be effective.

Note: Cedar must be "renewed" every year or two to be effective. If the pungent cedar smell dissipates, then so does the protection. Cedar must be re-sanded, or fresh cedar oil must be reapplied.

◆ Storing Clothing Outside Your Home

Now that you know what you are facing, ask yourself if your clothing is a good candidate for a storage service outside of your home. Keep in mind that not all clothing must be stored in a temperature-controlled environment, and many garments may still be fine in your home under improved conditions.

Do not lose sight of the fact that the clothing you deem worth storing represents a sizeable investment of time and money; but the cost of cleaning and storing your clothing is a drop in the bucket compared to the cost of repairing or replacing clothing that is damaged by moisture, light, or insects.

Types of Storage

The drycleaning industry generally offers two types of storage. Fur, leather, suede, and individual garments (such as a single cashmere coat) are usually stored on hangers.

Most woolens—such as sweaters, suits, dresses, and overcoats—are usually folded and stored in boxes. However, some companies have more linear space and choose to store all clothing on hangers. If a company offers only hanging storage, then you should ask for knitted and other similarly constructed clothing (that may stretch during long-term storage), to be separated, folded, and stored in boxes.

All garments are stored in a building that is monitored for temperature and humidity. Some cleaners have temperature-controlled storage space on their property, and some send the items out. You can consider both environments to be dependable.

Fur and Hanging Storage

The fur-storage process is "store-specific" within each drycleaners, but most cleaners have you fill out a form detailing the type of fur, the label, and the value. The form may ask if the fur piece is insured by your homeowner's policy. Some cleaners still offer insurance, but it is rare and expensive. It is much better to have a "rider" on your home policy.

Most furriers and many department stores that sell furs offer cleaning and storage services. If you have both clothing and furs to store, the drycleaner can offer you one-stop service, which may be more convenient. In some cases, retail stores and drycleaners send the furs to the same storage facility.

> **Fur Facts**
> In today's environment, with fur not being as popular as it once was and not being worn each season, many people are leaving their furs in storage for years at a time.

Most drycleaners and furriers suggest that you have the fur cleaned and glazed each year. (Glazing is a process that adds a soft, vibrant sheen to the coat.) You should use the "check-in process" to thoroughly inspect the item for repairs. Check the hooks, seams, lining, and the condition of the pelt. (See Chapter 24 for more on fur cleaning and restyling.)

The fur will be in storage for the whole season, so it is a good time to consider any restyling, alterations, and reconditioning that may be needed. It is also a good time to have a monogram sewn onto your fur lining. Monograms personalize your fur and make identification easier at coat checks, parties, and formal events.

Some cleaners will allow you to store the fur without cleaning it, providing it was not worn more than a few times during the past season. But don't be surprised if they ask for it to be cleaned first. Furs are stored in a controlled environment, and storage companies are very concerned about contaminating other garments with insects or bacteria.

Box Storage for Woolens

Administratively, the initial acceptance procedure for storing woolens is similar to that of hanging storage. The difference is that box storage is often a year-round service. Depending on the size of your wardrobe and the space restrictions in your home, you may need to store your woolens in the warmer months and your spring and summer clothing in the colder months.

Typically, the clothing is brought to the drycleaners (or picked up by the delivery driver), inventoried, inspected, and cleaned. It is folded for boxing or hung (depending on the facility) and then stored in a temperature-controlled building. You may receive a detailed listing of the clothing. If you're concerned about this matter, you may want to make a list by hand—or preferably by computer (you will then have the list ready for the next year)—for your records.

> **Don't Forget**
> Check all your clothing for personal property and jewelry before you store it. Stick pins and ornaments that are pinned to a garment are often overlooked.

This process presents a rare opportunity for you to see your wardrobe in its entirety. You can decide if you still identify with all this clothing, if it still fits properly, and if it is worth paying to have all of it cleaned and stored.

You can also use the opportunity to check for needed repairs: linings, zippers, open seams, hems, frayed areas, buttons, kick pleats, shoulder pads, and inside pockets (look to repair holes and to empty valuables and personal possessions). If you have particular concerns about stains or finishing issues, now is the time to convey these thoughts.

Note: Every storage season we have people calling, sometimes in a panic, looking for belongings that they believe have been left in their clothing. We search every pocket and inspect every garment before cleaning and storage, and we have found government ID's, jewelry, passports, medicine, and credit cards.

◆ At the Cleaners

If there are holes to repair on any of your woolens or sweaters, then try to discern whether they are the result of insect damage or from a snag or tear. If they are from an insect, then check the clothing very closely for more holes. Hold the garment up to the light and look through the surface for either holes or partially eaten or thinned areas.

If the garment is lined and you cannot see through the fabric, then check the surface closely. If the fabric has a print or a texture, then check even closer. If you find more holes, then mark them with safety pins and have the garment cleaned before repairing. If there are additional holes after cleaning, then the cost of repairs may eclipse the cost of the clothing. If you are going to repair any holes, then ask about the quality of the sewing, reknitting, and reweaving. If the holes are in an obvious location, then be particular about the finished product.

> **Repairing Holes**
> Reweaving is an excellent way to restore holes from insect damage. See Chapter 27 for more about reweaving.

Professional long-term storage in a temperature-controlled environment can be used to store wedding gowns and other family heirlooms. They can be effectively stored for years at a time for relatively little money. It is also a good way to store valuable household items such as draperies and bedding that you wish to save for your children or wish to use in your next home.

If you travel, or work out of the country for six months or more, temporary storage is a good option and a viable alternative to public storage lockers, which many times are not temperature controlled and do not offer protection from the elements.

Chapter 29

Drycleaning 101

The term "drycleaning" is a misnomer. Drycleaning solution, of which there are several types, appears "wet" like water, but has virtually no water in it other than the humidity in the air. Drycleaning solvent is not water soluble, and it does not dissolve most water-based stains, hence the word "dry" in drycleaning. In its virgin state, solvent is as clear as water, but once a detergent is added, it takes on a champagne-colored hue. Solvent is, however, very effective in dissolving most oily stains.

◆ What Is Drycleaning?

The solution, or solvent, is contained in a large front-load type machine, similar to a commercial washer in a laundromat. Through the glass door, the solvent looks almost identical to soap and water. The machines often have two or three storage tanks for solvent: one for light clothing; one for dark clothing; and one that stores the clean, or distilled, solvent. After the solvent is used to clean the clothes and absorbs impurities from them, it is transferred to a "still," which purifies the solvent and readies it for reuse. Most drycleaning machines today clean, spin, and dry the clothing in one continuous process known in the industry as "dry to dry."

What Does Drycleaning Solvent Do Best?

Drycleaning solvent, because of its oily nature, naturally removes oily stains, such as food and body oils. Solvent also serves as an effective vehicle for flushing out pre-spotting chemicals and lubricants used during stain removal. Drycleaning solvent provides a predominantly safe environment for colors and fabrics, minimizing dye bleeding problems and, un-like water, causing little-to-no shrinkage (roughly 1% on average) with most materials.

Pressing, Ironing, Blocking

Pressing, ironing, and blocking—steps performed after the cleaning process—are called "finishing." Finishing is as important as the cleaning and, in some cases, requires more skill than the cleaning does. (See Chapter 9 for the complete story on finishing.)

◆ Characteristics of Drycleaning

Little Shrinkage

Although most clothing will show little-to-no shrinkage from drycleaning, it is possible over time to experience as much as 2% shrinkage in some garments, which is enough for you to notice in the fit of your clothing. It's best to buy clothing with a little "wiggle room" for safe measure. Many times minor tightening can be "eased out" during the finishing process. Garments such as a favorite pair of blue jeans that may be a bit snug already cannot afford additional shrinkage from washing. This predictable shrinkage is especially valuable when cleaning slipcovers and drapery (2% to 4% shrinkage is common with household items).

> **Good Pressing**
> Did you know that the finishing process can permanently alter the look and feel of a garment— for better or for worse?

Good Removal of Oily Stains

Drycleaning solvent naturally removes body oils, food oils, wax, and gasoline from fabric, without the need of additional additives. When detergents are added, along with a pre-treatment chemical such as an oily-stain remover, drycleaning solvent can improve or remove lipstick, makeup, certain paints and dyes, typewriter correction fluid, and many other oily stains.

Poor Removal of Water-Based Stains

Because there is virtually no water in drycleaning solvent, most water-based stains are not removed during the drycleaning process. Liquid spills of all varieties— and blood, food dyes, sugar stains, and some perspiration—can be removed only with pre-treatment and pre-spotting using water-soluble stain removers. (See Chapter 8 for more information on stain removal.)

Color Fading

Colors may fade in both machine washing and drycleaning, but in most cases drycleaning is safer. A red linen blouse or a pair of navy blue jeans that fades when washed at home most likely will not fade when drycleaned.

> **Drycleaning**
> If a whole cup of olive oil were to spill on your clothing and it was drycleaned within a few days, then the oil should be easily removed.

Many colors that bleed when hand or machine washed may be safe in drycleaning. "High" colors—such as red, purple, or green, often used as trim (which technicians try to test first)—are usually safer in drycleaning than in washing, as are some hand-painted designs and surface prints (these items should be tested before cleaning).

Texture Improvements

Most garments that are drycleaned and properly pressed should have a soft texture when finished. Washed garments, even after softeners have been used, are rarely as soft as a drycleaned item. If a garment has become rough or stiff from washing at home and if the softness has not been restored after tumbling or fluffing, then drycleaning and steaming may improve the texture. Poor finishing can also stiffen a fabric, so be aware of this possibility when selecting a drycleaner.

Insect Damage

Many households will, at some point, have problems associated with insect damage. When mysterious holes appear in clothing, they are most often the result of insect damage—be it moths, crickets, carpet beetles, or silverfish. Most drycleaning solvents will kill the larvae associated with these insects.

In Summary: It pays to have favorite or expensive clothing drycleaned. To maintain color, texture, and size continuity, always consider drycleaning before automatically washing any fine garment. (And always check the care label before proceeding.)

◆ Drycleaning Solvents

You have choices for cleaning solvents: hydrocarbon, perchloroethylene (perc), CO_2 (carbon dioxide), and water … If you are concerned about the cleaning solutions that drycleaners use, then read on. Some solutions are more sensitive to finer clothing, some are better for environmental reasons, and some are more suited to people who are chemically sensitive.

Hydrocarbon

More and more drycleaners are using the new "organic" solvent, commonly called hydrocarbon. This solvent is, to some degree, an incarnation of a petroleum distillate that for many years was a mainstay. Petroleum was a "natural" solvent, and widely used, before perc became the popular synthetic, non-flammable, and faster-drying alternative.

The new hydrocarbon solvents have become safer because they have raised the "flash point," which governs flammability. This flash-point improvement has allowed drycleaners to have stores in shopping centers and other restricted areas that were previously unable to allow the more flammable petroleum cleaning machines.

What Makes This Solvent So Great?

Hydrocarbon is mild on clothing and allergies. On a scale of one to ten—one being weak and ten being strong—to rate degreasing and aggressiveness of solvents, hydrocarbon is roughly a three, compared to perc, which is roughly a nine. Hydrocarbon allows drycleaners to more responsively process fragile garments that have glued-on beads, pearls, sequins, and sensitive dyes, without the constant concern for damage. It is also mild on fabric dyes, which means less fading.

Hydrocarbon has proven to be an effective alternative for people with chemical sensitivity. Some customers who have had problems with other solvents have found hydrocarbon to be the answer to their concerns, whether it be skin, respiratory, or environmental. On occasion, a person's sensitivity may not only be to the solvent, but also to the soap and the fragrance that may be used with the hydrocarbon. Be patient when searching for a solvent that works for you.

Perchloroethylene

As stated earlier, "perc," the mainstay for many years because of its fast drying and its excellent cleaning ability, is slowly being phased out. It will take years to make the transition because the new equipment alternatives are very expensive and, to some degree, are still in the developmental stage. The majority of the cleaners in this country are still using perc. Many safeguards have been put in place through improved technology that will allow drycleaners, during the transition, to retain their current perc equipment for the foreseeable future. Still, many consumers have rallied around the industry in its move toward hydrocarbon and other alternatives, for environmental reasons.

Because perc is a chlorinated solvent, it is more toxic than hydrocarbon and it is subject to more stringent government regulation. Most drycleaners are focusing their efforts on proper machine maintenance, careful and legal removal of waste, and proper ventilation within their buildings. I expect the transition from perc to alternative, lower-maintenance solvents, to be a slow but constant movement.

Liquid CO2, Rynex, and Green Earth

The newest solvents embrace emerging technology. Liquid CO_2 and Rynex (glycol ether) are both being used in a limited capacity in the United States. These installations, though up and running, will take years to make it into the mainstream, and are being examined for cleaning, drying, colorfastness, and environmental aspects. They are on the cutting edge of the industry.

Cyclic silotanes, a silicone-based solution, being sold under the name "Green Earth," is said to be ready for trial across America. It is purported to permit safe cleaning without the need to separate dark and light colors.

As you select a drycleaner, ask about the methods and technological improvements in place, and then make your own choices.

The Greener Cleaner: Water

Greener Cleaner is one of the "names" given to fabricare centers that process clothing, in part or completely, with water. There is a growing contingent, albeit a small one, that advocates cleaning with water. Clothing made of wool, silk, cotton, and rayon is now being processed in this way. The cleaners are careful when accepting clothing with regard to shrinkage problems, but they are making strides. Wet cleaning is not a new technology, but it is one that requires exceptional "hands-on" care when processing clothing with dryclean-only care labels. For people with allergies and sensitivity issues, this option may be an excellent one, but, for some, it may be necessary to use a fragrance-free detergent and conditioner, as well.

◆ What Is Wet Cleaning?

Wet cleaning is the term used by professionals for washing clothing in water when it would normally be drycleaned. The process is performed under a controlled environment. It utilizes specially designed equipment, specially formulated soaps, and is often aided by the use of special bleaches. Clothing can be wet cleaned by machine or by hand.

> **Water Sense**
> The cup of oil that came out in drycleaning would not come out in washing. Very few oily stains can be removed in washing.

Water temperature is an important ingredient, as is agitation. Gentle hand agitation is necessary for some fabrics, while machine washing is necessary for others. Agitation can play an active role in stain removal, dye-bleed control, and shrinkage. Spinning or extraction speed, the amount of time the clothing spins, and moisture retention at the end of the cycle can affect fabric pilling, wrinkling, distortion, and drying time.

What Does Wet Cleaning Do Best?

Wet cleaning is performed by using water, which means that it removes water-based stains most effectively. Drink spills, food coloring, perspiration, blood, urine, and many other water-soluble stains are best removed by wet cleaning. Water, however, can "set" oily-type stains, making further removal in drycleaning more difficult. It is important to identify the nature of a stain before you automatically wash an item. (See Chapter 8 for information on stain identification.)

Wet cleaning is especially effective in the removal of large water-based stains such as soda spills. Drycleaning provides limited removal for small water-based stains and is even less effective for larger water-based stains and spills.

◆ Do-It-Yourself Washing

Wet cleaning does a very good job with water-based stains, especially large stains. You should consider pretreating certain stains before washing. If the stain improves in the first washing, then try it again for further improvement. If you wash an oil-stained item—which is easily recognizable because the stain usually remains after washing—then be sure to air dry it. The heat from the dryer could further "set" the stain or limit future removal in drycleaning.

Shrinkage and Distortion

Sometimes clothing shrinks when you wash it. Why? Water swells fibers, which can contribute to shrinkage. Agitation and the heat from drying can cause shrinkage. Tumble drying at too high a temperature can shrink clothing, weaken elastic, and contribute to static electricity. If done improperly, then the option of air drying can stretch or distort knitted fabrics. Most wool clothing, regardless of what the care label says, is better drycleaned than washed if you want to control shrinkage. Once a woolen shrinks in water, depending on the severity, it may be beyond restoration.

On the Bright Side: If a wool sweater is too large, tumble drying at too high a temperature may help to shrink it. This process can also cause felting (extreme shrinkage that cannot be reversed), so the restoration process must include pre-measurement and blocking, and must be closely monitored during drying.

Colorfastness and Dye Bleeding

Wet cleaning can be tricky when it comes to dyes. You certainly have seen more than one piece of clothing fade in the washing machine. You have probably seen some dye bleeding, too. Color classification is important and so is keeping dark colors together, as well as washing them in cold water. The skill comes in identifying which of the dark colors or trims may bleed, either onto the garment itself or onto another garment.

Some Care Tips

If a garment bleeds during hand washing, then it is best to drain the water immediately and re-rinse the garment a few times. If the garment is a dark color and is being machine washed for the first time, then your best option is to wash it alone, let the excess dye wash down the drain, and then dry it by itself. Most of these same dyes would not bleed in drycleaning, which makes the drycleaning process preferable for "high colors," such as red, purple, and green. Silk garments, which tend to bleed very easily in water, are definitely candidates for drycleaning.

Texture

Wet cleaning, even under professional conditions, can affect the texture of certain fabrics. Linen, silk, certain cottons, rayon, and wool are all susceptible to changes. Fabric softeners are helpful, but not all fabrics respond to them. If you do fluff or tumble-dry these fabrics, then remember to avoid overdrying them. They can be removed from the dryer a bit damp and then air-dried, which will make them softer. Remember, drycleaning and steaming can restore the soft feel to many fabrics that have become rough.

You now probably know more about drycleaning than you ever thought necessary!

For many years, every time that I went to a party or social event, and people found out that I was the owner of a custom drycleaners, I had all the attention I could ever want! As it turns out, the whole drycleaning process is a relative mystery to almost everyone. Almost every person has questions because, at some point, either their clothing or their drycleaner has had a problem, albeit even a minor one. But rarely is there a "live" representative, such as me, to openly answer questions. Clothing can be such a passion and expense that people often do have burning questions.

There may be a roomful of interesting and very qualified professionals from all walks of life and, funny enough, having a well-known drycleaner available to query is just as captivating for some people as someone from a more romantic or glorified profession.

I wrote this book for many reasons, but it was experiences like those mentioned above which helped me see the real need for it.

Chapter 30

Selecting a Drycleaner
Hints, Lists, and Tests

The following description of the drycleaning "business" is detailed, but it will open your eyes and help you to understand the choices available to you. This book is predicated on the belief that people want to know more.

The term "drycleaner" is really a misnomer. The proper term should be "fabric care specialist," because "drycleaner" is too limiting and doesn't really reflect the scope of services available at many establishments.

From the moment that you walk into the drycleaners or give your clothing to the delivery driver (be it from your home or office), the process begins. Before you choose a drycleaner, read this description of the process. It outlines the work that actually takes place in most drycleaners. These steps can vary depending on the quality of the business and the scope of the skills. Let us use an at-the-counter customer as an example.

◆ The Whole Process

Possibly you have little idea about how involved the drycleaning procedure is and, really, why should you care? You do need to know the fine points—enough to allow you to have *control over your clothing investment.*

At the Counter

You want to feel that the clerk is responsive when you point out a stain or discuss a problem. The clerk should do a thorough inspection of your clothing to identify any condition, be it faded, frayed, or in need of any particular repairs. The clerk should check the integral parts such as zippers, shoulder pads, and linings. If the garment has been badly pressed or has been shined, then the clerk should notice this condition and explain how gentle steaming may improve it. Conversely, if the hem or lapels should be softly rolled, then it is important that you convey these details to the clerk so that he or she can communicate them to the production department, in turn.

Drycleaners have two choices when accepting your clothing: the clerk can do a thorough inspection at the counter while you wait, which encourages you to voice any concerns you may have; or the clerk can issue you a "mini-ticket," which is simply a piece count with no detail. If the cleaner uses the mini-ticket method, then the inspection should be done by a "behind-the-scenes" detail person after you leave.

If the cleaner's policy is to inspect your clothing at the counter, then the clerk should read the care label (if a garment is distinctive in any way), discuss any unusual aspects, and alert you to any stains that need special attention. If the stains are so small that they are difficult to see, then the areas should be marked with red or yellow tape to alert the technician. In some operations, the clerk may be knowledgeable enough to discuss the different ways of cleaning or restoring your garment.

> **Be Helpful**
> If you are aware of certain stains, then you should point them out.

The Cleaning Process

Before cleaning, the clothing is "tagged" for identification (hopefully your cleaner removes these tags before your clothing is returned to you), and the staff members check and empty pockets. A good cleaner will safeguard and return to you any valuables found. If the buttons are breakable or unusual, then they should be protected or removed.

The technicians will consider the method of care and, using experience and the statement on the care label, will make six basic decisions: which stains need to be pre-treated; the length of the cleaning cycle necessary to remove soil and stains; the length of the cycle with regard to fragility; whether the garment requires a gentle cycle; possible air drying (if permitted) to control shrinkage or protect trims; and, finally, if it should be wet cleaned rather than drycleaned for more dramatic improvement.

It's possible that the technician may choose to process the garment *contrary* to the care label, such as wet cleaning a "dingy" white linen blouse (which has a "dryclean-only" instruction) to make the blouse whiter.

In determining whether drycleaning or wet cleaning is appropriate, the technician will evaluate whether texture, shrinkage, fading, or dye bleeding is a concern, and testing may be necessary before proceeding. The technician may ask the clerk to call you for additional information or permission. Once the garment has been cleaned and dried, it may be re-treated for stains that were not removed by the cleaning process and then it may be re-cleaned if needed. After this final inspection, the garment is ready for "finishing."

> **Wet Cleaning**
> Wet cleaning is a method of restoration that involves hand or machine washing with the possible addition of bleaches.

The Finishing Process

"Finishing" is the term professionals use for machine pressing or hand ironing. A typical garment may need both processes. Pressing by machine will impart a firm finish, while a hand iron may be used for the detail work or to impart a softer finish on more delicate clothing. An experienced finisher knows which approach will improve unsightly shine, button impressions, and hard wrinkles.

The finisher makes assessments the same way that the cleaning technician does: Should the jacket be "soft pressed" and lightly steamed to avoid creasing a rolled lapel? Should the hem be pressed or rolled? Should the linen blouse be lightly starched to achieve a crisp finish? Should the slacks have a sharp crease or a soft roll? These daily decisions are part of the finishing process.

> **Finishing Touch**
> The finisher may use a spray sizing or starch to add body or drape to the garment. This touch can add a "formality" to the garment or make a collar stand up.

Final Inspection

After the garment is finished, the last inspection takes place. This "nuance control," as I like to call it, falls under the "ready-to-wear" rule, which means that all the minute details have been fulfilled: threads snipped, loose buttons or hooks and eyes resewn, shoulder pads tacked, and hems and vents resewn. Thus, the garment should be returned in a "ready-to-wear" condition.

◆ In Conclusion

The "one-stop" process of dropping your clothing at the drycleaner is really not so simple. The drycleaner's job is to make it look simple. Proper acceptance starts with a skilled and caring counter clerk. A satisfying conclusion depends on the vigilance of skilled and intuitive people in the production department. Proper care for your clothing requires continuing education and awareness on your part, as well.

Consider the time and commitment that the average person invests each time he or she visits a salon for hair care or body work. A good drycleaner recognizes your investment in your wardrobe and needs your understanding of the often difficult task it is to protect that investment. Mutual respect and an eye toward the same goal combine as important ingredients for a successful relationship.

There can be great disparity among drycleaners—as with restaurants—and there are many different attitudes toward perfection. You know what your comfort level is. Assess yourself, decide what is best for you, and then set out to find the drycleaner that offers you the best fit.

◆ Story Time ...

A man had taken his Canali tuxedo to a drycleaner for a routine cleaning and to have a stain removed from the lapel. When he picked up his tux, he noticed that the stained area on the satin lapel was discolored or damaged, he wasn't sure which. He showed the counter clerk, and she told him that it was nothing that the cleaners had done. He was miffed, but he wasn't interested in a confrontation. For him, it was like trying to spar with a car mechanic over a repair when he knew nothing about car repair. He apparently wanted a second opinion, so he came to us.

What surprised me was that he did not insist on seeing a manager or an owner and had simply accepted the clerk's response. This problem is an all-too-familiar story by an ex-patron of another drycleaner, and is one that embarrasses me about my industry.

What Should Have Occurred?
The drycleaner, probably knowing that damage had occurred during cleaning or pressing, should have called the customer before he showed up, described the situation, and suggested a resolution. If that step was missed, then at the time of pickup, the clerk should have asked the man to wait while she brought a supervisor to address the situation. Very often, drycleaners know that damage has occurred.

The Next Step?
This man then came to our store because we have a reputation for being responsible and knowledgeable. He needed a diagnosis and a solution. To me, it looked as if the satin had been marred during spot removal by a tool that uses high-pressure steam or by a hand iron. I told him to go back to the drycleaner to see the owner, but he wasn't interested.

I gave him what I think is sage advice. I steered him to an excellent tailor at a specialty store, which was coincidentally the place where he had purchased the tuxedo. The tailor could remake one or both of the satin lapels, and the solution would cost much less than replacing a Canali tux. He followed my lead. Similar customer service will make a tangible difference when you choose a drycleaner.

A Lesson Learned Along the Way
When a person is at a social event and gets a food or drink stain on a prominent area of his or her clothing, he or she typically wipes it off with the nearest napkin, which my client fortunately refrained from doing. While we were talking, he asked me if there is a proper approach to self-stain removal. I told him that satin lapels

are very fragile, and if he had taken a white napkin and innocently wiped the stain, then he would have most likely roughed the fabric, delustered it, and caused permanent damage. He was literally speechless. This book was written to educate and to help prevent situations such as this.

◆ Nuts and Bolts of a Decision

Selecting a drycleaner is a personal issue. It is not necessarily an easy decision nor one that can be made without experiencing the drycleaner's service for weeks or even months. Many times people select a service provider, such as a drycleaner, for the wrong reasons or without thinking it through. Your drycleaner, to some extent, should be a reflection of your personality. I am hoping that this chapter will help you focus on your individual needs.

Drycleaners and restaurants are both service businesses. If you were to eat at a favorite restaurant once or twice a week for months, or years at a stretch, how many times would you have to send your meal back due to some detail? Think about that factor as you assess your drycleaning service.

In considering your drycleaning needs, you must find the balance of several elements: convenience, price, quality, services offered, and customer care.

Convenience

▸ Remember that rush hour, both morning and night, is a high-traffic time at your drycleaner's counter. If time is a consideration, then ask if the cleaner promotes a "quick-drop" method.

▸ Is free parking with easy access available? Looking for an empty parking meter for a quick transaction can be frustrating.

▸ If you pick up and drop off on your way to work or play, then consider these issues: some clothing can fade if left in direct sunlight for an extended period, the heat of a closed car can diminish a crisp finish on your clothing, and security may also be a consideration if the clothing is visible in your car.

▸ Will the drycleaners have flexible early-morning and evening hours? Drycleaners are typically open early, but few are open late.

▸ If Saturday is your preference, then you may need to wait in long lines. Does the cleaner offer Sunday hours? (Personally, I hope not.)

Price of Cleaning

Price is usually dictated by quality. Do you wear clothing that demands hand ironing and excellent spot removal at a higher price, or will a mainstream or, perhaps, a discount cleaner satisfy your needs?

Will you need two different cleaners—one for your regular clothing and one for your more delicate clothing? Sometimes men use a different cleaner just for their shirts.

Fact: Depending on the volume, a high-priced cleaner can cost an average customer $75 a week, or more. You can do the math from here.

Discount Drycleaners

When using a discount or "one-price" cleaner, you make sacrifices. These stores offer basic cleaning and basic spot removal for a "niche" clientele. They are not trying to be everything to everyone. Depending on the proprietor, their standard for pressing may allow seam and button impressions, subtle wrinkles, and minimal attention to details and subtleties. The clothing is still cleaned and pressed. (Some operations use a steam tunnel which does not impart as crisp a finish as pressing does.)

This service is meant to be utilitarian; don't try to complicate it. The goal is to offer a basic service for a low price and, in most cases, a quick turnaround for either the same day or within 24 hours. Some cleaners offer a discount if the orders are prepaid. Their scope of services may be limited depending on the operation.

> **Limitations**
> If you have a large spill or a serious pressing issue, a discount cleaner, admittedly, is not going to satisfy your needs. This concern is not their primary focus.

Mainstream Drycleaners

Mainstream drycleaners clearly offer a more full-service menu than discount cleaners do. They may offer pick-up and delivery, and they are generally focused on customer service issues. Their prices, though higher than a discounter's, should be competitive with other mainstream services. They will do some hand ironing, which guarantees fewer impressions, and they will give more attention to detail. The stain removal, by virtue of time and intent, will be more thorough. They can honor more special requests and may still be able to offer same-day service. If a garment needs a higher level of service than they can provide and if there is a well-known "specialty" drycleaner in the area, then the mainstream cleaners may openly refer you there.

Custom Drycleaners

Low price is not the forum of the custom drycleaner. These stores should be very focused on: individual care, at whatever cost; on customer service for the dis-criminating customer; on unparalleled quality; and on convenience. A hand iron, gentle steam, a subtle touch —all should guarantee no seam or button impressions and no shine. A sharp clothing inspector will catch the loose threads, minor repairs, and design nuances. For expensive designer and couture clothing, you should look nowhere else.

> **Scope of Service**
> Custom dry-cleaners also do blue jeans and casual wear. They may even offer a two-tiered price structure.

If you have a major restoration—be it a second-gener-ation wedding gown, a large stain, or difficult repairs and alterations—or you just want "the best," then con-sider a specialty or custom drycleaner. Like the discount cleaner at the other end of the spectrum, custom drycleaners have their niche, too. Customers often seek out a custom drycleaner to clean or restore a special garment in their wardrobe.

These cleaners also do a fair amount of restoration for garments that have been "mistreated" by other cleaners. (This sensitive subject is, nonetheless, true.) This is not to say that custom drycleaners do not make mistakes—they do—but they generally make fewer mistakes because of their skill and exceptional quality control.

> **Money and Quality**
> Does money really buy perfection? This is a question for the ages. When it comes to drycleaning, there are tangible differ-ences. Do the taste test yourself.

Note: If you collect vintage clothing and wish to have it restored, then a custom drycleaner should have the experience to process it properly.

◆ Services Offered

Services May Vary at Each Drycleaners
(This is a checklist—there is nothing to score.)

▸ Knowledgeable staff   ____

▸ Shirt laundry on the premises   ____

▸ Seamstress or tailor on the premises   ____

▸ Pick-up and delivery   ____

▸ Suede, leather, and fur cleaning   ____

▸ Reweaving   ____

▸ Flatwork—sheets and linens   ____

▸ Seasonal storage for clothing and fur   ____

▸ Shoe repair   ____

▸ Rug cleaning   ____

▸ Pillow cleaning and re-ticking   ____

▸ Upholstery cleaning (in-home service)   ____

▸ Drapery cleaning—take down and rehang service   ____

See the next page to fill out a quality rating chart about your drycleaner.

◆ How Does Your Drycleaner Rate?

Are your clothes ready-to-wear? Enter "Y" for yes and "N" for no.
(This chart contains issues for men's and women's clothing. Fill it out with a friend.)

▸ Dress shirts are returned with no cracked or missing buttons and no missing collar stays.　　　＿＿＿

▸ Dress shirts are returned free of wrinkles on the collar, cuffs, and pockets.　　　＿＿＿

▸ Dress shirts are starched to your liking.　　　＿＿＿

▸ Clothing is pressed without shine, button impressions, or double creases.　　　＿＿＿

▸ Stains are removed to your satisfaction and without damage to the color or fabric.　　　＿＿＿

▸ Skirt hems, lapels, and the edges of neckties are softly rolled.　　　＿＿＿

▸ Both shoulder pads are sewn in, smooth, and in correct position.　＿＿＿

▸ All seams and hems are sewn properly—none are hanging.　　　＿＿＿

▸ Clothing is free of objectionable odors.　　　＿＿＿

▸ Clothing is stuffed with tissue or packaged without wrinkles, and ＿＿＿ it is ready to wear.

Enter Your Total (all Y's is a perfect 10)　　　＿＿＿

9–10 You are getting most of what you deserve, and your clothing should be ready to wear. Tell your friends and your drycleaner.

7–8　If you like your drycleaner, then share your complaints with them and see if they can improve.

5–6　Find another drycleaner.

Quality: Is there a more mis-used term?
Everyone's vision of "quality" is different. Quality is examined quite thoroughly throughout this book. There are priorities and interpretations but, after cleaning, the basics should be summed up in three words: *ready to wear.*

◆ Business Relations

Responsiveness

When you have a complaint about quality; you have a lost garment; you need something in a rush; or you need a special favor, such as a quick repair or a special delivery, is your drycleaner there for you? Most services that drycleaners offer are labor oriented. Whether discount or custom, the cleaner should "bend over backward" for you. Expect no less.

Customer Service

The title, "customer service," implies a service standard. We take many aspects of service for granted: service with a smile, responsiveness, politeness, and caring. Have we forgotten about knowledge of services sold? A customer-service person should be an informed representative of the company and should be able to impart well-thought-out answers and accurate data. Is the manager—who may not always be available—the only true professional "go-to" person?

◆ Claims for Damaged or Lost Clothing

Lost or damaged items are, unfortunately, a reality in the drycleaning industry. This fact doesn't mean that *cleaner-caused* damage runs rampant, but it happens to every drycleaner. You are at a disadvantage when this problem occurs, which is when you can judge the true commitment of your service provider. Although it is important that the garment be found or fixed, how he or she responds to you in your time of need is what matters. A positive response and a speedy resolution are what you should expect.

Damage

Damage may be easy to recognize, but it can be difficult to assess. If the garment is torn by a machine, then the responsibility is reasonably clear. If the garment is new or is in excellent condition, then the full replacement cost should be refunded to you. But what if the garment tore easily because it was weakened by perspiration, stains, or age? The garment was still damaged by a machine while in the drycleaner's possession. Should you accept an adjusted value because of age or condition? And how should that value be assessed?

Loss

The same theory applies for lost clothing. If the garment was in excellent condition when it was misplaced, then the full replacement cost should be refunded to you. But if the garment was not new, then what is the appropriate value? If the garment is lost, then how can the value be accurately appraised?

These are all good questions. Such situations can really test the business-client relationship.

Resolving Damaged Clothing

Allow your drycleaner to explain and try to be open-minded and patient. The cleaner is probably as upset as you are. You have trusted your cleaner to care for your clothing; you should trust him or her to be honest in assessing the value of your damaged garment. Unfortunately, this is sometimes easier said than done.

It's helpful if you have an original sales receipt for the purchase of the garment. If not, then give the cleaner your best recollection. Arriving at a proper value is much easier with two understanding parties.

Resolving Lost Clothing

No one enjoys being the bearer of bad news, so you can be reasonably certain that if the garment is lost, the manager or owner has already researched all of the possibilities.

It is common practice for the manager to ask you for the exact size, color, design, brand name, and, perhaps, age of the "missing" garment. Again, he or she may ask for the original sales receipt. Be thorough in your description of the garment, and give an accurate account of the condition of the item. When you're done, ask for a copy of the drycleaner's notes or the "claim" form. You should allow the cleaner two to three weeks to research the situation because many missing garments do find their way back.

> **Lost Clothing**
> In many cases the missing garment has been mis-assembled into another customer's order, and it is returned within a few weeks.

Value Assessment

There is a guideline for assessing clothing value, called "The Fair Claims Guide," which is nationally recognized. The guide establishes the life expectancy of a garment, factors in the condition of the garment, and then applies the rules of depreciation (similar to how cars are depreciated).

I have used the guide before, but in most cases the customer and I were able to agree on an equitable value without it.

Note: Laundered shirts require a slightly different approach to valuing, which is examined in detail in Chapter 19, "Shirt Loss or Damage."

There is a saying in business that goes something like this, "Do a good job, and the person will tell a friend; do a bad job, and the person tells ten friends." Well, people don't generally rave about a drycleaner the way they do about clothing stores, hair stylists, or restaurants, but do a bad job, and all that will change! So, if you find a drycleaner through a referral, then consider it to be a strong endorsement.

The International Fabricare Institute, located outside of Washington, D.C., is a world renown testing laboratory for clothing and textiles. After examining more than 13,000 garments and household textiles submitted by drycleaners, for the year 2001, the lab reported the results of damage as follows:

Manufacturer Defects: 45%

Consumer Mistakes: 35%

Drycleaner/Launderer Mistakes: 11%

Not Damaged or Fault Not Determined: 9%

(Source: IFI International Textile Analysis Laboratory)

Glossary

All of the following terms have been "doctored" to apply to our subject matter.

Acid

For our use, an "acid condition" will refer to the effect it had on fabric. Perspiration starts out as an acid and turns alkaline with time. Strong spotting chemicals can affect vegetable fibers such as cotton and linen. On the pH scale, acid is at the opposite end of the spectrum from alkaline. Vinegar is a mild acid. The chemical, oxalic acid, is effective in the removal of rust.

Alkaline

Alkaline chemicals such as chlorine bleach (Clorox®), ammonia, and many hair-care products can harm clothing. Once perspiration turns alkaline, it too can harm fabrics, especially protein fibers such as silk and wool. Alkalinity can weaken and change the color of fabric.

Bias Cut

"A dress is cut on the bias." This common use of the word describes the diagonal of a woven fabric. All neckties are cut on a bias. Garments that are cut on a bias present a challenge when altering and pressing. Any fabric that is cut on a bias will have the greatest stretch and can distort most easily.

Bleach

There are many types of bleach. Drycleaners typically use peroxide, sodium bisulphite, and sodium perborate. Some may even use chlorine bleach (we hope under guarded conditions). Some bleaches are considered "color-safe," but all bleaches, if misused, can damage fabrics.

Caramelized

Drycleaners use this term to describe a sugar-based stain that has aged, which is evidenced by it turning the fabric brown. These caramelized stains are often permanent.

Colorfast

A term that implies that the color in a fabric will not bleed or change in washing or drycleaning, if the garment is processed as instructed on the care label.

Commercial Laundry

This is a laundry that processes shirts and washable household items. The term can also be associated with a laundry that is within a drycleaning plant.

Cotton Broadcloth
This closely woven fabric is used for shirts and dresses and, in our case, is typically associated with shirt material. Broadcloth usually has a very fine, lustrous finish.

CO_2
Liquid carbon dioxide is being tested and can be used as a cleaning solvent for clothing. It is nontoxic, noncorrosive, and nonflammable. It is similar to hydrocarbon in its cleaning strength.

Deluster
When a shiny lustrous fabric is rubbed or abraded and when the surface fibers have become rough, the sheen is dulled. This condition is common with silk, satin, polished cotton, and acetate fabrics.

De-pill
This process removes pills (pill balls) from the surface of a fabric. These pills can be removed by hand tools and battery-operated tools.

Drycleaning
Drycleaning is not dry at all. The solvents appear wet, but there is no water in virgin drycleaning solution. The process is performed in a closed machine, similar to a front-load washing machine. Drycleaning involves the use of solvents to remove soil, paint, tar, oil, and grease from fabric. Drycleaning causes very little, if any, shrinkage.

Dye Strip
This is the term used to remove dyes from a garment. The process is commonly used in commercial laundries. Dye stripper can remove the dye from most garments on contact, but it is typically used to remove loose or fugitive (from another source) dye from a garment, such as dye that deposits under the arms as a result of dye bleed from a dark garment onto a lighter garment.

Enzymes
Enzymes occur naturally in the body, and they aid in digestion. Enzymes are also used, in powder form, for breaking down food stains. They work best when mixed with warm water below 115 degrees F. Time is also an important ingredient; the longer the garment is exposed to the warm-water solution, the better the stain removal.

Faille (Pronounced: File)

Faille is a woven fabric with horizontal ribbing. The fabric is often used for neckties and is commonly used as dress fabric with a moiré finish.

Finisher

This is a more formal word used to describe a "presser" at a drycleaners or laundry.

Flash Point

At this temperature, a substance (such as drycleaning solvent) will ignite when exposed to an open flame. Very few, if any, solvents used in drycleaning today have a flash point low enough to ignite when exposed to an open flame.

Fused

This process heats and bonds together the layers of fabric or interfacing. When a fused fabric breaks down, bubbles may form. These bubbles look like raindrops sitting on glass.

Fusible Fabric

This fabric has an adhesive coating that can be "bonded" to another fabric by applying heat, moisture, and pressure.

Glazing

This process is used in the restoration of fur. A heated wheel is used to "electrify" the hair on a fur pelt, a process that lifts the hair on end while it restores the sheen.

Grosgrain (Pronounced: Gro-grain)

This fabric is typically used for dresses and neckties and has pronounced ribs, which are more rounded than those on faille fabric. It is a sturdy heavy fabric with a dull luster.

Hand Finished

This term is used to describe the ironing or steaming of a garment and is performed by hand rather than by machine. Such finishing is commonly used for fragile fabrics and hand-ironed shirts.

Hard Press

This term is used by drycleaners to describe the amount of pressure and heat used for a firm pressing on a garment or household item. The term can also have negative meaning, as in: "This fabric has been hard pressed and is now shined."

Hot Head

This type of press is used to impart a firm finish on cotton, linen, and silk. The top surface is made of chrome metal. A hot-head press is commonly used for tablecloths and shirts in a commercial laundry.

Hydrocarbon

This solvent is a reincarnation of petroleum and is popular among drycleaners. It is chemically treated to make it odorless. Hydrocarbon solvent is a mild de-greaser with a flash point of 140 to 149 degrees F.

Measure and Block

This term is used by the drycleaning industry to maintain the correct size for knitted and woven garments. The garment or textile is measured before drycleaning or wet cleaning and is reblocked to the premeasured dimensions during the finishing process.

Oxford Cloth

This absorbent, sturdy fabric is commonly used for shirts. It is woven in a basket weave with a white filling. Oxford cloth shirts were never made in the city of Oxford!

Oxidized Oil

Oil stains on clothing start out colorless. Heat and time can cause the stain to oxidize and turn a yellow hue. Once oxidized, the stain becomes very difficult to remove.

Percholoroethylene (perc)

Perc is a nonflammable synthetic solvent used for drycleaning. It has highly evaporative qualities and is an aggressive de-greaser. It is still used in many of the drycleaning plants in the United States, but is being phased out in favor of new and alternative solvents that are less toxic.

Pigmented

This insoluble colored matter is used in paints, enamels, and oil colors. The term is typically associated with the dyes that are sprayed on some leather garments.

Pile

This woven fabric may have cut or uncut loops that make up the surface and produce a "hairlike" texture. Fabrics with pile are typically used for velvet and corduroy.

Pills (Fabric pills)

When the end of a fiber is rubbed and the loose ends form small pills, pill balls are created. The length of the fiber and the twist of the yarn will affect pilling.

Placket

This term is commonly used to describe the front center part of an upper garment that may contain the buttons or zipper (like the button-down section of a dress shirt). This term is also used to describe the opening or slit of a skirt.

Preservation

This is the process during which a textile, bridal, or christening gown is actually packaged or boxed into an acid-free box (neutral pH environment) with acid-free tissue. This technique is the most effective way to reduce aging and discoloration.

Reweaving

This is the term used to describe the process of weaving threads to repair holes and tears in fabrics. During this process, threads are woven by hand, one thread at a time, in a crisscross fashion. The goal is to duplicate the weave that was originally done by the machine. The threads are taken from a hidden area such as a seam, cuff, or from inside the pocket of the garment.

Rolled Finish

This soft finish is used for the edge of a hem, lapel, pleat, bow, and any other fabric that is rolled rather than pressed flat or creased.

Rynex

This organic chemical is used for drycleaning and is not regulated by the Environmental Protection Agency (EPA). Propylene Glycol Ether (Rynex) carries its own moisture to break down water-soluble stains. It is nontoxic, noncarcinogenic, and biodegradable. (*Source: Rynex Environmental Business Solutions*)

Sizing

These materials are used to give a fabric stiffness, luster, or firmness. Sizing can also give additional strength and weight. Some sizing is soluble in water or solvent and can be diluted during the cleaning process. Sizing can also be added to drycleaning solution or sprayed directly on clothing, but rarely does it match the quality used during manufacturing. Sizing can stain certain fabrics if sprayed topically.

Soft Press

This term is used to describe how to press a garment without leaving impressions, shine, or hard creases. The term may refer to hand ironing, steaming or, in some cases, even machine pressing—or whichever process is necessary to create a soft finish.

Soluble

This term describes a substance capable of being dissolved in liquid. Water-based stains are soluble in water, and oily-based stains are soluble in cleaning solvents.

Spotter

This is the name given to the person in a drycleaners or laundry who removes stains from clothing before and after drycleaning or wet cleaning. This same person could be the one who actually cleans the clothing in the machine or launders the shirts.

Starch

Like sizing, starch is intended to give a fabric stiffness. It is soluble in water and is regularly used for shirts and linens. It can be sprayed topically or dissolved in a washing machine to starch a "load" of shirts. It can stain certain fabrics if sprayed topically and can be hard to remove from dryclean-only garments.

Wet Cleaning

Wet cleaning is the term used by professionals for washing clothing in water when it would normally be drycleaned. The process is performed under a controlled environment. It uses specially designed equipment and specially formulated soaps, and is often aided by special bleaches. This process could even include enzymes and dye strippers, but it does not include any drycleaning solvents.

Worsted

This lightly twisted woolen yarn is used to make smooth fabrics, such as gabardine and tropical-weight wool.

Yarn Slippage

This is the shifting or separation of yarns or fibers. This "slippage," which is most common with silk, satin, chiffon, and organza, results in open spaces between yarns. Slippage is mostly seen in stress areas such as the underarms, waist, and across the back. This condition can sometimes be improved by carefully re-aligning the individual yarns with a straight pin.

Wedding Gown Inspection Sheet

Give this sheet to your "designated person" to take to the cleaners.

Any Invisible Stains? (white wine, champagne, clear soda, spills) _____

_____

_____

_____

Any Unusual Food Stains? _____

_____

_____

_____

Heavy Soil on Hem, Neck, or Other Area _____

_____

_____

_____

Tears, Loose Seams, Dangling Beads on Gown or Veil _____

_____

_____

_____

Specific Wishes to Convey to Cleaner _____

_____

_____

_____

Inventory all pieces: Gown ___ Veil ___ Headpiece ___ Gloves___ Slip ___ Other _____

cut here

✂ cut here

Stain Diagram for Gown, Veil, and Headpiece

Put an "X" wherever the stains are and a "Y" wherever sewing is needed.

Front of gown

Back of gown

Veil and headpiece

Slip or crinoline

cut here

◆ Christening Day Diary

The _____ Family Diary

Date _____ Time _____ Day _____

Name of Newborn_____

Siblings _____

Parents _____

Grandparents_____

Other Family/Guests _____

_____

Family Thoughts _____

_____

_____

_____

_____

◆ Christening Outfit Preservation Diary
Cleaning, Care, and Preservation

Date _____ Time _____

◆ Cleaning and Repairs

Date of Ceremony _____

Name of Newborn _____

Who Took Outfit for Cleaning _____

Where It Is to Be Cleaned _____

Drycleaned _____ Wet Cleaned _____

Remarks/Condition _____

Repairs Needed _____

◆ Boxing and Preservation

Inventory: Gown _____ Slip _____ Bonnet _____ Gloves _____

Booties _____ Other _____

Any New Clothing Added _____

Reboxed with Acid-Free Tissue _____

Diary Included with Box _____

Other _____

◆ Questions for a Key Person at the Cleaners

▸ What kind of stain removal should I expect?

▸ Will the leather cleaner be able to properly match the original dye? If it needs to be re-dyed, will the dye look natural?

▸ Do you think that my garment requires hand cleaning in order to maintain the body, texture, and color?

▸ If it is machine cleaned, then will the size, color, or texture change?

▸ Should I expect any shrinkage from cleaning? If there is shrinkage, then can the skin be stretched? If so, how much?

▸ If there are scars, belly wrinkles, or imperfections that have been filled in and covered by the tannery during manufacture, how badly will they show after those fillers and resins fall out during the cleaning process?

Note: The answers to these questions can only be approximated by the cleaner because they are not privy to what occurred during the tanning process.

▸ If a hem has come down, will the leather cleaner routinely glue it back up?

▸ Will the leather cleaner automatically reglue the nicks and touch-up the scuff marks?

▸ Will the buttons, zipper, and trims be safe in cleaning?

▸ Will the leather cleaner protect heavy buttons and clasps on my shearling coat, if needed?

A Necessary Step: Even with their best and most earnest efforts, cleaners cannot always predict the condition of a skin after cleaning. Most cleaners will ask that you sign an agreement before they accept your leather or suede for cleaning.

◆ Questions for Salespeople

Standard questions that apply to most clothing purchases will help you make the best of your investment. I would wager that you already have clothing in your closet that you don't wear because of the style or the color—why add improper fit, fragile elastic, or possible shrinkage to the list? Ask more questions.

▸ When buying a suit or a sport jacket, ask about fusible construction.

▸ Ask for extra buttons when you buy nice clothing because the buttons may not be available later.

▸ When buying dress shirts, ask how much shrinkage should be expected in the collar. You would be surprised at the amount of progressive shrinkage in the collars of designer and custom shirts.

▸ For expensive or unique clothing, ask for any care information the salesperson can share about washing or drycleaning. Ask whether the buyer has said anything specific or whether the salesperson has heard feedback from customers.

◆ The Next Step: Assessing Your Personal Needs

Sit down, relax, and take some quality time (maybe in the restaurant at the department store where you shop) to ask yourself some questions.

▸ Assess your wardrobe needs. You've shopped your whole life, and you have some definite likes and dislikes.

▸ Write down your favorite colors and fabrics. Write down your least favorite colors and fabrics. Think about what people have commented on and complimented you on.

▸ Your body has probably found its natural weight by now—maybe not your ideal weight, but its natural weight (the one that you philosophically accept, even if your ego doesn't)—and you have a sense of what looks good on you. Or maybe you could use some fashion guidance, and that's all right, too. Write down what styles make you feel good.

▸ Do you have the interest and the inner strength to spend two to three hours with one salesperson? Is the time you will invest with this person worth any more than the hours you spend looking through racks and racks of clothes to find the right style at the right price?

▸ Have you had enough of the shopping rat-race, the traffic, the people, the time invested, the frustration of shopping numerous locations for hours on end and leaving with nothing or little of what you set out to find? Is it really worth all that?

cut here

I

M

R

Index: The Ultimate Guide to Shopping & Caring for Clothing

Index: The Ultimate Guide to Shopping & Caring for Clothing

◆ *Resources*

The list that follows contains the names of people and companies that were kind enough to lend their thoughts and expertise on a variety of subjects.

Men's Clothing Insights

Mike Colen—James Limited, Mclean, VA.

Tito Vargas—Bergdorf Goodman, New York, NY

Fred Anderson—Tom James Co., Franklin, TN

Shirt Care and Construction

Fred Anderson—Tom James Co., Franklin, TN

Gambert Custom Shirts—Millburn, NJ

Moda Georgio Custom Clothing—Phoenix, AZ

Necktie Care and Construction

Lee Allison—Lee Allison Necktie Co., Chicago, IL

Brian Targovnic—Kings Choice Neckwear, New York, NY

Andy Tarshis—Tiecrafters, New York, NY

Leather and Suede Care and Cleaning

Paul Kantor and Burt Feldman—Ram Leather Care, Manassas, VA

Joe Hallak—Hallak Cleaners, New York, NY

John Conway—Kirk's Suede Life, Inc., Willowbrook, IL

Clothing Protection—Insect Insights

Bob Orrence—Able Termite and Pest Control, Lanham, MD

Reweaving Specialist

Barbara Gibson—Washington, D.C.

Your Online Resource

www.clothingdoctor.com

•Exclusive Interviews

The Ultimate Guide to Shopping and Caring for Clothing started the ball rolling with Nordstrom, Neiman Marcus, Saks Fifth Avenue, and Bergdorf Goodman.

I will have more useful shopping advice and valuable insights as I continue my exclusive interviews with these and other famous clothiers.

•Free Reports

Each month I will post free reports, focusing on a "fabric of the month," groundbreaking fabric and clothing news, and hints for the care of your household items.

•Monthly Fabricare Tips

Life goes on, even after the book is written. Education is an ongoing goal and new information is constantly forthcoming. I will share it as I get it.

•Question and Answer Forum

You can post any questions you have and I will answer them as soon as possible.

•Shopping Updates

As the deals and opportunities arise—you will be the first to hear about them. Check my website regularly for the latest information.

•Steve's Peeves

As I see them, you will read them!

•Tour Dates

All of my book signings, fabric seminars, and lectures will be listed by date and location.